MURDER IN THE CHURCHYARD

Shirley B. Garrett

Shirley B. Garrett

This is a work of fiction. All the characters, organizations, locations, and events portrayed in this novel are either products of the author's imagination or used fictitiously. Any similarity to anyone is purely coincidental.

MURDER IN THE CHURCHYARD
Copyright 2022 by Shirley B. Garrett, Psy.D.

All rights reserved. No part of this publication may be reproduced, stored in a retrieval system, or transmitted in any form or by any means, electronic, mechanical, photocopying, recording, or otherwise, without the written permission of the publisher.

ISBN: 978-1-943065-14-1

Published by Positive Directions, LLC

Cover design by Shirley B. Garrett. Original cover art by Dan Pritchett.

Previous Novels by SHIRLEY B. GARRETT

THE CHARLIE STONE CRIME THRILLER SERIES

Deadly Compulsion
Deadly Lessons
Deadly Obsessions

THE PHOENIX O'LEARY HOT FLASH SERIES

Hot Flash Divas
Hot Flash Desires
Hot Flash Decisions

Nonfiction Books by SHIRLEY B. GARRETT, PSY.D.

Stop the Craziness: Simple Life Solutions
5 Steps to a More Confident You: Quick Tips for Life Series
5 Steps to Adapting to Change: Quick Tips for Life Series

DEDICATION

This book is dedicated to my husband, Bob, the man who loves me, supports my creativity, and always has my back.
Thanks, Sweetie.

MURDER IN THE CHURCHYARD

Table of Contents

DEDICATION .... *iv*

ACKNOWLEDGEMENTS .... *i*

CHAPTER 1 .... *1*

CHAPTER 2 .... *7*

CHAPTER 3 .... *12*

CHAPTER 4 .... *29*

CHAPTER 5 .... *36*

CHAPTER 6 .... *49*

CHAPTER 7 .... *55*

CHAPTER 8 .... *59*

CHAPTER 9 .... *66*

CHAPTER 10 .... *73*

CHAPTER 11 .... *76*

CHAPTER 12 .... *88*

CHAPTER 13 .... *94*

CHAPTER 14 .... *97*

CHAPTER 15 .... *100*

CHAPTER 16 .... *109*

CHAPTER 17 .... *115*

CHAPTER 18 .... *127*

CHAPTER 19 .... *135*

CHAPTER 20	140
CHAPTER 21	146
CHAPTER 22	151
CHAPTER 23	156
CHAPTER 24	167
CHAPTER 25	171
CHAPTER 26	174
CHAPTER 27	181
CHAPTER 28	191
CHAPTER 29	198
CHAPTER 30	206
CHAPTER 31	210
CHAPTER 32	216
CHAPTER 33	221
CHAPTER 34	223
CHAPTER 35	236
ABOUT THE AUTHOR	239

ACKNOWLEDGEMENTS

Special thanks to the following beta readers who gave their valuable time and expertise to improve this novel. Elaine Anderson, Yvette McCoy, Edie Peterson, Genett Baines, Kenny Emmanuel, and Jared Austin.

The following writer's groups also offered their guidance: The Huntsville Literary Association and North Alabama Mystery Writers.

My appreciation to my family and friends who helped to inspire me.

Kudos to Huntsville, Alabama for providing such a wonderful place to live. The city and community inspire my creative efforts.

There are no words to express my gratitude to my editor Lisa Prince, who has helped me weather the many renditions of this novel. It has been a journey.

MURDER IN THE CHURCHYARD

CHAPTER 1

A ghost wearing a suit and top hat stepped in front of my car while I was tooling around Huntsville's courthouse square.

The hulking black truck in the next lane prevented a course correction. I cringed when we glided through the spook.

"Sorry."

Mid-hood, his eyes widened before he dissipated like fog. I knew he was dead but it still felt disrespectful.

Good thing he's ectoplasmic or I'd have creamed him for sure.

Prissy, my fur baby, planted her tiny paws on the dash and barked. The cute Chihuahua in the movie *Legally Blonde* couldn't compare to my loving, yet sassy, little girl.

"Calm down," I told her.

Prissy glanced over at me and resumed her guard duties in silence.

I'm Brianna Kelly, and seeing disembodied spirits is one of my psychic abilities. I see this power as a blessing, a curse, and a responsibility to help earthbound spirits to cross over. It is not always as easy as it sounds.

I keep my gifts hidden, except with a few trusted people. I've suffered enough verbal abuse and rejection from my father and others to drive home the disadvantages of being different.

I parked Hot Stuff, my red Tesla Model 3, on Eustis Avenue. I was meeting my friend, Mystery Jones, for an early Monday morning walk.

My store, Chocolates and Delights, is next door to her business, and she holds me personally responsible for her frequent consumption of dark chocolate with almonds. Mystery has researched the properties of dark chocolate and is convinced it is a health food that combats stress, depression, and any other excuse she needs to rationalize her enjoyment of one of her favorite treats. Since I sell her the chocolate, she feels it's my moral responsibility to help her avoid the dreaded bubble butt by walking with her three mornings a week. I call this Mystery logic.

We come from different cultural backgrounds, which in our case means we complement each other's strengths and weaknesses. Mystery's the fifth-generation, African American daughter of two Alabama A&M University professors whose family have lived in Huntsville, Alabama, for five generations.

I'm an interesting combination of Irish and Italian lineage. I inherited my Mediterranean complexion and curves from my mother, Olivia; and my dark copper hair and emerald green eyes, from my dad, Sean Kelly. Dad divorced Mom, a renowned psychic, when I was five. She told me the combination of his logical approach and her intuitive nature created unhealthy vibrations. He claimed she'd hidden her weirdness before they married, and all the psychic mumbo-jumbo creeped him out. This, of course, means my psychic gifts also give him the heebie jeebies.

Mystery parked her blue Prius behind me. Unlike my dad, she has a longing for anything supernatural. This makes for an interesting friendship.

When I looked in my rearview mirror, she shot me a radiant smile and waved.

I waved back. *How can she be perky at this time of the morning?*

She's an early bird, while I'm more like a bat who can't fall asleep until midnight.

Since I don't have to arrive at my shop until nine-thirty most mornings, my sleep pattern usually isn't a problem—except on the days I walk with Mystery.

Prissy spotted Mystery getting out of the car and went into a tail-wagging frenzy.

Though she's generally well-behaved, my dog has a passion for chasing squirrels and no amount of yelling will bring her to heel; so as a precaution, I clipped on a leash. Once her paws hit the pavement, she pranced toward my friend.

"Come here, Sugar, and give me a snuggle." Mystery picked up Prissy and loved on her before putting her down. Then she rubbed her hands together with apparent anticipation. "I wanted to start our walk here, so I could tell you about this Episcopal Church."

The brick church had a pleasant grassed side-yard with a few small trees and shrubbery, surrounded by a decorative black iron fence.

Mystery's deceased husband, Tyree, was an accomplished architect who loved historic buildings. They had often strolled through Huntsville's Twickenham District, where he'd educated her about the different styles and features of the lovely historic buildings and homes. Hence, she considers herself to be knowledgeable on the topic of historic architecture. This has been an advantage when she leads ghost tours.

I pointed. "Let's start in the churchyard. It should be safe for Prissy to romp inside the fenced area while we talk."

The iron gate's rusty hinges squealed at a nerve-grating pitch. I ushered the dog through, and Mystery closed it with a clang. After I unhooked the leash, Prissy spotted a low-flying butterfly and began a pursuit punctuated by leaps.

We stayed on the brick walk, since the grass was damp from a brief early morning April sprinkle. The refreshing scent of rain still lingered on the cool breeze.

Mystery said with the authority of a docent, "This church was built in 1859 with a Gothic Revival architectural style. I've never been inside, but I've heard the pews are a pain to the bootie, if you know what I mean." Her scrunched-nose expression served as an exclamation mark.

I squinted up at the tall octagonal bell tower that cast a long shadow across the church's verdant lawn. "How tall is that thing?"

"Tyree told me the tower is 151 feet tall."

"Wow!" I never took the time to learn much of the city's history until I was asked to lead a series of Halloween ghost walks. I met Mystery on the Twickenham District walk, and we've been friends since.

Prissy's whimper drew my attention. She stood stiff, sniffing the air, before shooting toward the bushes that ran along the side of the church.

"Prissy! You better not be chasing another squirrel." I pointed at the brick walk by my side and commanded, "Heel."

Prissy reached the shrubs and scooted out of sight between them.

Mystery cocked a hip, placed a hand on it, and chuckled. "Like that worked."

Dang-blasted dog. I strode, arms swinging, to where she'd disappeared.

Mystery trailed close behind me.

I noticed something sticking out from behind the shrub on the end.

"Is that a foot? Did someone faint?" Concerned, I pushed my way behind the prickly holly bushes which grabbed at my clothes.

"Who is it?" Mystery asked, peering over the thigh-high bushes.

I covered my mouth, but it didn't stop the scream.

A woman lay behind the hedge, her gray hair crusted with blood. Her face had a peculiar mask-like appearance, and her lower jaw drooped open. Wide-open eyes with dilated pupils stared up at the cloudless blue sky.

With bile inching up my throat, I picked up Prissy, who was sniffing the woman's hand, and turned to run. I smashed into Mystery, causing both of us to tumble to the ground on the other side of the bushes.

Mystery landed with an "Oomph." She sat up and shook her head as if trying to restore order to her neural network. "Bree, was that woman… dead?"

I struggled to my feet, brushed off my clothes, and leashed Prissy. "I don't know." My words dripped sarcasm when I said, "Why don't you go check for a pulse?"

I felt immediate remorse. "Sorry." I extended a hand and helped her up.

"Me?" Her eyes narrowed. "Brianna Olivia Kelly, you know how I hate dead bodies." She shuddered and ran her hands through her short, dark curls. "I don't even like to look at them dressed up and in coffins at the funeral home." She pointed a trembling finger. "You go back and check. You're the one who sees haints all the time."

"What does that have to do with it?" I asked.

"Haints are dead, aren't they?"

"So, why do you like ghosts and not dead bodies?"

She huffed and crossed her arms. "It's different."

I handed her Prissy's leash, shored up my resolve, and squeezed back through the damp bushes. I knelt and checked for a pulse on the woman's cold, wet neck. Nothing. When I looked up, Mystery was peering over the bushes, her brown eyes filled with a tender expression of concern.

"Well?" she asked.

I stood and shook my head. "She's passed." My stomach did flips while I reached into my belt purse for my phone.

"Sweet Baby Jesus!" Mystery clutched her throat with one hand and laid the other across her large bosom.

"What's wrong?" I rushed to her side.

She started hyperventilating. "I…can't…breathe." Panic widened her eyes. She staggered to her left.

I reached out to steady her. "Take some deep breaths, or you're gonna have another panic attack and pass out like you did at Tyree's funeral."

When Mystery's husband died two years ago, it threw my formerly unflappable friend off the road of stability and deep into the emotional weeds. To this day she keeps a tenacious emotional grip on Tyree and her grief.

"I'll count your inhales and exhales for you," I said while rubbing circles on her back the way my mother had soothe me as a child. For some reason, calming her helped me to cope with the situation.

It took a few moments, but she regained control. "I think I'm all right. I wish I was a steel camellia like you."

I rolled my eyes. "If you only knew the number of times, I've been terrified almost witless in my life. It's a miracle my brains aren't addled and I don't have ulcers." I rubbed my pounding temples and looked around. "This may be a crime scene. Maybe we should wait outside the fence."

She nodded and seemed to be regaining some of her composure.

I was wrestling with the rusty gate latch when I noticed a man with red hair sprinting from the corner to cross the street. He disappeared behind a nearby building.

Once we were on the sidewalk, I phoned 911 and explained the situation to the emergency operator. I declined to stay on the phone and disconnected the call. "The police are on the way."

"Sweet Baby Jesus." Mystery grasped the fence like the earth was shifting beneath her feet. "Bree, I recognized the dead woman. It was hard to tell at first with her so pale and laying half under a bush." Her chest rose and fell as she took several deep breaths. "I went to a meeting once with Tyree, and she was there raising Cain about something or another. Lordy, that was years ago, so I can't be sure."

I waved my hand in a circle. "And…"

"I believe it's Victoria Spellman, the president of the Historic Preservation Board."

CHAPTER 2

Uniformed officers had strung yellow crime scene tape along the wrought iron fence. Police cars filled all the available on-the-street parking, and one of the officers stood guard at the gate, holding a clipboard.

I cuddled Prissy close and deep breathed to remain calm while Detectives Anthony Ricci and Chris Haddington with the Huntsville Police Department took our statements.

The younger detective, Haddington, smiled at me while Mystery told them, with broad gestures, how she recognized the victim. He was a tall, attractive man with dark hair and broad shoulders.

I refocused my attention on the senior partner, who ran a hand through his salt and pepper hair. He carried the faint aroma of bacon, which may be why Prissy kept sniffing in his direction.

Keep breathing, slow and steady.

"So, you saw a man running from the scene. Can you describe him?" Detective Ricci's brown eyes focused on me like ocular lie detectors.

"He wasn't running from the churchyard. He ran from the corner." I pointed to the area, surprised to see my hand still quivered like my insides. "He had short red hair and wore blue shorts with a white tee shirt."

Haddington's gaze stroked over my hair and asked, "Was his hair a dark copper color like yours?"

Something about the look felt intimate. My face flooded with heat. "No. It was bright, carrot-top red."

Ricci jotted down my description. "Did you see his face?"

"All I saw was his back."

"How tall was this guy?" Ricci shifted his weight back onto his heels.

"Maybe six feet or so."

He ran his hand down a Micky Mouse tie and patted his slight paunch. "Was he heavy or slender?"

"Fit like a runner."

Prissy started squirming. Since she was leashed, I placed her on the ground.

He nodded again and wrote the information into a small black book. "Now tell me again, how you found this body?"

I recounted the story once more before adding, "Prissy's my first line of defense, but I never thought she'd find a dead body." The memory sent shivers over me.

Both detectives looked down at my dog with raised brows. Ricci stifled a chuckle and cleared his throat. "This tiny dog is your first line of defense?" He sounded incredulous.

Bristling with indignation, I drew myself up to my full five-foot-seven. With a steel-reinforced tone, I said, "This dog has heightened senses. She barks when there's danger, attacks if I'm threatened, and is an excellent judge of character."

Ricci's eyes popped wide before he dropped to one knee and held out his hand.

Prissy eased forward and sniffed it. She wagged her tail with enthusiasm before licking his hand like it was coated with bacon grease.

Grinning with clear delight, he scratched her behind the ears. "My grandkids would love you. You're such a cutie."

Prissy closed her eyes and tilted her head to a better angle for petting.

"Well, you passed the Prissy test, despite insulting her," I said with a gruff tone. I crossed my arms to emphasize my displeasure.

Mystery crossed hers, too. "You've done it now."

Ricci stood, winced, and rubbed his right knee. "Didn't mean to insult anyone."

After a few more redundant questions, Ricci handed a card apiece to Mystery and me. "Call me if you think of anything else." He hurried toward a white van with "Forensics" printed on the side that had pulled into the Health Department lot across the street.

Haddington looked down at me with twinkling blue eyes. "You'll have to come in for a line-up if we locate the suspect."

Mystery wiped her forehead as if relieved. "Thank goodness I didn't see him. I wouldn't want to pinpoint a suspect in a line-up. Sounds dangerous."

"It's safe. Ms. Kelley will look at the suspects through a one-way mirror, so they won't be able to identify her." He turned to face me; his look intent. "Is it Miss or Mrs?"

"I'm not married." I felt heat flood my face. "I'm not sure I'll be much help. I only saw him from the back."

Prissy planted her paws on the detective's pants leg. He picked her up and tucked her in close while rubbing her head. "You'd be surprised."

His ease with my fur baby didn't escape my attention. "Okay, let me know when you need me. I have a business in the Five Points area, so a little notice would be helpful."

He watched me for a moment, then flicked his gaze over to Mystery. With a concerned look, he asked, "Are you ladies, okay?"

Mystery blurted, "I don't know about Bree, but I'm like, one-hundred-percent freaked out, if you know what I mean."

Haddington nodded and with a reassuring tone said, "It's normal. Many people would be upset. After all, most folks don't see dead people every day."

Mystery looked over at me and opened her mouth to speak.

I shot her a zip-it look. The last thing I wanted this cop to know is I see earthbound spirits.

She closed her mouth and took a step back.

His gaze tracked the silent interchange. He cocked a brow, but before he could pursue the matter, Ricci called for him to come to the van across the street.

Haddington placed Prissy back on the sidewalk and smiled before saying, "Excuse me, ladies." He nodded toward me. "Call me if you remember anything?" He handed me his card before jogging toward his partner.

Mystery sidled closer. "I wish a hot man would smile at me like I was a beautiful red-headed goddess."

I cocked a brow. "You'd change your hair color?"

"If the guy was good looking enough, I'd consider dying it."

I flipped a dismissive hand. "He was being nice."

"I may not be psychic, but he's definitely interested in you. He didn't give *me* his card. If he asks you for a date, accept. That way you'll be able to wheedle information out of him to help solve this crime."

I took a step back. "Have you lost your ever-lovin' mind? You're freaked out about finding a dead body, and you want to investigate the crime? Seeing the dead and helping their spirits cross over doesn't qualify me to track down a cold-blooded killer." I pointed at her. "In case you've forgotten, running ghost tours and selling ghost-hunting and spy equipment doesn't qualify you, either."

She crossed her arms and jutted her chin forward. "Bree, are you telling me that murdered woman won't need our help to cross over? How can that haint manage it with her killer running free? Besides, I'm like you. I can't resist a mystery."

"What makes you think she's earthbound? Not every murder victim becomes a ghost." I looked toward the crime scene. To my surprise, Victoria Spellman's ghost was floating erratically above the bushes, holding her head. "Good grief, you're right. She's a ghost."

Mystery looked confused. "When did her haint show up? You didn't mention her when we found the body."

"I suspect she was trying to gain enough power to manifest. She would need a source of energy to do so. Our emotional distress probably helped to fuel her."

"Girl, you make her sound like a supernatural battery pack."

"I think of her like a wireless receiver that stores energy, sorta like a rechargeable battery." I shrugged. "It's a simplified version of how spirits operate."

Eyes widening, Mystery asked, "Is her haint scary looking?"

"She looks to be about five-foot-six and toothpick thin. Her hair is gray, styled in a pageboy that frames her narrow face, which has thin lips and a long nose. There's nothing scary about her at present. She looks confused. I hope it stays that way."

"Are you worried that could change?" she asked, looking concerned.

I nodded. "Right now, she's fading in and out like a faulty electrical circuit. If she finds a good source of emotional energy, she could grow powerful. From what you said, she wasn't a nice person.

Personality traits can continue into ghosthood."

"Lordy, I hope you're wrong, because she was a piece of work."

CHAPTER 3

Struggling to fight off my pre-lunch slump, I slit open a box of lingerie from France and handed it to my assistant to unpack. Kaya Mendez is a petite, second-generation Mexican-American with plump cheeks, doe-like brown eyes, and long dark hair that she usually wears in a sassy, swinging ponytail.

"Do you want these on the bra rack up front or the one toward the back?" Kaya asked.

"The front one. These are too lovely to hide in the back. In two weeks, we'll shift them to a new location. My plan for product promotion is to move the merchandise in the store on a regular basis."

"Why?"

"It makes it look to our regular customers like we always have new merchandise. How did your statistics exam go?" I asked, before standing and brushing the dust off the knees of my slacks.

Kaya's a University of Alabama Huntsville student who's majoring in accounting. Besides helping to run the store, she also does my bookkeeping. It's a win-win for us both, since she plans to add this employment to her resume after graduation.

"I think I aced it." She crossed her fingers before grabbing the box and heading to the front.

I hadn't told her about the dead body I'd found that morning, nor does she know about my gifts. She's superstitious, so I didn't want to make her uncomfortable. One of my major fears as a psychic is rejection by people who don't understand my gifts or my goal in life. It may sound silly, but it's a real concern to me.

I'm not sure what was worse in my childhood, trying to cope with seeing ghosts or dealing with other people's unkind words and reactions to my abilities. I still remember what happened when I was five, after I told my closest friend about the ghost floating in the corner of my room. She blabbed about it to all the other kids. Over the years, my nicknames have included ghost girl, spooky girl, and weirdo, among others. The consequences spread past the name calling. Many parents wouldn't allow their children to play with me.

That was when my mom took me to the Humane Society shelter to pick out a puppy. That loving, yet fierce, little dog saved my mental health and guarded me from the spooks. I've often wondered if my parents' arguments over Speckles was the final crack that collapsed their earthquake of a marriage.

Sighing, I glanced around to see what needed to be done. My shop and Mystery's have the same basic layout. The space is a large rectangle. A long hall divides the front and rear areas of the store, and all the interior doorways open onto it. The back section contains the storeroom, two small offices, a restroom, and a large room that I use as a combination lunch and conference room.

The front retail area has huge plate glass windows across the front. Large gold script lettering announces **Lingerie** on one window and **Chocolates** on the other. The centered front entrance says **Chocolates and Delights**.

The other three walls have counters with locked drawers or cabinets underneath. Lingerie is displayed on the counters and walls, along with some large color photos of models displaying my wares. In the center is a smaller rectangle of four glass display cases that holds chocolates from around the world. This is where my register is located. The rest of the area is full of racks holding all the pretty lingerie and support garments a lady needs to feel special and look awesome.

I changed out all the electrical fixtures for spot lighting and an assortment of crystal chandeliers I'd purchased at yard sales and the Habitat for Humanity ReStore.

A recording of French instrumental music played softly in the background while I sprayed vinegar and water on a display case, and wiped.

Prissy, who was in her bed on a low shelf under the register, sneezed. She stood and shook her head, clanging the tags on her collar.

"How is your grandmother?" I asked Kaya. She'd recently been hospitalized with pneumonia.

"Since she's been home, she's improved and is almost well." Kaya chuckled. "She thought the cooks were trying to poison her with the bland hospital food."

I laughed. "I've never met anyone who likes hospital food."

"Me either. Papá smuggled hot sauce into her room." She giggled. "Mamá told him he has to confess this to the Padre because he broke the hospital rules." She made the sign of the cross. Her family are devout Catholics.

Kaya fluttered her eyelashes. "I've met the cutest guy in my accounting principles class."

"I thought you liked Zach Stanner."

Zach is an electrical engineering major at UAH who works part-time for Mystery as an installation tech.

She looked down, her cheeks turning pink. "I do, but he acts like I'm invisible or something."

I finished wiping and said, "Let me guess, the new guy is blond with blue eyes."

Her eyes widened. "You must be psychic! How did you know?"

I inwardly cringed at the psychic reference. "All the guys you like match that description."

"Oh." She shrugged. "I guess everyone has a type."

I thought of Detective Chris Haddington. *He is definitely my type.*

Thinking of him led to remembering the murder, which sent a flurry of questions racing through my mind. *What type of person was Victoria Spellman? Why was she in the churchyard? Was she murdered there, or was she murdered elsewhere and then dumped behind those bushes? More importantly, who killed her, and why? So many dang questions.*

The strange thing was, I felt an intense need to solve the mystery of Victoria Spellman's death. Part of it was my insatiable love for solving puzzles and mysteries of any kind, but I also had a feeling that solving her murder would be the only way to help her spirit cross over.

I was having second thoughts about keeping the murder from

Kaya. She and Jasmine Williams, who works for Mystery, are friends. Not only is Jasmine too nosy for her own good, but she isn't the type to keep this type of juicy tidbit to herself.

"Kaya, I hope this doesn't creep you out, but I think you need to know what happened before work this morning."

She stopped what she was doing, and her gaze focused on me like a laser beam.

I told her about the incident, minus the ghost aspects. The longer I spoke, the wider her eyes became.

She rushed over and gave me a quick hug. "How awful. Are you okay?"

I nodded, touched by her concern.

I'm pretty much on my own. Dad lives in town, but I hardly ever see him. He remarried a boring zealous woman who treats me like I'm the Devil's spawn. My mother resides in Savannah, Georgia, one of the most haunted cities in the South.

"Kaya, I'm going next door. I think I need to talk this through with Mystery and make sure she's all right."

She offered an encouraging smile. "I've got things covered."

"Call me if you need me. I'm taking Prissy." I hooked her up. "Let's make a little pit stop first."

When we stepped outside, the breeze fluttered my pink awning with bold black script that reminded me of my trip to Paris several years ago. We turned right and strolled to one end of the strip mall, past a small pet supply business and a musical instrument store. Prissy dug in, pulling me to the small patch of grass. After a thorough sniffing, she circled twice and then did her business.

We backtracked to The Mystery Shop. When I opened the door, the merry jingle of a bell announced my arrival, and the smell of strong coffee gave my flagging spirits a lift.

"Girl, I wondered when you'd show up. It's not every ole day we find a dadgum murder victim." Mystery looked down at Prissy. "I see you brought my favorite fur baby."

"Mystery, I've got all these questions and no answers," I said, pulling my hair off my neck into a ponytail, before releasing it.

Jasmine walked in from the employee area in the back. She also attends UAH and is in one of Kaya's classes. I dread the day that Jasmine slips and asks Kaya how she likes working for a psychic.

"Hey, Prissy!" Jasmine reached down.

My dog pranced over, tail wagging to greet her.

"You're such a good girl. Yes, you are." Jasmine gave her a thorough loving and tucked her under an arm.

Tight jeans and a form-fitting top made Jasmine hard to miss. She has a male-magnet body and a perfect sepia complexion. Her physical assets camouflage a mind that is wicked smart when it comes to electronics and computers, but defective when picking the right guy.

She comes by both honestly. Her mother, Chantel, has married some doozies and recently kicked out her fourth husband.

"Are y'all okay?" Jasmine asked, her brow furrowing. "You both look punked-out." She pinned Mystery with a knowing look. "Your needs aren't getting met. I can tell 'cause you have that deprived look."

I looked at Mystery, trying to decide what made her look needy.

Do I look deprived, too?

Jasmine gyrated her neck from side to side in a way that would send me to a chiropractor. "You'd be happier if you were dating some nice guy."

Mystery stiffened and raised her chin. "My needs are just fine, thank you very much."

Jasmine then cast her assessing gaze on me. She eyed me up and down as if doing a CT scan for emotional deprivation. "Want me to set you both up on some dating sites? Some of my friends' moms are using them."

The thought horrified me more than any apparition. "Absolutely not!" My brief experiences on a dating site were a nightmare of epic proportions. The mere memories caused me to shudder.

Mystery pointed at Jasmine. "Don't you dare."

The doorbell jingled, cutting our conversation short. A haggard-looking young woman entered carrying a squirming toddler.

Mystery greeted her with a welcoming smile.

The dark-haired, cherub-cheeked tyke grabbed the jingling bell on the door in a vise-like grip and wouldn't let go.

"Gabriel, stop it!" The mother pried his chubby fingers loose before placing the boy down. He took off like a kid under the influence of high-octane cotton candy.

Jasmine handed me Prissy and leaped to supervise the future Olympic sprinter. How any kid could reach such an acceleration rate while wearing diapers was beyond my understanding.

I backed out of reach behind a counter. I didn't want him to spot Prissy.

In response to the customer's request, Mystery showed her a recording device to place in her husband's car. They discussed in hushed tones the woman's suspicions. Both women ignored the child, who ran laps around the store.

Sounds like another cheating husband. So sad. I could feel the waves of pain emanating from her.

In addition to my ability to see ghosts, God has blessed me with clairsentience, the ability to receive intuitive messages through feelings, emotions, or physical sensations. I call it "empathy on a rocket launcher," an appropriate definition considering I was born in the Rocket City.

I entertained myself by watching Jasmine's useless attempts to corral the child. Before she could stop him, he'd smeared an enormous quantity of snot across the front of one of the clean glass cases full of expensive infrared cameras.

I winced. *Yuck. Glad I don't have to clean that glass.*

Purchase completed, the mother clutched the bag close to her chest, took a deep breath, and visibly steeled herself before taking Gabriel by the hand.

He shrieked like his pull-ups were on fire all the way out the door. We watched his teary, red-faced tantrum until his mother managed to wrestle him into a car seat.

"Wow! Remind me to never have kids." Jasmine looked rattled. She was still panting from the chase.

Mystery patted her shoulder. "Not all kids are holy terrors, but Gabriel sure wasn't an angel. I need coffee."

"I'll join you," I said. Mystery bought a Keurig coffee machine that puts my office coffeemaker to shame. *I need to unclench my purse strings and visit Costco next time they are on sale.*

We'd returned to the front of the shop with our mugs of java when the jarring sounds of squealing tires and honking horns drew our attention. I craned my neck for a better view out the windows.

"What in Sam Hill is going on?" Mystery asked, placing her mug on the counter in front of her.

A white Volvo SUV shot in front of a UPS truck and rocketed straight for The Mystery Shop.

I backed toward the rear of the store, sloshing hot coffee over my hand as I went.

"Sweet Baby Jesus!" Mystery stood frozen as the car raced toward her.

Jasmine looked up from the counter she was cleaning. "What the heck?"

"Run!" I yelled.

Jasmine dropped her spray bottle of cleaner and shot around the end of the counter, screaming as she ran toward me.

The Volvo screeched into the parking space that Gabriel's mom had just vacated and rocked to an abrupt stop.

From somewhere behind me, Jasmine said, "At least she didn't drive through the front window like that old fool did in October. People need to quit driving when they can't tell the difference between the accelerator and the brake."

I nodded, clutching my chest as though I could hold in my pounding heart. "That was a mess."

Mystery said, "Be glad you weren't here when the drunk guy drove through it last month. That one was even worse. I'm sick and tired of filing insurance claims."

"I'm tired of sweeping up broken glass." Jasmine turned and glared at me. "Why doesn't anyone drive through your windows?"

I shrugged. I didn't mention that I pray for protection around my store.

My phone rang. I placed it on speaker. Sounding breathless, Kaya said, "Brianna, did you see that car rocketing in just now? If she comes in here to shop, will you come back? She could be high or something."

"Yeah, I thought Mystery's window was a goner for sure. Don't worry. I've got you covered."

I put my phone away and peered through the pollen-caked windows at the woman in the Volvo.

Volvo Woman tucked a strand of her long, blonde hair behind one ear and sat looking somewhat dazed as she inspected the shop.

The scalloped edges of Mystery's new black-and-white striped awning fluttered, creating a dancing pattern of sun and shade on the window's signage. After the latest drive-through, Mystery had replaced the clear plate glass windows with tinted ones like mine, to lessen the intense rays of the sun. The art student she hired used bold white lettering. The door says THE MYSTERY SHOP. The window to the left says GHOST TOURS and PARANORMAL INVESTIGATIONS, and the one on the right says SPY EQUIPMENT and PARANORMAL DEVICES. After she purchased the store, she crammed a bunch more merchandise inside, but she still only has so much window space. The spy and security equipment remain her best sellers. She discovered early that the supernatural didn't pay all the bills, although she tells me the ghost tours are picking up.

"Volvo Woman looks glued to the seat." I ran a hand through my hair. "I wonder if she's okay?"

Jasmine returned to the front and pulled a phone from her back jeans pocket. "Good one, Bree. Who knows? Volvo woman drives like she's demon-possessed!" She leaned against a display case and checked her phone while gnawing on a thumbnail.

Mystery shrugged. "Right now, she's gripping the steering wheel like a life preserver. At least she can't cause a wreck while she's parked. Who knows, Kaya may be right, she could be planning to visit your place next door."

Jasmine smirked. "Yeah, like she has a lingerie emergency."

Mystery chuckled at her quip. "She could be in chocolate withdrawal. I know how bad that feels."

The Mystery Shop sits between my store and Craft's Antiques. The old-fashioned shopping strip is separated from the street by a row of front-space parking. Past the antique store is a gift shop, and past that is a Thai restaurant named Garuda, which makes the seventh establishment. The strip is part of the Five Points shopping district, which lies nestled between the elegant homes of Huntsville's oldest historic district and a neighborhood of quaint cottages that aspire to become future landmarks.

Jasmine glanced out the window and frowned. "I think Volvo Woman's out there mooching our free WiFi. See, she has her phone out." She rolled her eyes. "The rich ones can be so chintzy."

I bit my lip to keep from chuckling. Jasmine is the worst WiFi scrounger I know. She's on a tight budget and does everything possible to stretch her paycheck.

Mystery tapped her long, bejeweled nail on the glass countertop. "Nope. Look at her face. She's working up her courage." She turned and crossed her arms. Clearing her throat, she shot a disapproving glare at Jasmine's phone. "Aren't you supposed to be working?"

Jasmine looked up and jammed her phone into a pocket. "Sorry. Guess I better finish cleaning up this mess in case she comes in to shop." She sprayed cleaner on the glass case Gabriel had smeared, pausing to sneeze as the vinegar smell filled the air. Then she scrubbed away the impressive array of snot art the runny-nosed toddler had finger-painted on the glass.

Nodding with satisfaction at her efforts, Jasmine grabbed the bottle of cleaner and tucked it behind the counter. "Look, Volvo Woman moved. Maybe she's decided to come in."

Curious, I again turned to look out the window.

The blonde stepped out of the vehicle, glanced left, then right, and scurried toward the shop's entrance. The bell on the door jingled as she entered. Her floral scent wafted in along with the warm breeze.

Mystery's polished smile showed no hint of the uneasiness I sensed from her.

"Welcome to The Mystery Shop, Sugar. What do you need? A haunted tour? Maybe you want me to investigate your haunted house?"

Volvo Woman's red-rimmed blue eyes seemed to dominate her pale face. Her distress was more powerful than her floral scent. "Dr. Stone sent me." Her gaze darted around the store. "She said you could help me with my, um, problem."

Dr. Charlene "Charlie" Stone, a local psychologist, has a private practice and does part-time forensic profiling for the Huntsville Police Department. She's gained some measure of fame after assisting the police in the apprehension of several killers. What she doesn't advertise is that on occasion, she can see ghosts.

My, my. This just got more interesting. I placed Prissy on the floor and stepped closer.

Mystery rested her elbows on the counter. "Doc is good people. What's up?"

Volvo Woman moved closer to the counter and lowered her voice. "I have an unusual situation. I almost didn't come inside because you'll think I'm stark raving mad."

Mystery flashed her a kind smile. "Well, Sugar, you came to the right place. We get unusual situations in here all the time."

I chuckled to myself. *If the walls could talk.*

"Mystery Jones." Straightening, she offered a hand over the counter. "I own this here joint, such as it is." She gave Volvo Woman's hand a reassuring squeeze.

"Tiffany Blake."

Mystery leaned on the counter and pointed at Jasmine. "This is Jasmine Williams. She's my computer expert. The queen of the machine." She nodded toward me. "This is Brianna Kelly, who owns the shop next door."

Tiffany's eyes widened, her open-mouthed stare settling on Jasmine's hair. It was cut short on the sides and back, providing a dark platform for the prominent frizzy top, which she had just dyed an obnoxious clown-red. It was purple the week before. I suspect she picks the colors she does to aggravate her mom.

"What?" Jasmine did her neck thing signaling her disapproval. "You ain't never seen red hair before?"

"Not quite like yours. I didn't mean to be rude, but I'm a little out of sorts. You see, I-I'm afraid I'm losing my mind. That's why I saw Dr. Stone." She gestured toward the Volvo. "I called her to bolster my courage, so that I could come inside."

I was glued-to-the-floor curious.

Mystery said, "Now take a few deep breaths, Sugar. Would you like to talk in private?"

"No, this is fine. It's just us ladies."

Mystery nodded. "If anyone comes in, we'll move the conversation to the conference room."

Tiffany gave Mystery a distracted nod and turned to look around the shop again. I noticed that her gaze lingered on the devices in the glass cases. "This place is bigger inside than it appears from the outside. It looks high tech."

With a pleased look, Mystery said, "I bought the business a year ago from a private detective who ran a spy shop. I've updated some of the stock. When you live in a city full of scientists, engineers, and computer nerds, it's a must to stay current on technology."

I took the opportunity to size up Mystery's potential new client. She reminded me of a guitar string stretched to capacity and ready to break. The energy emanating from her felt like a vibrating electrical charge, sending tendrils of her anxiety along my nerve endings. The itchy sensation was overloading my system.

I took a few steps back, inhaled a deep breath, and raised my shields. I do this often when hounded by emotionally overwrought people or spirits with poor boundaries. It's a survival mechanism Mom taught me.

Mystery said, "Now start at the beginning. Jasmine, pull up a stool for Ms. Blake. This could take a while."

"Call me Tiffany." She perched on the stool that Jasmine had brought and fiddled with her wedding ring. "How do you know Dr. Stone?"

"Doc helped my second cousin get her life straightened out. Monique was headed down the slippery slide to destruction when Doc helped her get clean and sober. She went the extra mile, even came to do an intervention at Monique's home to convince her to go into an inpatient program."

"That's impressive," Tiffany said, her shoulders lowering back to a normal state.

"Later on, I sold Doc the video equipment that helped catch a guy who was stalking her. Jasmine and my technician, Zach, installed everything."

At the mention of her name, Jasmine stood taller.

Tiffany placed her Prada purse on the counter. "I hope between Dr. Stone's services and y'all's, my life will get back on track. I have a definite man problem and possibly...," she leaned forward and whispered, "a ghost in my house."

That caught my attention. What kind of ghost? I moved closer.

"Huh. Like I said, you're in the right place if you have a haint." Mystery gave me a conspiratorial wink before saying, "Tell us your story and start at the beginning."

Tiffany continued to finger her wedding band. "Ten years ago, I inherited my family home in the Twickenham District. Wendell and I moved in and did some minor renovations. We were happily married until he died three years ago. You couldn't ask for a better husband." Tiffany's eyes glistened with tears. "It was so quick. When he left to go to work, all was right in my world. That night, a policeman came to the door and told me he'd been in a car accident and had died on the scene."

Mystery patted her hand. "Sorry to hear that, Sugar. I'm a widow, myself."

I slid the box of tissues closer, glad that I had my shields in place, or I'd be crying with her.

"Then you know how it feels," Tiffany said.

"Sugar, when my Tyree died, it felt like someone reached inside me and ripped out my heart."

Tiffany nodded. "Wendell was such a good man, which makes what's happening now feel even worse." Tiffany pulled a tissue and dabbed under her lashes. "I love my home. It's always been such a comfort...until lately."

"Is it one of those historic houses with the little signs out front that tells the ... whatchamacallit?" Jasmine asked.

"Provenance," Mystery said.

I added, "Whatchamacallit is a candy bar."

Tiffany sniffled and nodded. "Yes, it's one of those. That's the other reason I'm off-kilter today. One of my neighbors, Victoria Spellman, was found murdered at the church downtown. You know, the one with the tall steeple. I heard somebody shot her on the front stairs of the church."

My stomach tumbled like an Olympic gymnast. My voice sounded raspy when I said, "Mystery and I found her."

Tiffany gasped. One hand shot up to cover her mouth.

"Say what?" Jasmine took a step forward. "Y'all didn't say anything about finding a dead body."

I ignored Jasmine's comment.

"Was it awful?" Tiffany asked with a mixed tone of curiosity and horror.

I picked up my fur baby for comfort. "It wasn't good. To be precise, my dog, Prissy, found her behind the bushes that grow along the side of the church. I don't know where you heard your information, but it's wrong. I didn't see any gunshot wounds, but she did have a gash on her head. Looked like someone hit her to me, but I'm not a medical examiner." I flipped my hair over one shoulder. "What do you know about her?"

Tiffany cast a quick glance toward the door before she leaned closer and lowered her voice. "I hate to speak ill of the dead, but I'm not surprised somebody murdered her."

A chill flowed over me like an icy rain, causing an involuntary shiver. "Why?" I asked, my curiosity piqued.

"Victoria was a first-rate busybody and tart as an unripe persimmon to boot. There's a rumor she used what she learned to blackmail folks into doing what she wanted. According to the

Camellia Express, that's how she landed the presidency on the Historic Preservation Board. It controls what homeowners in the Twickenham District can and can't do to their homes."

Jasmine did her neck thing. "What the heck is the Camellia Express? I know the camellia is Alabama's state flower, but I've never heard of this other thing."

"It's the nickname for the underground information network in the historic district. Not much happens that doesn't get discussed." Tiffany winked. "We're a gossipy bunch."

"If your information about the murder came from that source, it proves it's not always accurate," I said, leaning back against a counter. "Has anyone had any recent tiffs with Victoria that you know about?"

"The list is long." She crossed her arms. "Even my husband, Jason, threatened to sue her because she wanted to block our plans for a patio extension and fountain in our back garden." She huffed, "I'm the secretary on the preservation board, but that woman still gave us grief."

"Surely there's one or two people who hated her more than the rest?" I asked, beginning to feel the enormity of the task to help this ghost.

"According to the local gossip, her biggest row is with Katie Abernathy," Tiffany said.

I straightened. "Tell me about it."

"Katie and Victoria have been in a feud about Katie's Yorkshire terrier, Phoebe, for years. The situation escalated when Victoria started calling the police and animal control."

Jasmine's brows bunched with clear disapproval. "Why has she been picking on poor little Phoebe?"

"They're next-door neighbors. Katie walks the little dear every morning and afternoon. Victoria claimed Phoebe did her business on her lawn numerous times. I've seen Katie clean up after her dog, so I'm not convinced. Lots of folks walk their dogs in our neighborhood."

"Unless she didn't clean up Victoria's yard out of spite," Jasmine said with a smirk.

I cocked a brow. "That's it? Doesn't sound like a good reason to kill a person."

"Victoria is…was a stickler for the rules. Of course, the dog issue was only the Hollandaise sauce on the broccoli." Tiffany shifted on the stool and crossed one leg over the other. "There's a long list of spats over this and that between the two women."

"You've given me something to think about," I said. *Perhaps Mystery's right. Maybe we do need to investigate this murder. Based on what I'm hearing, Victoria was a doozie when she was alive, and she may become a troublesome spirit. She'll probably stick around until her murderer is caught.* I tapped my chin with a forefinger. *After all, Prissy and I did find the body.*

Mystery tapped her finger on the glass counter and looked impatient. This is interesting, but what did you want to see me about?"

Tiffany licked her dry lips and then continued. "I remarried a year ago." She shook her head. "Big mistake."

We all leaned closer and asked in unison, "Why?"

Tiffany exhaled a sigh drenched with regret. "Jason seemed nice at first. He whisked me into a whirlwind romance and proposed to me in Paris. I got swept up in the fantasy and said, 'yes.'"

"Brilliant," said Jasmine. "That's like, major romantic."

Tiffany shrugged and fingered the tissue. "I thought so at the time. How could I say no, with Jason on one knee on the top floor of the Eiffel Tower at sunset?" She held her wedding rings out for Jasmine to see. The two-carat ensemble twinkled. "He even arranged for flowers and a bottle of champagne with two glasses. It was straight out of a romance novel."

"My mama would say Jason swept you off your feet," Mystery said.

Jasmine slipped into the back and returned with a bottle of water, which she placed in front of Tiffany. "It's not champagne, but it's cold and wet, and you look thirsty."

"Thanks, my mouth is dry as a boll of cotton." She uncapped it and took a swallow. "After the honeymoon, Jason wasn't so nice."

"What did he do?" I scraped a stool over the tile floor and perched.

Tiffany scrunched her face in apparent concentration. "It started with little things. You know, small, nasty putdowns in private."

Jasmine frowned and leaned in closer. "Yeah, like what?"

"It was mainly a constant barrage of remarks like, 'I can't believe you did something so stupid,' or 'Only a nitwit would say something like that.' Then he began to say meaner things to me in front of our friends and his business associates. Jason's an attorney, so we attend all these social functions." Tiffany looked down at her clenched hands.

I felt the heat of anger rising to my face. "How long has this verbal abuse been going on?"

"It started a month after we married."

"So, he's been dissing you all this time?" Jasmine asked. Her brown eyes darkened to black.

"She means he was disrespectful," Mystery said, shooting Jasmine *the look*. I don't know where she learned it, but it can sear flesh off bones.

Tiffany looked a tad confused, but nodded. Tears once again glistened in her eyes. "The last couple of months, Jason has started drinking more and coming home late. He says he's working, but he didn't work that late when we were dating. I'm sure he's having an affair, but I need solid proof."

"Do you suspect someone in particular?" Mystery asked, pulling her notepad closer.

"My best guess is his new paralegal, Sierra Locke, but I'm not certain." She reached for the crumpled tissue and blotted under her lashes.

Mystery jotted down the name. "What else is going on?"

Tiffany gulped more water. "Well, I've been feeling kinda depressed lately. Jason's been calling me more names, like 'crazy' and 'loony' ever since I accused him of having an affair. I know it sounds silly, but the constant haranguing is wearing me down."

Mystery reached over and patted her hand again. "Sugar, that would wear anyone down."

"True." I steepled my fingers. "Where does the ghost come into the equation?" Maybe there's more than one. Jasmine would love it. A true ghostaholic, she's read tons of information about earthbound spirits. Too bad a good bit of it isn't true.

Tiffany leaned in again and lowered her voice. "Two weeks ago, strange things started happening in the house."

Wide-eyed, Jasmine moved closer and whispered, "Yeah? What?"

Why is everybody whispering? I mused. Tiffany seems more ashamed of a possible haunting than her husband's bad behavior.

"Noises, like doors opening and closing during the night."

Excitement shot through my body like static electricity. Sounds like a ghost. "Anything else?"

"Things aren't in their usual places. It's like someone keeps moving things out of place all over the first floor of the house."

I exchanged a what-do-you-think glance with Mystery and Jasmine.

Mystery shrugged.

"Have you seen these objects move?" Jasmine asked, her eyes bright with curiosity.

"No. I come downstairs in the morning and find them out of place." Tiffany ran both hands through her hair and tugged. "I'm afraid I'm losing my mind."

Mystery patted her arm. "Doc wouldn't send you to me if she thought you were ready for a mental hospital. Has anything like this ever happened before?"

"No."

"I'm not a licensed private detective, but we can run background checks or set up spy equipment for you," Mystery said.

I knew Mystery had to be careful not to cross any lines, since unlike her former boss, she's not a licensed private investigator. When she purchased the store from her, she inherited all the equipment, search engines, and disguises, but there are legal limits she can't cross.

"Jasmine will give you a copy of our contract and some forms to fill out about Jason and Sierra. Once she has all the data, she'll do her magic with the computer. When do you want us to start checking your house to see if it's haunted?" She pulled out her trusty black appointment book from under the counter and grabbed a pen.

"Jason's going to a legal conference in Nashville, Tennessee, this coming Monday. He'll be gone until Friday. I think the weasel may be taking Sierra with him because he didn't invite me like usual." Tiffany looked at Mystery with pleading eyes. "Can't you set up some spy equipment in his hotel room to catch him?"

She nodded while writing notes in the schedule book. "Like I said, I'm not a detective, but I can set up spy equipment at your request."

Tiffany nodded. "Good. I've spoken to an attorney. Some video or photos would be best."

Jasmine spoke up, excitement dancing in her eyes. "If you're interested in learning more about hauntings, the Rocket City Paranormal Society is having a newcomers' meeting here tonight. Brianna will be talking about earthbound spirits."

Tiffany's head whipped in my direction. "Are you a psychic?"

I nodded. "I try to keep a low profile."

She twirled her wedding ring again. "I guess it would be good to learn more about ghosts, since my house may be haunted. What time is the meeting?"

"Eight. We close at seven, so it gives us time to set up," Jasmine said.

"Tiffany, I've scheduled you. The conference should give us plenty of time to get the goods on Jason and check out your possible haunting while he's out of the house." Mystery leaned closer with a conspiratorial smile. "With your permission, here's what we're gonna do."

CHAPTER 4

Tiffany backed out of the parking space like a robber from a bank heist being chased by the cops.

A Volkswagen Beetle swerved to avoid ramming the Volvo and beeped its squeaky horn.

I winced, feeling my stomach contract with disbelief. "Tiffany didn't even look before she backed up."

Mystery shook her head. "If she keeps driving that way, she's not gonna live long enough to pay my bill."

"She's driving a Volvo. They have great safety ratings," said Jasmine. "Man, she didn't even flinch when you told her our rates." A Cha-ching grin spread across her face while she did a happy dance. "I love rich clients."

"I love paying the rent on time." Mystery rubbed the back of her neck.

"Since I'll be consulting on the haunting aspect, I'm looking forward to the commission check." I lowered my shields. While they protect me, they do require an energy output that is fatiguing.

Jasmine cocked her head. "Brianna, why do you keep such a low profile about your psychic gifts?"

I held Jasmine's gaze and used my *this-is-serious-business* tone of voice. "If you envy me for my gifts, Jasmine, you shouldn't. I've learned the hard way that a lot of people aren't comfortable with them. My store is how I make a living, and I don't want to scare off potential customers. Some folks might see my God-given talents to help earthbound spirits cross over as evil. Others would think I'm plumb crazy. This could not only affect my sales, but even who would want to work for me."

"With her business, Bree's right to keep a low profile. Now, if she owned this place, it would be an asset." Mystery shot me a concerned look. "I'm feeling a bit uncomfortable about this case. I'm not a PI." She tapped her fingers on her display case like a hyperactive woodpecker.

Jasmine waved a dismissive hand. "We've set up spy equipment for folks in the past. Besides, how can investigating a naughty ghost be much different than checking out a wayward spouse? They're both misbehavin'." Jasmine sharpened her grin and leaned against a counter. "Since Tiffany's gone, you can answer the question I had before that snotty demon toddler came in with his mom." She shook her head with amazement. "I never knew a kid could scream so loud."

"What question?" Mystery feigned ignorance and wandered toward the other side of the store.

Jasmine cocked a hip. "When are you going to start dating again? I'm not trying to be nosy or anything, but don't you two ever get…you know?"

"What?" Mystery asked.

"Lonely." Jasmine turned and fastened her gaze on me like Velcro. "You're just as bad. Girl, you're hot with that mass of red hair and those green eyes. You should have men lining up around the block to go out with you. Don't you get lonesome, too?

"Why would I? I've got Prissy."

Hearing her name, the dog trotted over to me, her tail fanning the air. I scooped her up. "This little tail-wagger is pure unconditional love."

"Yeah, she's great, but don't you ever miss, you know, a guy?" Jasmine gave a hip wiggle.

I pretended not to see the suggestive body gesture and clipped on the dog's leash in case I needed to make a quick escape.

Mystery crossed her arms. "Sugar, you ask too many personal questions."

"Come on, Mystery. It's been almost two years since Tyree's death. Don't you miss having a guy around?"

"Sugar, are you going to bug me about this again? How many

times do I have to tell you I don't need another man in my life?"

Jasmine pushed out her lower lip, "If it weren't for a man, you wouldn't be born, and I wouldn't be working for such a pittance."

The word-of-the-day calendar Mystery had given Jasmine on her twenty-first birthday sat on the counter near me. Pittance was today's word.

I could tell by the tightening of Mystery's jaw that this was going to get interesting. Switching from defense to offense, Mystery crossed her arms and shot a hot glare of disapproval at her saucy employee to put her in her place.

"Girl, you've had some raises. Who else would've talked Vera into hiring you at sixteen? Who taught you about the spy equipment? Maybe I should've included some marketing lessons. If we don't get more business soon, you may be looking for employment instead of asking for a raise."

This surprised me. I knew the business was only a year old, but I didn't realize my friend was having financial woes.

With the persistence of a rabid terrier, Jasmine ignored Mystery's attempt to change the subject and returned to her interrogation. "You still haven't answered me. Don't you miss hot sex?"

"You should know by now that getting sweaty is not my thing," Mystery scoffed and flipped away the comment with a dismissive gesture. "That's your problem. You're too hung up on 'needing a man.' You don't need one if he's not good for you. You're smart and you can take care of yourself. Besides, the guys you've dated were pure trouble."

Uh, oh. Jasmine's jutting her chin. Not a good sign. I backed up to stay out of the fray and to avoid some of Jasmine's angry vibrations. That young woman has a heart as big as our solar system, but her fiery temper can burn like the sun.

Jasmine stood taller, raising her bosom like a shield. "Hey, they weren't all that bad."

Mystery held up an index finger. "First, there was DeWayne."

Jasmine's shoulders slumped and her anger faded. "I didn't know he was in trouble with the law. Honest."

Mystery held up a second finger. "Then, there was Marcus. What about him?"

"Stop." Jasmine held up both hands like a flag of surrender. "You've made your point. My picker's broken."

"Sugar, you're the Bermuda Triangle of Love. The only person I know who's worse at picking the wrong guy is your mother, Chantel, bless her heart."

"I have to agree." Jasmine's shoulders slumped even more. "Mom has married some losers."

"I don't mean any disrespect to you or your mother, but I want something better for you."

Jasmine heaved a dramatic sigh. "Don't think I'm not grateful for my job, because I am. I need a place without so much drama, which means I need more money. It's time. Besides, Mom's seeing a new loser. I didn't think she could do worse than Clarence, but this Damien guy doesn't even have a job." She walked over to the supply closet and put away the spray bottle. Her eyes widened with desperation. "He's always asking me for money."

I nodded my understanding and offered a conciliatory smile. "Now you know why we're so careful. Some of those guys on dating sites are scary." *She has no idea how creepy.*

"And married," Mystery said, before leveling a steady gaze toward Jasmine. "You should understand by now. I had a good man. He is the love of my life."

Jasmine pursed her lips before saying, "Was. Tyree *was* the love of your life. It's time to let go."

Her words were true.

Mystery's feelings flooded her face. She turned and strode toward the break room, blinking back the tears she clearly didn't want Jasmine to see. "I need more coffee. Keep an eye out for customers."

I placed Prissy in Jasmine's hands and followed my friend.

With a hand that she couldn't seem to will to stay steady, Mystery added cream to her mug of coffee. When she saw me, she said, "Heck, I thought I was past crying over that man."

We hugged. I stepped away. "She's right. It's time to let go and move forward with your life."

She frowned, puckering her brow. "Not you, too? Give me a break." She glanced at her watch. "It's time for the Adam Craft show. You gonna stay? The view's better from over here."

"Sure. Then I have to spell Kaya, so she can go to lunch." We returned to the front and I sat on the nearest stool, only to leap to my feet and rub my backside. Eww! Is this the stool Tiffany used?" It was vibrating with yucky energy, like someone had a nervous breakdown."

Mystery nodded. "That's the one. What's the problem? You saw what an emotional mess that poor woman was while she was here."

"Yeah, but I wasn't feeling it on a sensitive area." I glared at the stool that had given me the negative vibes. "The woman's energy reads like someone experiencing an emotional earthquake."

"I can't wait until we check out her haunted house," Jasmine said, bursting with enthusiasm.

"We don't know that it's haunted, yet." I pointed out the front window. "Mr. Craft sighting."

We lined up facing the street, ready to spy on Adam Craft, who owns the antique shop next door. Mr. Craft often contracts with Mystery to research certain antiques' ownership and to clear spirit freeloaders from objects he's purchased. That's where I've come in as a consultant.

Hawk-nosed with expressive brows like furry caterpillars, Craft moseyed out the door at the stroke of noon. Leaning on his ebony cane, he waited outside his door like an ancient wolf, ready to pounce on anyone willing to park in his reserved spaces. Garuda's volume of business at lunch and dinner gobbles up most of the parking. Only three designated spaces are allotted to each of the smaller stores. Mr. Craft guards his three with ferocity.

Within minutes, a carload of teens whipped into one of the slots in front of his store. They piled from the vehicle and headed toward Garuda.

"Come back here," Mr. Craft yelled, tapping his cane on one of the signs he'd installed. The sign warned, Violators Will Be Towed. "If you don't move this vehicle, it won't be here when you come back."

The teens laughed, and the driver shot him a rude gesture before continuing toward the restaurant.

Jasmine did her neck thing. "Oh, they shouldn't have done that. Mr. C will tow that car for sure now."

Mr. Craft watched them go, peering from under his brows. He pulled a phone from his suit pocket and spoke into it. After completing his call, he shuffled toward Mystery's shop.

We scrambled, and by the time he pushed open the door, we stood behind the counter wearing angelic expressions and pretending we weren't watching him.

He muttered, "Those kids have no respect." He made it to the counter and held on with bony fingers. "I want to show you my newest acquisition."

Mystery rushed to place a pad on the glass countertop so he wouldn't scratch it.

Mr. Craft placed his walking stick on the pad. The silver wolf's head atop the polished ebony cane gleamed under the fluorescent lights.

"Jasmine, get Mr. C a seat," Mystery said as she pulled her mug closer. Steam rose from it, spreading the pleasant aroma of coffee.

After he'd planted his backside on the stool Tiffany had used, Mr. Craft adjusted the knot of his tie to make sure it was straight. He didn't seem to noticed Tiffany's energy traces.

Lucky him.

The mingled scents of Old Spice and moth balls made my nose twitch. After glancing at him for permission, I caressed the gleaming surface of the wolf's head and smiled as its cold energy flowed into my hand.

"It's pure silver. Provenance goes back to the 1700's in Bulgaria. The legend is the owner used it during full moons to repel werewolves," Mr. Craft said with a twinkle in his eyes.

I removed my hand, which tingled. "Its energy is powerful." I winked and gave him a knowing grin. "And tonight's a full moon."

"Mystery, I came over to tell you the security floodlights y'all installed need to be adjusted. Can you send over Zach?" he asked.

Mystery picked up her phone. "I'll text him right now."

He turned and gave me a poor-pitiable-me, look as he rubbed his hip. "My arthritis has been kicking up lately. Brianna, will you take a photo of the plaque at Maple Hill Cemetery that lists the Alabama Governors buried there? It's for a Historical Society project."

"Sure Mr. C. I'll do it sometime this week, if that's okay?"

His smile creased his face. "No hurry. Thank you."

Yellow lights flashed outside the window.

Mr. Craft straightened and pulled his cane off the counter. "Excuse me, ladies. The tow truck I called has arrived. Leaning on his cane, he exited the shop and pointed at the teens' car.

The tow truck driver nodded and maneuvered his truck into position.

"Time to discuss this morning's, um, incident," I said, pulling my attention away from the drama outside the windows.

Jasmine's eyes grew round as she listened to our discussion.

When we finished rehashing what we'd seen, I said, "You're right, Mystery, we should investigate. I believe her spirit isn't going to be in a rush to cross over from what I've heard. I'm sure the church's priest won't want a disturbance during church services."

"I told you that haint might be a problem. You should have heard the way she was carrying on at that meeting when she was alive. She was downright rude and uppity."

Jasmine stepped forward. "If it's okay with Mystery, I can do research on the computer."

I nodded. "It will take a team effort to solve this, since I don't know what the heck I'm doing when it comes to an investigation." Seeing my opportunity for escape before Jasmine provided another needs assessment regarding my lackluster love life, I said, "Prissy will need a quick walk before Kaya leaves for lunch."

I made a beeline for the door and escaped outside, with Prissy scampering to keep up. I took her around back, where she sniffed the grassy area near the dumpster. A stiff breeze ruffled my hair, sending the smell of rotting fruit my way. *Phew. I'll be glad when they empty that stinky thing.*

A truck delivered a piece of furniture to Craft's Antiques next door. It looked like a 1950's table and chairs. A female specter decked out in classic sock hop apparel followed the furniture into Mr. Craft's storage area.

It won't be long before he contacts us to clear that ghost.

CHAPTER 5

After I closed my shop, I took Prissy home and fed her, before returning to Mystery's store. I needed to prepare for my presentation to the Rocket City Paranormal Society, known by its members as RCPS.

Jasmine followed me around the conference room, bubbling with excited chatter about the event. She paused and turned to locate Mystery's whereabouts before whispering, "This is the first time Mystery has sponsored an event like this or has allowed any of the general public beyond the retail showroom. She's worried it might be a mistake."

"Let's hope not," I said.

Mystery and I had assured Chantel that we wouldn't involve her daughter, in any paranormal work until she turned twenty-one. We'd kept the promise, despite Jasmine's constant pleas to participate in ghost investigations. When Mystery wouldn't bend on her promise, that girl haunted me worse than any ghost. The day after her twenty-first birthday, she confided to me that she'd joined the RCPS the night before.

I fiddled with the projector connected to my laptop and adjusted the image to better fit the screen. The light blinked on and off. "Don't get hinky on me," I said to the machine. It does this every time I use it. It's probably a loose wire, but if I didn't know better, I'd think it was possessed.

I'd given this presentation to most of the paranormal groups across North Alabama. Despite this, my stomach still felt like bats stirring to leave a cave.

I don't advertise my gifts, but word has spread across the small paranormal community of Alabama and Southern Tennessee. Most of that community also keeps a low profile to avoid harassment, with the exception of a few known attention-seekers, like a certain parapsychologist teaching at a nearby state university.

Mystery books our ghost investigation gigs, and we split the profits. The arrangement has suited us both. It allows me to separate what my dad calls my psychic mumbo jumbo from Chocolates and Delights, and she sells more ghost-hunting equipment.

With a loud clatter, Jasmine emptied part of a bag of ice into a large bowl and added tongs. "That should do it. We have water, soda, chips, cookies, and chocolate."

"Lordy, I can smell the chocolate from across the room. I hope I can resist until the break." Mystery eyed the treat table. "You know I'm a stress eater."

I chuckled. "If there were Thin Mint Girl Scout cookies over there, you'd be a goner."

Mystery's hand covered her throat. "So true. We'd have to walk four days next week to help me ward off the dreaded bubble butt."

My jaw dropped. "I have no responsibility for cellulite added to your backside by Thin Mint cookies. You'll need to contact your local Girl Scouts about that matter."

Jasmine looked at us like we were daft and shook her head.

Eddie Smithers walked in, disrupting the conversation. He's a mechanical engineer who works on Redstone Arsenal for a defense contractor. He serves as the RCPS's president in his spare time and is always the first to arrive. I suspect he was born on schedule.

Eddie had the unkempt look of a divorced man trying to adjust to the absence of a woman's touch. His wrinkled clothes stretched tight over his egg-shaped physique in some places, while hanging loose in others. He ran a hand through his thinning brown hair, which needed a trim, as he worked his way toward me. I could feel the amorous waves flowing from him.

His intelligent blue eyes sparkled with enthusiasm behind his steel-rimmed glasses. "Thanks so much for letting us meet here tonight." His smile revealed a space between his front teeth.

"You're welcome, but you need to thank Mystery."

When Mystery heard her name, she joined us. "Hey, Eddie. I have a new infrared camera in stock that you might want to see."

"Sure." He widened his smile. "RCPS would love to make this our regular meeting spot." He wiggled his brows, trying to seal the deal.

Mystery's smile tightened. "I don't know, Eddie. It makes for a long day." She rubbed her lower back. "We'll see how tonight goes, and I'll get back to you."

After he walked away, she whispered to me, "I hosted this meeting so Jasmine would stop hassling me. You know how she gets." She quirked a shoulder. "It doesn't hurt that the recruits often buy their ghost-hunting equipment from me."

"Sounds like a win-win situation."

"We'll see," she said.

Eddie looked around. "Jasmine, you did a fine job of setting this up. I appreciate it." He licked his chapped lips. "I've been at my wits' end since the divorce." His gaze slid over to me and stayed. "It's been a hard adjustment. I've been thinking about dating. It would be nice to find a lady who shares my interests."

His ears turned a bright pink. Shuffling to a nearby table, he pulled a pen from his pocket and placed it next to a legal pad.

"Can you help me make sure everyone signs in and provides their contact information?"

"Sure." Jasmine grabbed the pen, which had an image of the space shuttle on the barrel, and signed her name on the list with a flourish before adding the rest of the information.

Eddie looked at the cookies with interest. "I'm expecting a light crowd tonight, since none of the regulars are attending."

"Why not?" I asked.

"They're checking out a report of a haunted barn in Hazel Green. Please, don't mention it tonight. We kept it on the down-low because we don't want people trying to attend who haven't had our required training."

"What other training do your new recruits have, other than this one?"

"I teach a class on our rules and safety procedures before they can participate in an investigation."

"That sounds responsible. Ghosts can be dangerous." I turned in time to see Tiffany stroll in. I greeted her with a smile and wave.

"Glad you could make it, Sugar." Mystery handed her Eddie's pen. "Sign in for us."

Tiffany nibbled a piece of dry skin on her lower lip and glanced around the room. "I feel a little silly being here, but it's exciting to do something out of my comfort zone." She leaned closer, lowering her voice. "I hope to learn something to help with my situation."

Mystery patted her on the shoulder. "I'm sure you will."

Two men in their early twenties came in behind Tiffany, one tall with blond hair and the other a redhead with a medium build and wearing a Roll Tide, Alabama cap.

They were followed by a middle-aged woman with highlighted hair in a pageboy hairstyle that looked glued in place.

Jasmine once named me "the queen of descriptive monikers." Living up to the label, I mentally named the woman with highlighted hair, Hairspray.

I eyed the blond guy, who had swaggered into the room with his chin thrust forward and his chest puffed out, and nicknamed him Trouble. *I hope he doesn't ruin the meeting for everyone.* I could feel the negative energy flowing off him.

Unlike his friend, the guy in the Alabama cap emanated the excited energy of a true believer. I named him Bama.

Eddie started the meeting at eight on the dot. "Welcome to our new member meeting."

A flustered-looking girl in her late teens slipped into the nearest seat while Eddie gave his opening remarks. She had pink hair and a matching tee shirt and jewelry.

I'll call her Pinky.

"I'm going to lock the front door," Mystery whispered.

"Good idea. If anyone else wants in, they can knock," I said.

She returned when Eddie said, "Now I'll turn the program over to the most knowledgeable person I know when it comes to ghosts, North Alabama's own Ghost Wrangler, Brianna Kelly."

I inwardly cringed, and my face flushed hot. The fame-seeking paranormal psychologist called me that once, and it has stuck to me like gum in my hair. I hate the moniker. It makes it sound like I go around saddling ghosts.

After a splattering of applause, I looked into each person's eyes and said, "Raise your hand if you can see a ghost or hear its conversation?"

The audience looked at each other, but no one raised a hand.

I went on to explain that I was psychic and able to do both.

Hairspray asked in a soft voice, "Have you always been psychic?"

"Yes, it runs through the women on my mother's side of the family."

Eddie cocked his head the way Prissy does when she's curious. "Do you know if it's genetic? It would be cool if they could isolate the specific gene or genes for psychic ability."

I shrugged and raised my palms in a who-knows gesture. Desperate to get the subject off me and onto the presentation, I said, "I'm sure you'll agree people are different."

The audience nodded, except Trouble. He sat as stiff as if he'd been dipped in heavy starch.

"Since ghosts are dead people, they are also unique and tend to maintain the personality they had in life."

I clicked the remote in my hand to change slides. "I categorize earthbound spirits into three categories."

My PowerPoint slide showed:

> Intelligent haunting
> Residual haunting
> Poltergeist

"What's the difference?" Hairspray asked, her gaze focused on the screen.

"When there's an intelligent haunting, the ghost can communicate in some way. It may moan or move objects. I once had a ghost write a message on a dirty car window. When the spirit can communicate, it's easier to help him or her cross over, *unless* it's a malicious poltergeist."

Bama asked, "Are most of the hauntings you encounter intelligent hauntings?"

"Yes," I said.

Trouble mumbled under his breath and shook his head.

"So, what's a residual haunting?" Tiffany leaned forward and squinted at the screen.

My shoulders drooped. This type of haunting always makes me sad. "Unfortunately, we can't do anything to help the situation if it's residual."

"Why not?" Tiffany asked.

"It's like a continuous loop on a video." I made a circular motion with my index finger. "The images play over and over at a specific time or date. They're like ghostly movies imprinted on time." I paused before asking, "Has anyone ever been to the Gettysburg battlefield?"

Eddie shot his hand in the air.

"That's a perfect example," I said. "Parts of the skirmishes are seen or heard at the estimated time of the battle. It's like someone took a movie and replays a holographic image of it on the anniversary of the event. It was such a horrific experience that it's become a stain on reality."

"Wow," Bama said, staring at me with an expression of wonder on his face.

"It's a sad ghostly record of the past." I was pleased he understood that there are marvels of this world which many can't experience.

"What about the poltergeist?" Pinky asked.

"Poltergeist is German for a loud spirit. They're naughty, sometimes vicious ghosts who can levitate objects, move them, and make noises like knocking on doors. The most malevolent ones can hurt people if they're strong enough." I looked each participant in the eye. It was important for me to make this point. "Not all earthbound spirits are lost and looking for help to cross over. Some are dangerous. You'd be wise to keep that in mind while ghost hunting, and *never* do it alone."

Tiffany shuddered and rubbed her arms. "How?"

I paused for effect. I wanted them to understand this hobby can be as dangerous as chasing a tornado and just as unpredictable. "Poltergeists can throw objects that injure people. There have even been reports of ghosts tripping people, or pushing unsuspecting people down staircases. When I visited Savannah, Georgia, one of the tour guides told me it wasn't uncommon for the tourists to be pinched or bitten by some of the local ghosts."

Jasmine said, with a wistful expression, "I want to go there someday."

"That was the most haunted place I've ever visited. I couldn't walk a hundred feet in downtown Savannah without encountering a ghost or residual haunting."

Discussing the city made me miss Mom. I wish she hadn't moved there after I finished college. She felt a city that embraced its history and supernatural aspects offered her more acceptance and economic advantages. Unlike me, she doesn't keep a low profile.

The group stared at me with wide eyes and slack jaws, except for Trouble. The leer on his face brought my thoughts back to the present.

He gave me a bawdy wink. "Did any of the ghosts pinch you?"

I ignored his question and refused to meet his gaze.

Eddie glared at him, tapping his pen on the table.

Oh, boy. Time to switch gears.

I turned off the projector and said, "If you're not like me, your best bet to locate a ghost is some up-to-date, reliable technology. We are fortunate tonight that Mystery Jones, the owner of this store, has agreed to demonstrate some of her equipment." I swept my hand like a game show model toward my friend.

Mystery and Jasmine walked to the table she'd set up with some of the store's stock. She introduced Jasmine and picked up a box. "If you're on a tight budget or only want to dabble, this pre-boxed Ghost Hunting Kit may be all you need."

The box was black with dramatic swirls of red and had yellow lettering. A white cartoon ghost occupied the right bottom corner.

"It contains a low-cost thermometer and electromagnetic sensor, along with a guide to identify the different types of ghosts." She produced a knowing smile. "*However*, if you're interested in doing professional investigations, we do have a variety of more advanced products."

The way Mystery said that last line made it sound like only a fool would want the basic equipment.

Jasmine held up a device that was about the size of her hand. "This is The Ghost Meter."

Trouble squinted. "A ghost-what?" He rolled his eyes and nudged Bama. "You've got to be kidding!"

Uh, oh. I fixed my gaze on him as if I could will my words into his mind. *If you're smart, Trouble, you won't light that firecracker's fuse. You may find that Ghost Meter in a place you won't appreciate.*

Jasmine's jaw jutted forward. If it tensed any more, I could raise a garage door with it. "This isn't any ole meter. It's designed for professional paranormal investigations. You see, a ghost emits energy that produces an EMF. When one shows up, the LED light will come on." Jasmine pointed at the meter. "I can tell the strength of the ghost's EMF emission by how far this needle moves."

Trouble sat back and crossed his arms, looking unconvinced.

"What's an EMF?" asked Tiffany, stretching her neck to see the device.

Eddie stood and smiled. "I'll take this question, if you don't mind. An EMF, or electromagnetic field, is a radiation field that surrounds a moving electrical charge. Jasmine is correct that a ghost will produce an EMF that will vary according to the strength of the spirit. Keep in mind, an EMF meter will react to these fields whether emitted by appliances, x-ray machines, or thunderstorms producing lightning, as well as ghosts. That's why you want to use more than one detection device and be aware of atmospheric phenomena when you're trying to verify a true haunting."

Spoken like an engineer. Clear, concise, and above a few people's heads, I thought.

Jasmine and Trouble were still glaring at each other.

He shot her a rude gesture.

She took a step toward him, looking ready to launch the device at his head.

Mystery scowled at Trouble before reaching for the meter.

Jasmine yielded it with some reluctance.

Phew, that was close.

Proceeding as if Trouble weren't there, Mystery said, "The analog scale on this model measures electromagnetic fields from 0 to 5 milligauss."

Tiffany asked, "What's a milligauss?"

Eddie stood. "A unit of magnetic flux density equal to one-thousandth of a gauss."

Tiffany shook her head. "Sorry I asked."

The spirit I had seen following the 1950's dinette set into Craft's Antiques ghosted through the wall into the room. She wore a black skirt with a pink poodle on the front, bobby socks, and saddle oxfords. Her hair was pulled back into a ponytail. She seemed just as surprised to see all of us as I was to see her.

I walked over and gave Mystery a discreet nudge before saying, "Did y'all know a ghost just entered this room?"

"Right now?" she asked, her eyes widening, as the others started looking around the room.

I nodded. "Don't just stand there. Demonstrate the meter," I whispered.

"Shall we see what happens?" Mystery said with an enthusiastic tone.

Bama's eyes sparkled with excitement, but Trouble looked skeptical. Pinky paled and licked her fuchsia tinted lips. Hairspray kept touching her hair while shifting her gaze left and right. Tiffany's mouth stretched into a maniacal grin that looked part excited, part terrified.

Mystery switched on the meter. The EMF signal flew to five milligauss. She turned it so the group could see the readout.

Eddie's mouth gaped. "Wow, five milligauss! That's a strong signal."

With a squeaky voice, Tiffany asked, "Is it male or female?"

Mystery adopted a serious look, but a twitch at the corner of her mouth revealed her pleasure at everyone's reactions.

I described the Sock Hop Spirit as she floated closer to Mystery and leaned over to look at the meter.

Sensing the ghost, Mystery shivered and whirled around.

The Sock Hop Spirit frowned at her reaction.

I asked, "Have you noticed it's cool in here, and can you smell the ghost's perfume?"

Jasmine, who had goosebumps prickling her bare arms, sniffed the air.

"I smell it." Pinky shifted in her seat and rubbed her arms.

Several others nodded, but not Trouble.

Mystery picked up the next device, which was black with orange accents and buttons, and announced to get everyone's attention, "This is a Ghost Thermometer."

Everyone's gaze snapped back toward her.

Trouble put his hand on Bama's shoulder. "This is stupid. Let's go."

Bama shrugged off his hand and said in a low voice, "Go if you want, but I'm staying."

Jasmine's gaze shifted from Bama to Trouble. Her eyes narrowed as she did her neck thing.

Uh, oh. I know that look. I nudged Jasmine, who looked ready to rip Trouble's tongue out, and whispered, "Ignore him."

Mystery continued, "You turn the device on with this button, and the digital display shows you the temperature. That's a type K thermocouple sensor plugged into the top." She held it closer to the group. "The display indicates the haint has lowered the room's temperature to 62.4 degrees Fahrenheit, which is well below our normal temperature setting of 76 degrees."

Pinky raised a shaky hand. She pointed at the metal probe. "Where do you insert that metal thingy on the ghost to take its temperature?"

The idea of sticking the probe into a ghost's ectoplasm forced me to bite my lower lip to stifle a giggle.

Jasmine tried to explain. "The thermometer measures the temperature of the air in the room. It's not a thermometer that you stick up your, um, that measures your body temperature."

Looking disturbed at the description, the ghost slipped through the back wall.

"Our ghost just left," I said, watching for everyone's reactions.

Jasmine's bottom lip protruded. "Where did she go?"

I pointed toward the back wall of the room.

"Why did she leave?" Tiffany asked.

I shrugged. "Ghosts tend to do what they want and are sometimes unpredictable. Maybe she was afraid of the thermometer."

Some of the group looked relieved, others disappointed.

Mystery and Jasmine handed the meter and thermometer to the people around the conference table to examine, while Jasmine went on to demonstrate a small selection of infrared cameras. I knew Eddie was interested in one of the high-end models on the table and Mystery had high hopes he would buy it tonight. She had told me earlier that she planned to do puppy marketing by placing it in his hands after Jasmine finished the demonstration. Engineers can't resist touching devices.

When Jasmine and Mystery finished, I took over.

"This is a good time to take a break. There are drinks and treats available. The restroom is to the left of this room in the hall, and all smoking needs to be outside the front door. Please place your butts in the container with sand."

Everyone lined up for the goodies except Bama and Trouble, who retreated to the front of the shop.

Mystery rushed to the front door with her key in hand and unlocked it, in case they wanted to leave or go outside to smoke. I joined her, in case there was a problem. That was how we became witnesses to the loud argument between the two men.

Trouble cursed and pushed Bama, whose face bloomed crimson with anger.

Mystery squeezed my arm and whispered, "Lordy, I hope they don't get into a fight and break something."

Using my best command tone, I said, "Cool it or I'll call the police."

Both turned to look at me with surprise.

Trouble's face contorted into a mask of malice. "Fine!" He cursed some more before shouting, "Stay if you want, but I'm outta here." He pulled the door open with such force that I feared he'd fling the bell off.

Eddie popped into the room and looked around. "I heard shouting. Is everything okay?"

"Our problem left. Thanks for checking," I said.

He looked at me with constellations in his eyes. "I wouldn't let anyone hurt you."

Mystery popped a fist on her hip. "What about me?"

He shuffled his feet. "Um, I'd keep you both safe. Excuse me." He nodded and returned to the conference room.

Bama looked more embarrassed than angry at this point. "I'm sorry. I shouldn't have brought him."

Mystery nodded in sympathy. "No problem, Sugar. No one can blame the sins of a nonbeliever on a believer."

He shifted his sneakered feet and slapped his forehead. "I just remembered; he drove me here. I don't have a way home."

Bless his heart. He's not having a good night.

Mystery patted him on the shoulder. "I'm sure someone will give you a ride, or you can call Uber. Meanwhile, we have some tasty goodies. Why don't you go load up a plate?"

His eyes twinkled with interest.

"In the Harry Potter books, chocolate counteracts a dementor attack," I said with a wheedling tone. "I'm sure it would also work in this situation."

This remark brought a quirky grin to his face, which was now only pink. "Thanks." He offered his hand to us. "I'm Clay Wilkes." He glanced around the showroom. "If you ever need some part-time help, I'd love to work here if you can work around my class schedule. I'm a computer engineering major at UAH."

Mystery's brows rose. "No kidding? Jasmine has the same major. You're welcome to come in and fill out an application. I have two other students working part-time, and it's hard to fill all the slots with the different class schedules. I need someone to create and maintain a website."

His face lit with enthusiasm. "I can handle that task."

"I'm also expanding my ghost tours." Mystery followed him back into the conference room.

When I joined them, Mystery nudged me. "I thought those two were going to come to blows. I plan on downing some dark chocolate with almonds to calm my nerves."

"Go for it." I noticed that Clay and Jasmine were in an animated conversation near the fridge. I was easing that way to eavesdrop when Eddie called the meeting to order.

"Please hurry and take your seats so we can finish by nine," Eddie said, making shooing motions.

Once everyone was seated, I asked, "Have you ever wondered why spirits get stuck on this plane of existence?" Pausing, I scanned the faces of my audience. "There are many reasons."

I flipped to a new slide.

The words *Unfinished business* filled the screen. "Most of my cases involve this principle."

"Like what?" Pinky asked, twirling a lock of hair around her finger.

"Mystery and I had one case where a man died in an auto accident. He had a secret deposit box full of cash. He didn't have life insurance, so he wanted his wife to have the money."

Mystery chuckled. "I'll never forget that one. His wife was fit to be tied when she found out. She said he made her miserable with his pinchpenny habits."

Pinky grinned. "I wish someone would leave me a box full of cash."

Several folks chuckled.

"Guilt is also a biggie," I said. "Mystery, remember the ghost who felt guilty because his son never returned home after an argument?"

She nodded.

"His wife never knew that he told his son to leave and never return. She grieved for years wondering what she'd done wrong," I said.

"That's sad," Hairspray said, wringing her hands. I could feel some personal regret flowing from her.

Clay raised his hand. "Do ghosts ever get stuck because they're confused?"

"Good question. After sudden accidental deaths, sometimes spirits don't realize they're dead. They see the light but don't know they should go to it. By the time they figure it out, the light is gone and they're earthbound," I said.

Pinky clapped both hands to her cheeks, looking appalled. "Can you help them reach the light?"

"Yes." I was too tired to go into further explanations. Like Mystery, I'd had a long day.

I briefly covered angry ghosts and the ones who become attached to people or objects. When I ended the talk, I was pleased that everyone appeared to have enjoyed the time.

Eddie stood and waved a hand to get everyone's attention. "I've asked Mystery to open her retail area for thirty minutes, so you can check out the other paranormal devices they carry, and to make purchases if you so desire." He chuckled and winked at Mystery. "I plan to check out a few items myself."

Mystery and Jasmine got busy helping those who wanted to purchase items while I packed my equipment. I peeked into the retail area and saw Eddie examining an infrared camera.

I took the opportunity to leave out the back door. He seemed to be working himself up to asking me for a date. He's a kind man but not my type. Chris Haddington's face flashed through my mind again. *Now, he's my type.*

At that moment, my only desire was to go home. My feet felt like they'd been kneaded and baked in an oven, and I felt down-to-the-bone-marrow tired. All I wanted was a long, hot soak with a sparkling glass of ginger ale and my latest Agatha Christie novel, *Big Four*.

CHAPTER 6

I woke, stretched, and stared up at the blue sky complete with clouds on the ceiling of my bedroom. The previous owner of my house had been an artist and was responsible for the mural. I yawned and stumbled half asleep from the bedroom into my large shower.

While washing my hair, I closed my eyes and hummed *Blue Skies*. After rinsing away the suds, I opened them to find the ghost of Pierre Garnier smiling as his gaze flowed over me like hot water.

My heart nearly leapt out of my chest, before I managed to snatch the shower curtain around me. "Out!"

"Ma chérie." His smile widened. "You do not mean this." He reached out to hug me.

I backed against the wall, the hard tile stopping my retreat. His touch produced the sensation of icy electrified rain. Nausea churned my stomach as he passed through me.

He staggered back, becoming more translucent.

Earthbound spirits who come in contact with humans find our lower vibrational level to be draining. At least that's the way Mom explained it to me when I was twelve.

I turned off the water and gathered my psychic energy. Pushing out with my hands, I released it while yelling, "You are banned from my home forever."

Pierre flew from my sight. Another neat trick Mom taught me when I was fifteen. I'm not sure I'd have survived childhood without my psychic mother.

I've always thought Pierre must've been an attractive man while alive. His oval face had soulful eyes, a strong chin, and a narrow nose. His well-trimmed loose curls that occasionally fell across his forehead added to his sex appeal. I felt sure his bohemian charm had enticed many a lady into his art studio when he was alive.

I grumbled to myself, "Dang blasted spirits. Talk about poor boundaries."

Prissy wagged her way into the steamy bathroom. She stopped, raised her nose, and growled.

"Yes, Sweetie, we had an early morning visitor, but he's gone now." I'm not sure how she senses disembodied spirits, but she does.

I dried off, took care of Prissy, and got ready for work. After a bagel with cream cheese and some coffee, I felt ready to take on the world.

Security conscious, I set the alarm and locked the door, before getting into the car with Prissy. The garage door rattled up, squeaking when it was close to the top. It was one of those ear-piercing sounds that set my teeth into grind mode. "Great, one more thing to have fixed." I love owning my home, but I'm not keen on the repairs. After backing out onto the driveway, I braked and hit the remote.

Prissy flew into a barking rampage, lunging toward the back seat.

I looked in the rearview mirror and jumped. "As I live and breathe!"

Holding my hand over my leaping heart, I said, "Pierre, we need to talk. Get in the passenger seat. I'm not your chauffeur. Prissy, come sit in my lap."

He floated through the seat and wagged his brows at me. "I have no need of a safety belt since I am already dead."

I may never get used to ghost humor. In particular, French ghost humor.

He reached a hand toward my growling dog.

She lunged forward and bit through his finger. Whining with alarm, she back-pedaled across my lap until her backside was against the door. She shook her head and shivered.

I glared at Pierre while rubbing her ears. With a soothing tone, I said, "That didn't feel good, did it?"

"Why are you angered against me? I did not bite her," he said with a wounded tone.

He was still misty, which told me he hadn't regained his full strength since hugging me.

Feeling disoriented by the morning's events, I backed into the street and headed toward my store. Like Mystery, I live in a bungalow in Five Points and love the quaint area. As a bonus, the drive to my shop takes only five minutes.

The sun twinkled between the bright green leaves of the mature trees that lined both sides of the street. Creative shadow art painted the road.

"Pierre, you have to stop pursuing me. You need to cross over."

"Je t'aime, ma chérie. How can I leave you?"

"No, you don't love me. It's only a bad case of ghostly infatuation."

On my first trip to Paris three years earlier, I avoided a collision with Pierre while strolling through the sculpture garden at the Musée Rodin. My evasive maneuver alerted him that I saw ghosts.

When I woke in the middle of the night, he was in my bed, propped on an elbow watching me sleep. I nearly had a heart attack. I banished him from my hotel room.

The next morning when I left my room, he was waiting for me. Pierre had been an artist when he was alive. He'd died at age thirty-four. A man had stabbed him to death during a mugging along the bank of the Seine. He'd lost his life over fifty Euros.

When I asked why he hadn't crossed over, he said with great fervor, "My killer still runs free. How can my soul have peace when I have no justice?"

That day, Pierre directed me to a small gallery where two of his paintings were for sale. One was a large oil painting in an elaborate gold frame. Imagine my shock when I stared at myself, red hair flying in the wind as I rode a green dragon, with a castle in the background.

The clerk looked at me, and then at the painting. "Mademoiselle, it is a striking likeness. Did you pose for Monsieur Garnier?"

I shook my head. "I've never met him." *Until yesterday.*

I bought the artwork and arranged to have it shipped home. It hangs over the fireplace in my living room.

Pierre followed me everywhere on that trip and became my unofficial tour guide. When I was ready to leave France, I managed to elude him. At least I thought I did. How he made it to Huntsville is beyond me, but I suspect he attached himself to the painting. He's not a constant presence in my life, but he shows up too often to suit me.

"Pierre, I don't love you. You're dead. A disembodied spirit. There can be no love affair between us."

He made a dismissive gesture. "C'est absurd. You will come to love me. I painted you before I met you. We are destined to be together."

I rolled my eyes. *He is one pigheaded ghost. Mom warned me to watch out for Frenchmen, but she neglected to mention the dead ones.*

I parked in the back lot of my store, next to Kaya's bright yellow VW Bug. After I opened the door, Prissy hopped down and paused to christen a patch of grass.

"I have to work. Goodbye, Pierre." I gave him a finger wave.

With a stubborn set to his chin, he followed us to the back door, despite Prissy's growls.

"Go away." I made shooing motions.

He glided past me into my shop.

I rushed to unlock the door. Pierre could be mischievous. *What if he does something to scare Kaya?*

I sprinted through the store room lit by a lone window and into the brightly illuminated hallway searching for him. *Dang blasted ghost! Where is he?*

I flipped on the lights of both offices.

No ghost.

I peeked into the conference room.

Nothing.

I slid to a stop in the retail area. Kaya was on her knees stocking chocolate bars into the case.

Three feet behind her, Pierre was holding aloft a lace bra, admiring it.

Without thinking, I said with steel in my tone, "Put that down!"

Kaya jumped, chocolates flying out of her hands.

Pierre grinned. "Pourquoi? I am not hurting it."

I prayed she wouldn't notice the bra, that to her, would be floating in midair.

"You would look belle in this one, ma chérie."

I shot him a look that should've evaporated him on the spot.

He rehung the bra, held up both hands, and backed away.

I sucked in a breath to regain some composure. "Kaya, I'm sorry. I didn't mean to frighten you."

She stood, a vulnerable expression cloaking her normally smiling face. With a trembling voice, she asked, "Did I do something wrong?"

My heart thumped a heavy beat that would make any Rock drummer proud. *Think fast.* "Uh, not a thing." I crossed my fingers behind my back. "I forgot you were coming in early. I thought someone had broken in and was stealing the chocolate."

I know it sounded ridiculous. How many chocolate junkies are there, besides Mystery?

Kaya leaned against the counter and placed a hand over her chest. She exhaled, a look of relief flooding her face. "I guess we scared each other." She frowned. "Didn't you see my car?"

Oops. Unsure what to say, I shrugged.

Pierre guffawed behind me. I wanted to banish him from my store, but he knew I couldn't do it with Kaya here. *She'd really think I was nuts and quit if I yelled, "I banish you from this store forever."*

She gave me an intense up and down. "Are you okay? You had a weird look on your face. Is there something wrong with one of the displays? You keep looking over there."

I waved away the observation. "I'm fine." Strolling to the rear of the store, I locked my purse into a deep drawer. I glared at Pierre as I passed him. After unlocking the front door, I turned on the open sign.

I'd made it back to the counter when the door pinged, alerting me to a possible customer.

Zach Stanner slouched into the room. Even with poor posture, he towered like a giraffe over me. "Mystery told me to tweak your security camera, so it covers a wider area before I clock out to go to class."

"Good." I handed Prissy to Kaya.

Pierre floated up behind Zach and poked one of his spiky blond tufts of hair.

A shudder worked down Zach's slender frame like a spreading earthquake. Bug-eyed, he spun around, running his hand over his hair, which sprang back into place.

I covered my mouth to stifle a giggle before aiming a reproving scowl at Pierre.

Kaya, who's had a year-long crush on Zach, gave me a conspiratorial wink and put down my fur baby. "Watch out! Here comes Prissy."

Prissy tail-wagged her way toward him offering him her most beguiling doggie smile.

Zach boosted himself onto a glass display case and wrapped his spindly arms around his lanky legs.

Pierre backed away, his brows shooting near his hairline.

I massaged the spot between my eyes to fight off the beginning of a headache before bellowing, "Zachary Alexander Stanner, get off of there before you break the glass!" I picked up Prissy. "You know this little dog loves you to pieces."

Zach cringed and slid off the case. "But she sneaks up behind me and barks."

Kaya convulsed with laughter. "She's playing with you."

Pierre levitated nearby, his shoulders hitching up and down with his laughter.

"I'll be out back working on that camera." Frowning, Zach tugged his tee-shirt over his lean hips.

Kaya offered a conciliatory smile. "I'll hold the ladder."

After they were both gone, I rounded on Pierre. "What the heck were you doing?"

He held up both hands. "I wanted to touch his spiky hair. I did not think he would feel it."

"Well, he did. Zach's sensitive, so don't do it again." I pointed at his chest. "If you don't leave now, I'll banish you forever from this shop."

He produced a suggestive grin. "Ma chérie, you would not do that. You must admit your attraction to me. Will you model some of this lovely lingerie for me?"

I was pulling in my energy when he noticed and ghosted out of sight. He knew I couldn't ban him if I couldn't see him.

"Drat, I should have acted faster."

CHAPTER 7

Kaya and I were steaming wrinkles out of some adorable pajamas designed to keep hot-flashing women cooler, when screeching brakes announced Tiffany's arrival in front of my store. I cringed, imagining my plate glass windows shattering into tiny glittering pieces.

"Please, Lord, stop her before she plows through the store," Kaya prayed, crossing herself.

"Amen!" I added. *Maybe I should renew my prayer protection.*

Tiffany popped out of her still rocking Volvo and looked both ways as if on a secret mission. She scuttled toward The Mystery Shop's door.

I wonder if she has an update on any paranormal activity in her house. "Kaya, can you finish up? I want to find out if Tiffany's neighbors have heard anything else about that woman's death."

Kaya's frown created a valley between her brows. "Sure. I hope they catch the killer." She shuddered. "It's scary knowing there's been a murder so close to the store. I hope you or the police solve it soon."

"I agree."

Huntsville has a low murder rate. Most homicides have occurred in the low-cost housing areas where the drug deals go down.

Prissy pranced over giving me her cutest doggie smile.

"Not this time, Sweetie. Stay here with Kaya. I'll only be gone a few minutes."

My fur baby sat and yipped her disapproval.

Kaya smiled and shook her head. "Sometimes I think she understands everything we say." She opened the jar full of Greenies on the counter, and said, "Treat."

Prissy ran to her and ignored me.

"Traitor!"

When I walked into Mystery's store, I was greeted by the jingling bell and Tiffany's floral scent.

Mystery, Jasmine, and Tiffany turned and smiled.

"Hey, y'all. Thought I'd check to see if you have any paranormal updates."

"Goodness, yes!" Tiffany's tone held excitement. "I woke up this morning to find all the chairs pulled away from the dining room table. It was as if everyone rose in a hurry from a dinner party and left. After listening to last night's talk, I'm beginning to think I may have a poltergeist."

Interesting. Before she was upset about a possible ghost and now, she sounds excited about it.

"That's freaky," Jasmine said, nearly bouncing with excitement. Wish I'd been there to see it when it happened.

A frown furrowed Tiffany's brow. "Of course, Jason accused me of moving all those chairs. He said the sleeping pill I took caused me to walk in my sleep." She ran a hand through her hair. "After that meeting last night, I was a tad overstimulated."

I stiffened. *Sleeping pill?*

"Do you take them on a regular basis?" I asked.

Tiffany stepped back, a startled look freezing her features.

"Um, not very often. Why?" Her tone was steeped in suspicion.

"Were you a sleepwalker as a child?" I followed them into the conference room.

"No, I don't think so. My parents never mentioned anything about it."

"What about as an adult or after you started taking the sleeping pills?" Jasmine asked.

"No." Tiffany crossed her arms and scowled first at Jasmine, then me. "Jason is trying to blame me for this haunting. Heck, he blames me for everything. I hope to goodness y'all aren't blaming me, too."

Jasmine's tone sounded conciliatory. "No, not at all. I was worried because my psych professor told our class that certain medications could cause sleepwalking and sleep-eating."

Tiffany's mouth dropped open. She looked as if she'd misheard. "Sleep-eating? Never heard of such."

Mystery pulled out a chair and sat. "Jasmine's right. There was even a case where a woman under the influence of a prescription sleep aid drove to Sonic and brought home a sack full of food to eat. She woke the next morning and found the wrappers along with the credit card receipt on the dining table. She had no memory of the incident."

"That is beyond strange to downright weird. I'll talk to my doctor about this during my appointment next week. I have enough problems without sleep-eating. Can you imagine the weight gain?" She opened her large purse and pulled out some papers. "I brought the rest of the information you requested on Jason."

"Perfect. Let's talk and make sure I have everything needed to do a complete background investigation," Jasmine said. "Mystery knew you were coming, so she brought in some doughnuts, and you can pick out the K-cup you want."

"Bree, get a doughnut and take one to Kaya. Lord knows, I don't need extra treats hanging around adding additional cellulite. We'd have to walk four days-a-week to prevent a bubble butt expansion."

I held up my hands, palms out. "Any extra cellulite due to doughnut consumption would need to be taken up with Krispy Kreme. Perhaps they could assign an employee to walk with you."

Mystery harrumphed.

As I grabbed two doughnuts with napkins, I couldn't help but wonder if Tiffany was sleepwalking and there was indeed no haunting. *If it's true, Jasmine will be bereft.* I smiled to myself realizing I'd used one of Jasmine's words of the day.

I waved. "Gotta go. See you later. Thanks for the treats."

An hour later, I was going over my vendor order for Swiss chocolates when the phone rang. "I've got it," I yelled to Kaya.

"Chocolates and Delights! Put some sweet and zesty back into your life. Brianna speaking."

A deep, gruff voice asked. "Do you have a good selection of Spanx?"

"Yes, we carry that brand."

"And do they come in all sizes and colors?"

Using my best upbeat and confident tone, I said, "We have a selection of beige and black ones in a variety of sizes."

"What? No red ones? My woman told me they come in red. She needs one in extra-large for tonight," he said sounding haughty.

"I assure you, sir, I've never seen that color in the Spanx catalog. Perhaps she means another brand." I gift-wrapped every word in a calm, reasonable tone. I could feel my face beginning to flush.

Using the forceful tone of a man used to getting his way, he said, "If *my* woman says they come in red, they do. You need to go look in your storeroom and find me one, right now. I'll wait."

Who does he think he is? I paused, trying to gain control over my rising ire.

A familiar giggle traveled over the phone line.

"Mystery Lucille Jones! Is that you?" Anger flamed my face.

She laughed.

"How old are you anyway? Twelve?" I spat the words with equal sarcasm and annoyance.

"Old enough to buy special order goodies from your store," Mystery said between chuckles.

"That was a favor for a friend," I said in my haughtiest tone.

"Sorry. Mama would say 'the devil made me do it.'" She chuckled again. "I called to talk about the murder case. When do you plan to talk to Katie Abernathy? I'm dying to know if she had an alibi."

Still feeling irked, I said, "That's on my agenda after lunch."

"Do you want me to go with you? Jasmine can watch the store."

After what you just pulled? Forget it. I took a calming breath and said, "I've got it."

"Good luck. Can't wait to hear what you find out. Can you get away for dinner tomorrow? We need to compare notes."

I guess that is necessary. "Let me check my schedule." I looked at my phone calendar. "It'd have to be around seven after we close."

"Works for me. Let's go to Bonefish Grill," she said.

"Good idea. I haven't had Bang Bang Shrimp in a long time. If anything changes, I'll call you back." I hung up and looked at Kaya, who was grinning.

"Mystery got you again, didn't she?"

CHAPTER 8

I grabbed my purse and Prissy before popping my head into Kaya's office. "Please watch the store. I'll be gone for about an hour."

"Sure thing," Kaya said while chewing a large bite of taco. Her cheeks puffed out like a chipmunk storing nuts.

The drive to Katie Abernathy's home in the Twickenham historic district was pleasant. The sun created dappled patterns of light and shade on her verdant lawn. A local lawncare company displayed its advertisement on a spike near the curb. *Wish my grass was this green.*

The Georgian-style architecture of the home had a structure and proportion that suited my sense of balance. The large, sand-colored house had six Doric columns supporting the roof that spanned the width of the two-story portion of the home. Single-story wings jutted from each side. The architect had surrounded the open porches on top with stone balustrades. Black shutters dressed a generous number of floor-to-ceiling windows in true Southern style.

I pulled into the circular drive and stopped in front of the residence. A woman was locking the door, and a tiny Yorkshire terrier sat beside her. It was apparent the woman hadn't heard my nearly silent electric car.

I opened my door, which triggered the dog to bark.

This caused the woman to look over her shoulder. When she saw the car, she took several steps back. "Hush, Phoebe."

I exited the car with Prissy in my arms. *Time to test my theory that dog lovers will be more open with other dog owners.*

"Is that a Tesla? It was so quiet I didn't hear you."

Noticing the hearing aids, I shouted, "Yes. I'm looking for Katie Abernathy."

"Well, you found her." She gave her dog a "stay" hand signal. "This is Phoebe."

I strolled closer, so I wouldn't have to yell. "I'm Brianna Kelly and this is Prissy. Is it okay to put her down? She's on a leash."

"Sure. Phoebe likes most dogs. Doesn't care much for cats."

I lowered Prissy to the porch. The two dogs circled, sniffing each other's backsides.

I'm so glad humans don't greet each other that way.

Katie beamed up at me. "See, they're getting along fine."

With her squat build and short gray curls, she could have played Mrs. Claus in any movie. Her vivid makeup complemented her brightly colored blouse that hung long over black pants. She displayed one foot to show off her bright pink canvas shoes tied with neon green laces.

"My youngest granddaughter gave me these shoes for Christmas." She cocked a thumb toward the neighboring house. Scrunching her nose, she said, "The snotty old biddy next door hated them."

"Do you mean Victoria Spellman?"

Katie thinned her wrinkled lips and looked at me with sudden disapproval. With a sharp tone, she asked, "You a friend of hers?"

I shook my head. "I've never met her." *Except after someone murdered her.* I thought a second. *Technically, I haven't even been introduced to her ghost.*

"So, what's your interest?" she asked, her tone spiked with suspicion.

I shrugged. "Mostly curiosity."

Katie looked up at me through slitted eyes. "Not the police?"

"Nope."

"You a reporter?"

"No, ma'am."

The woman gave me an assessing look that stripped away all pretense.

"Ms. Abernathy, I was hoping you could tell me something about your neighbor, maybe help me understand who'd want to kill her?"

"Why are you so curious?"

I paused. "I found her body at the church. I know it sounds silly, but I have to know what happened." I looked down studying her pink shoes and then up to meet her gaze. "I've never found a murder victim before."

Her gaze softened. "I imagine that was hard for you. It would be for most folks." She smiled down at the two dogs, licking each other's faces. "Call me Katie. Let's walk the dogs. Gotta keep moving when you're my age, or your joints freeze up."

We walked in silence for a bit. The delicate pink and white blossoms of dogwoods provided a lace of color amid the bright green new growth of the oaks and maples. Azaleas created a riot of reds, pinks, and whites in the elaborate landscapes of the historic homes.

The tension in my shoulders loosened. "I love this time of year. I noticed some beautiful yellow flowers on your fence. What are they?"

"Carolina jasmine. It has such a lovely fragrance." She looked down at Prissy and frowned. "Do you intend to plant some?"

"No, probably not." I gave a dismissive gesture. "I'm way too busy to care for plants and flowers." I steered Prissy away from a flower bed surrounding a mailbox.

Katie gave a decisive nod, jiggling her second chin. "Good, because it's poisonous, especially to dogs. I had to put up a special fence to keep Phoebe away from it." She gave me a pointed look. "You can't be too careful when it comes to the safety of your pets."

I nodded. "True."

A male ghost wearing clothes from the forties sat on the porch of a house across the street. I slowed to get a better look. When he noticed that I saw him, he smiled and tipped his cap.

I smiled and nodded before he faded from view.

Prissy tugged at the leash, forcing me to catch up. Phoebe had taken the lead, and Prissy didn't like it one little bit.

"Do you have any theories about the murder?" I asked, trying to decide on an approach to the tougher questions.

Katie cackled like a plump hen. "Heck, I would've shot her myself if I could've gotten away with it. The woman was a knife in my gizzard. Miss High and Mighty thought she was too good for everyone."

So, she's heard the rumor that Victoria was shot. Either she doesn't know about the head wound or she's covering her tracks.

"Were you the only one who disliked her?" I asked, surprised by Katie's frankness.

"Heck, no. That woman managed to insult nearly everyone she met. Even her daughter couldn't stand her. Poor Darlene once told me the only reason she visited at all was so her mother wouldn't cut her out of the will. I can't imagine what it was like to grow up with such a wretched mother."

The word *will* nudged me to ask, "Did Victoria cut Darlene out of her will?"

"Don't know for sure. Last week, they were screeching at each other like two feral cats in heat. I heard Vickie yell that she would."

"Vickie?" I asked. The ghost I'd seen didn't look like she would ever accept a nickname.

Katie cackled again.

On second assessment, her laugh was part chicken and part crow.

"I'm the only one who ever called her Vickie. She hated nicknames. It made her spitting mad." Katie screwed up her face, making it a roadmap of lines. "That prude insisted on calling me Kathleen."

"I'd like to talk to her daughter. Maybe she might have some information. Do you know her last name and how to reach her?" I asked.

"Sure. It's Darlene Hennessey. The funeral is on Thursday at the church where Vickie died. Darlene told me she wanted it over and done. They're going to plant the cantankerous old biddy at Maple Hill Cemetery." She slowed and cackled again. "Rumor is she left strict orders on how to arrange things and paid for everything in advance."

Ahh, the famous Camellia Express. Wonder if it's true? "Are you going to the funeral?"

"Wouldn't miss it for the world. Knowing Vickie's need to control everything, she'll stick around for the funeral to make sure everyone follows her exact orders. Besides, I always liked Darlene and her daughter, Susie. I'm looking forward to having them as neighbors."

Surprised by Katie's reason for attending the funeral, I asked, "Do you believe in ghosts?"

"You bet. If you live in the historic district and don't believe, you're a dang fool. Old houses and ghosts go together like thunderstorms and lightning."

We turned right onto Franklin Street and slowed to navigate the uneven herringbone brick sidewalk. It didn't seem to bother the dogs.

"Watch your step," Katie said, looking down. "The tree roots have buckled the bricks into a dang obstacle course."

"I never realized this walk wasn't concrete. It's not obvious when driving past."

We stopped to let the dogs sniff a wrought iron fence.

"This is my favorite home in the district," Katie said, looking up at the majestic two-story home.

The sign in the landscaped front garden said, "Van Valkenburg House, 1902."

I gave an admiring smile, ignoring Prissy's tug on the leash.

Katie said, "It's a beautiful example of Classic Revival architecture. Herbert Cowell was the architect."

Surprised, I asked, "How did you know?"

She gave my shoulder a brief squeeze. "I'm a widow. I lost my Henry five years ago to a sudden illness. He was a botanist and a lover of old houses. You know what they say, you can't throw a stone around here without hitting a scientist of some dadgum kind."

We rounded the corner to Williams Street and stopped to admire the large stained-glass window on the north side of the Van Valkenburg House.

Tears welled in Katie's eyes. "Henry told me about this window. It's a copy of one made by Louis Tiffany that depicts the story of Hero and Leander in Greek mythology."

I nodded. "I didn't know the part about the Greek legend. It's beautiful."

"I walk Phoebe this way most days to see it. My daughter wants me to avoid those treacherous bricks, but I can't resist seeing this lovely home."

When we resumed walking, I decided to shift the conversation to throw Katie off balance. "If you don't mind telling me, what did Victoria do that made you hate her so much?"

Katie lurched to a stop, looking suddenly exhausted. Sweat gathered above her upper lip. "It's more like what she didn't do.

When Vickie thought I wasn't looking, she'd create all kinds of havoc. She was the meanest woman I've ever met. She'd cut her nose off to spite her face.

The local gossips circulated all kinds of rumors about me over the years; most were started by that old biddy's lies." She paused and took a breath. "I know it's silly, but my reputation is important to me." She raised a fist in the air. "Her attacks on my sanity varied from screaming at my grandkids if they touched a blade of grass on her lawn, to dumping her branches and such over the fence into my backyard. That vindictive old woman even stole the baked goods right off my front porch when I put them out to cool."

"That's awful", I said.

Her blue eyes darkened. "That's only the half of it. The worst was her campaign of hate against my Phoebe!" She pointed at the dog, who wagged her tail and smiled up at me. "That woman called the police and animal control on the poor little dear, I don't know how many times." Katie slammed her clenched fist into the other palm. "I tell you that woman was evil!"

"How horrible. How long did you live next door to each other?" I asked, keeping an eye on her fist.

"She moved in fifteen miserable years ago. My previous neighbors sold the house when it became too much for them, bless their hearts."

She certainly has a motive. "I hate to ask, but where were you on Monday?" I watched for her reaction.

Katie pursed her lips. "You sure are a nosy one." The line deepened between her brows. "So, you think I offed her, too? Is that what you've heard from that dang Camellia Express?"

She was such a character that a chuckle bubbled out before I could stop it. "Not really, but an alibi would prove your innocence and put a stop to some of the gossip. I have a friend who lives in the historic district. I could have her pass the word that you have an alibi." *If you do.*

Katie pulled a phone out of her pants pocket and said, "Siri, call Charlotte."

Like many hard of hearing folks, she had the speaker on and the volume on high. I listened to her daughter's cheerful greeting.

"I'm putting someone on the phone. Tell her who you are and about our recent trip." Katie handed me the phone.

I took it and introduced myself.

"I'm her daughter. My family took Mom to Gatlinburg, where we rented a cabin to celebrate her seventy-fifth birthday."

Katie looked smug.

"Sounds like a fun outing. When did y'all leave and return?" I asked.

"We left for Tennessee before noon on Friday and didn't get home until around nine on Monday night. What's this about?" her daughter asked.

I nodded at Katie, who had a satisfied smirk on her face. "I'll let your mom explain it," I said, before handing Katie the phone.

"I'll call you when I get back to the house. Love you." She disconnected the call.

"Happy birthday." My timer chimed on my watch. "Oh my, I need to go back to work. My assistant has a class in an hour." I handed Katie my card. "Call me if you hear anything that will help me find Victoria's killer. At least now I have a better understanding of why she died. It seems like the list of possible suspects may be long."

Katie looked at the card, then me. "Chocolates and Delights?" She frowned and slipped the card into her pocket. "You'd be better off leaving this to the police, if you ask me." She eyed me from top to bottom. "I suspect you won't take my advice."

I opted to change the subject. "I'd like to bring Prissy back to walk with Phoebe sometime, if that's all right."

The two dogs were licking each other's faces.

Katie smiled and nodded. "I'd like that. Maybe you can catch me up on the case. I wouldn't put it past that old biddy to come back as a ghost."

If you only knew.

CHAPTER 9

At seven-thirty, Mystery and I pushed through the rotating door of Bonefish Grill. The delicious scents of cooking food made my stomach growl like a Doberman on guard duty.

Mystery's gaze locked on my face, then traveled down to my stomach. She smirked. "Someone's hungry."

The bar and the communal tables were already full. I yelled to be heard over a loud group of guys slouched around a communal hightop. "Mystery, it's a good thing you made a reservation."

Pierre soared into the restaurant with a smug grin. "You cannot banish me from here, ma chérie. It is too public."

I rolled my eyes. "Oh, great. Just what I needed."

"What?" Mystery looked around with a confused look.

"Pierre." I jabbed a thumb in his direction.

"Here? At this moment?"

"Yep."

The perky hostess strode up and led us to a booth in the back corner of the restaurant section next to the window. We slid into opposite sides. I chose to sit with my back to the wall. The place buzzed with conversation. I noticed that the elderly couple seated in the booth behind Mystery wore hearing aids. *If they're like my grandmother, they'll have turned them off because of all the noise. In this racket, our chat should be somewhat private.*

Mystery picked up the menu, eyes twinkling like she was being super naughty. "Let's start with Bang Bang Shrimp." She glanced around. "I can't believe this place is so busy tonight."

"I love that appetizer. It's the right amount of spicy," I said, my stomach grumbling in agreement. *Goodness, I ate lunch. My gut is acting like I'm starving.*

Pierre floated in the aisle near Mystery and looked over her shoulder at the menu.

Mystery said through clenched teeth, "Back off, Pierre. I know you're there because I'm turning into a fudgesicle."

He looked up at me with a rueful expression. "I keep forgetting. Please offer my apologies." He eased back a foot or two, right into the path of the approaching waitress, who walked through him and yelped.

Mystery turned to locate the sound.

Looking stunned, Pierre glided backward, straight through a waiter who carried two glasses of iced tea. The young man stumbled, dumping the glasses' contents into the lap of a stylishly dressed woman. She shrieked and jumped to her feet, knocking over her chair and toppling her wine glass. The man dining with her leaped out of his seat to avoid the red liquid spreading across the white tablecloth.

"Excuse me," our pale waitress managed to say before covering her mouth with a hand.

Mystery watched her stumble out of sight. "I think she's gonna be sick."

I shook my head. "I'm not surprised. She walked straight through Pierre, who then collided with the other waiter. Now he's weaving like a drunk dog, and he's almost faded from view."

I jerked my head for him to come back to the booth and pointed at the seat beside me. When he arrived, I whispered, "Look what you did. Get in this booth before you run off the rest of the waitstaff and fade away to nothing. You're flickering like a lamp with an exposed wire."

The restaurant's noise lowered to the level of visitation at a funeral home as the other patrons craned their necks to see what had happened.

A flock of waiters fluttered around the woman, handing her dry napkins, busing the table, and righting her chair. With repeated apologies, the manager moved the couple to a new table. The woman disappeared into the ladies' room, and a cacophony of discussion exploded through the restaurant.

Mystery had unwrapped her flatware and was dabbing under her eyes with the black cloth napkin. Unable to control her laughter, she rocked in the booth, shoulders heaving up and down.

It was contagious. I began laughing so hard that tears sprang to my eyes.

Pierre stared at us as if we were insane. "That was *not* amusing! Americans have a strange humor."

His French accent made his declaration even more hilarious. I imitated it for Mystery.

He crossed his arms and turned away from me.

When we were able to control ourselves, we settled back into our seats to catch our breath. Conversation in the place had returned to a steady, low roar.

Pierre turned back toward us glaring his disapproval down his narrow nose.

A new waitress arrived. "I'm Annabel. Would y'all like to start with drinks or perhaps a starter?"

"I'll have ice water with lemon," I said, ignoring Pierre's sulk.

"Perfect," the waitress said, with a tip-seeking smile.

"I'll have the same, and we want to start with an order of Bang Bang Shrimp to share," Mystery said.

"Perfect. I'll be back with your drinks and some bread."

Pierre still looked somewhat translucent but appeared calmer. He'd uncrossed his arms and his jaw muscle had stopped flexing. "What is Bang Bang Shrimp?"

I placed the menu in front of him so he could read the description.

He nodded. "It sounds enticing. I wish I could enjoy the texture and taste of food, and not just the smell. Being a ghost has its... how do you say...limitations."

I shared his remarks with Mystery.

"If you could eat, then you'd have to complete the digestive process." I could see Mystery working through the idea. "You'd create haint poops. I wonder if they would stink?" She cocked her head. "Then you'd need a haint toilet."

Pierre slapped a hand over his eyes and slid down in the booth.

I whispered, "Come on, Pierre. You have to love a woman who thinks like a combination of an internal medicine physician and sanitation engineer."

"Mon Dieu," he said with a pleading tone, "save me from these indignités."

"God would if you'd cross over," I said.

Annabel returned with two water glasses, a small loaf of bread with olive oil with a small container of pesto on the side, and the shrimp. She recorded our entrée orders onto her pad and said, "Perfect."

After she left, I pulled off a slice of bread. My stomach was spinning like a whirlwind. "Tonight is a *perfect* example of my point."

Mystery reached for the bread. "What point?"

"Sorry, I was talking to Pierre. You are *not* meant to be on this plane of existence. The three of us are out to dinner, and so far, you've managed to zing two of the waitstaff, ruin a lady's dress, wreck the couple's dinner, and disrupt the entire restaurant."

Pierre jutted his jaw and recrossed his arms. "It was not ma faute. That waitress walked through me."

Mystery leaned closer. "What was his reply?"

I told her.

She huffed. "Just like a man."

I held up both hands in a placating gesture. "This is in no way meant to hurt your feelings, Pierre. Spirits have a difficult time existing in a world where most people can't see or hear them, so things happen." I looked at Pierre. "As for your plans to seduce me, you can't hold me, kiss me, or make love to me because you're dead and should no longer be part of this world."

"So true," said Mystery. "Heck, you can't even eat Bang Bang Shrimp." To emphasize her point, she speared one and waved it on her fork.

"Forget the guy who stabbed you to death. Karma will take care of him," I said.

"I'll think about it, ma chérie. Bonsoir. Enjoy your meal." He dissipated to nothingness.

"Good night." I had to admit, I was warming up now that he'd left.

"Is he gone?" Mystery asked while transferring some of the shrimp onto her plate.

"Yep."

"Things have been so crazy with finding Victoria's body, the RCPS meeting, and that guy carrying on at my shop. I've been kinda freaked out about the whole thing. It's like haints are everywhere, only I can't see them. You know, like nasty little dust mites. If I think about it too much, it makes me feel squirrelly."

I chuckled in an empathetic way. "Now you know why I keep my shields up when needed. Ghosts sense when you can see them. That's how I met Pierre in France. Spirits pop up in the most unlikely places, and many have lousy boundaries." I told her about the shower incident with Pierre.

"You're kidding me. Were you naked?"

"Of course, I was. Do you wear clothes in the shower?" I asked.

"Don't be silly." She speared another shrimp. "Mmm. These are so good. You're so lucky. I've wanted to see ghosts since something moved the planchette around the Ouija Board when I was ten."

I swallowed and reached for my ice water. "It's a blessing and a curse."

"You keep saying that." She stopped, narrowed her eyes, and asked, "Are you keeping Pierre earthbound?" Her gaze softened, and she looked concerned.

"I hope not. He claims his soul won't rest until his killer is caught by the police and convicted."

Mystery nodded and wiped her hands. "I get all that, but why isn't he back in France haunting his killer?"

Good question. I thought a minute. "You've seen the painting above my fireplace."

"It's beautiful. The woman riding the dragon looks like you. I've always wondered about it."

"Pierre painted it before he was killed."

Mystery sat back in the booth; her eyes wide with surprise. "That was before he met you. That's like, freaky fate."

I nodded. "He thinks he's in love with me."

"Do you love him?"

I shook my head. "I like him, but I don't love him."

"Poor haint. I wonder if you two were fated to meet, but the killer messed with the plan by murdering Pierre."

I shrugged. "Who knows?" Deciding it was time to change the subject, I said, "I met with Katie Abernathy." I chuckled, remembering the spry little woman and her hot pink sneakers with neon green laces. "She's a hoot." I gave Mystery a detailed description of Katie and what I'd learned.

Mystery put more shrimp on her plate. "That takes her off the suspect list. I guess Darlene is the next suspect to investigate. Maybe she got fed up and killed her mother before she could change her will."

"People have been murdered for less," I said. "The funeral is tomorrow at the church."

Mystery gulped some water. "Is it my imagination, or do these shrimp get hotter the more you eat?"

"Seems that way."

Mystery waved at the waitress and pointed at her glass. "I think we should go to the funeral and check out Darlene. Jasmine wants more hours to pay for her ghost hunting toys. I'll ask her to work so we can attend."

"I'm game. Kaya is working tomorrow, so my store is covered. She's *almost* the perfect employee." I also downed some water, trying to quench my fiery tongue.

"What's the problem?"

I explained the situation. "I'm afraid she'll quit when she discovers I'm psychic. She's so superstitious."

Mystery waved her hands in a dismissive gesture. "Jasmine talks to her about ghost hunting all the time, and they're still friends."

I felt a presence next to me and looked up into the kind blue eyes of Detective Chris Haddington. I was so surprised that I sucked in a breath, sending the bite of shrimp down my windpipe.

I couldn't breathe.

Mystery's eyes popped wide. "Are you all right?"

I shook my head while holding my throat.

"Can you breathe?" Chris asked in an urgent tone.

I shook my head again.

He pulled me from the booth and did the Heimlich maneuver. This was not the way I'd dreamed that he'd wrap me in his strong arms. When he squeezed, I felt sure his hands went clear to my backbone. The offending shrimp shot two feet through the air and landed on the floor.

The place became quiet while all eyes focused on me.

Dear Lord, let me disappear now.

Coughing and gasping for breath, I managed to croak, "Excuse me." I staggered to the restroom, feeling the gazes of the patrons tracking my progress. Tears welled in my eyes while I locked myself into a stall. *The cutest guy I've met in months, and I pick this time to suck a piece of shrimp down my windpipe.* I stood in there for five minutes trying to regain my composure. I rubbed the tender spot where he'd pressed. *You have to face him sooner or later.*

I washed and dried my hands and fluffed my hair. Head held high, I left the restroom and strode to our table, ignoring the other patrons' stares. Mystery looked up. "Good, she's back." A mischievous grin spread across her face. "I asked Chris to join us for dinner. It would be a shame if he had to eat alone." She winked. "Especially since he saved your life."

CHAPTER 10

Chris slid out of the booth and stood. "Are you feeling better? I hope you won't have a bruise."

"Me, too. Thank you sooo much. I might have died if you hadn't been here." I felt my face heating under his gaze. My emotions straddled the line between humiliation and attraction.

He gave me an aw-shucks look.

"A true hero," Mystery said with a wide grin.

Then it hit me. Placing my hand over my tender spot, I said, "If you hadn't surprised me, I wouldn't have choked on the shrimp."

He looked sheepish, jamming his hands in his pockets. "Sorry about that."

Deciding to forgive him, I slid into the booth and he sat next to me. His warm energy field was calm and soothing.

"I didn't think you'd want any more of the shrimp, so Chris helped me finish them off," Mystery said.

Annabel arrived with our entrees. She looked at Chris with a where-did-you-come-from expression.

"I placed a to-go order under the name of Haddington. Could I have it plated to eat here?"

Annabel smiled. "Perfect. What would you like to drink?"

"Sweet tea."

After Annabel left to retrieve Chris's dinner, Mystery turned to him with a don't-lie-to-me look. "Have you ruled Bree and me out as suspects yet?"

She has an astonishing gift of getting to the point, except when she wants to drag things out to torture me.

Chris' mouth dropped open.

"My mama would say, no use beating around the bush. Since we found the bodies, we had to be on the suspect list. That's the only reason I can see that you haven't called Bree for a date."

My face felt as hot as an iron skillet sitting on high heat. *I'm gonna kill her.*

Chris started laughing.

I turned to look at him. His neck was pink.

"Busted!" he said. "Yes, we ruled you out, but don't tell my partner I told you. Have to admit, I didn't think my first date with this lovely lady would be a double date."

Mystery giggled like a school girl. "Does that mean you're picking up the bill?"

"Mystery!" I said, wishing I could slide under the table and disappear.

"My treat. I get tired of eating alone," he said.

"Thank you," we said in unison.

The scents of my Chilean sea bass, steamed asparagus and garlic mashed potatoes wafted in warm waves toward my face, making my mouth water. I hated to eat before Chris' food arrived, so I waited.

Within minutes, Annabel returned with his plate. "Here you go."

We ate in silence for a while. I enjoyed the melody of flavors that tantalized my taste buds. The neutral interior furnishings created a soft and tasteful seafood décor, unlike most tacky nautical ones I've seen in the past. My only complaint was the noise level. *Why can't restaurants do something to deaden the sound, so people can talk without yelling?*

While Chris was cutting up something on his plate, Mystery was giving me an ask-him look while making encouraging movements with her head.

I took a sip of water and cleared my throat. "How's the case going?"

"Fine."

"Have they established a time of death?" I asked, loading my fork with garlic mashed potatoes.

He gave me a serious look. "That's confidential information."

Mystery huffed. "Come on, we have a right to know, 'cause we found her."

I gave him my best Prissy look. "Please."

He shook his head and rubbed his hand over his mouth and chin. His seven-o'clock shadow made a rasping sound. "Don't look at me like that with those beautiful green eyes." He sighed. "It's estimated between one and four in the morning."

My jaw dropped. "What's a little old lady doing out at that time of night?"

He shrugged. "Beats me. Strange, isn't it?"

I tried to rub the tension from the back of my neck. "What was the cause of death?"

"Until we get the autopsy report back, they're assuming it was a blow to the head with a blunt object."

What kind of blunt object?" Mystery asked. If she leaned over the table any more, her bosom would drag through her salmon pasta.

"I suspect a baseball bat. We should know more in a day or two."

CHAPTER 11

I stood mesmerized at the gate of the Episcopal Church, watching as Victoria's ghost terrorized unsuspecting funeral attendees. Victoria had a vicious look of glee every time she pinched someone.

A shiver raced down my spine and did a return journey. *Good grief! That ghost is out of control.* Swallowing the urge to yell at her to stop, I shaded my eyes with a hand and told Mystery what was happening. I knew Mystery could only see people jumping or whirling around to look for who had assaulted them.

"Well, that's not nice," Mystery said, hands on her hips.

"Victoria's getting stronger and meaner. She's feeding off the emotions of the mourners."

"According to Tiffany, most folks didn't like her, so I don't know how much mourning is going on." Mystery removed her sunglasses.

"Doesn't matter whether it's love or hate; both create energy that can sustain a disembodied spirit. I think we now have a poltergeist on our hands."

It was a pleasant sunny day with a mild breeze, so the churchyard was full of people conversing.

I pointed. "See that woman wearing hot pink? That's Katie Abernathy."

"She's the one Tiffany told us was a sworn enemy of this haint," Mystery said, opening the creaky iron gate.

Katie jumped and whirled around to see who had accosted her.

Victoria laughed, looking pleased with herself.

"What happened? Why is Katie looking around?" Mystery asked.

"Victoria pinched her," I said, never taking my gaze off the naughty poltergeist.

"Let's go inside before Victoria spots you watching her." Mystery looked around like she might be pinched any moment.

"Good idea. We don't want her focused on us." I took her arm and propelled her at a brisk pace down the brick walk to the church's entrance.

I blinked several times once we stepped inside, waiting for my eyes to adjust to the gloom. The combination of the dark wood arched ceiling, the planked oak floor, and the brown wooden pews seemed to swallow the light. The many stained-glass windows and the ornate cylindrical hanging lights did little to brighten the interior. A red runner drew my eye down the sanctuary's long, narrow nave. Toward the end, a curved apse contained the altar and three narrow stained-glass windows.

A cherry casket, covered by an impressive spray of red roses with a tasteful scattering of baby's breath, rested in front of the altar.

Mystery followed me into a pew that was midway down. I planted my backside in the middle, hoping people wouldn't be crawling over me. I whispered, "I've never seen the inside of this sanctuary before." I tried to get comfortable on the hard wooden bench and looked up. "If they'd painted the ceiling a lighter color, it wouldn't be so gloomy in here."

"I think so, too," Someone whispered from behind me.

Already on high ghost alert, we both jumped, before twisting in the pew to find Katie sitting behind us.

"Vickie squashed any mention of changing anything in the church," Katie added, leaning forward so her whisper could be better heard.

I introduced Mystery to the older woman, who looked dressed for a celebration instead of a funeral. *I guess to her, it is something to celebrate.*

"Wouldn't the priest or the congregation have the final word on changes in the church?" Mystery asked.

"The church is listed as a National Historic Landmark because it was built in 1843. Vickie was the president of the Historic Preservation Board, so she had a good deal of control."

A round-faced woman sporting a short, trendy haircut walked toward the front, with her arm around a girl whose hair was the same dark brown. I guessed the girl was about ten years old.

Katie touched my shoulder, "That's Darlene and her daughter Susie. I've spoken to her about our conversation the other day. She wants to meet with you for a moment after the funeral."

Surprised that Katie had mentioned our discussion, I said, "Thanks."

Katie shrugged off my response and slid back in the pew.

I faced the front. *Wonder what she told Darlene?*

The Eucharist seemed to take forever. I squirmed, unable to get comfortable. I'd never thought kneeling would be preferable to sitting. Shifting closer to Mystery, I whispered, "These are the most uncomfortable pews I've ever encountered. Girl, my backside is numb."

Mystery nodded. "The ones in Mama's church at least have padded cushions."

With a subdued chuckle, I said. "The pain keeps the congregation awake during the sermon."

The organ music mounted to a crescendo, signaling something important.

Victoria's ghost glided with majestic grace down the aisle, with her chin held high. She glanced from one side to the other, glaring at certain people as she passed. When she reached the coffin, she floated in a sitting position over the flowers, one ethereal leg crossed over the other. Her head rotated to track the priest as he approached the podium.

Showtime. I wonder what he'll say about such a disliked woman?

Katie tapped me again. Her hot breath warmed my ear and the scent of mint followed. "That's Father Garrison. Can't wait to hear what he has to say about the old biddy."

He held a white envelope up for the congregation to see. "Victoria asked me to read the contents of this envelope during the service."

The spirit raised her chin again and looked down her long nose at the congregation. She seemed to glow with energy, clearly anticipating the reaction to the letter.

I shuddered when I saw the malice in her expression. *I bet that woman was a pain when she was alive. I pray she will cross over without causing any more harm.*

The priest opened it, perused the letter inside, and frowned before shaking his head with a disapproving expression. With tight lips, he folded the paper, returned it to the envelope, and laid it on the podium.

Katie leaned forward and whispered in my ear, "He's not going to read it. If she's here, she won't like it one little bit."

The priest began, "Victoria Spellman served on many boards in our community."

Victoria screamed like a banshee on steroids. "How dare you not read my letter!"

She zoomed upright and flung the roses off the casket. They landed several feet down the center aisle.

Everyone gasped and froze.

Father Garrison's eyes bulged as he stared at the flowers.

A trembling Mystery grabbed my elbow. "Sweet Baby Jesus. Did you see those flowers fly off the casket? Can she do that in a church?"

"She's a disembodied spirit, not a demon."

Gripping harder, she asked, "What's she doing now?"

A roar of conversation punctuated with a few screams reverberated in the sanctuary. Some mourners cringed, shrinking from view. The more curious ones stood for a better view.

Katie said with a cackle, "I told you so. I knew she was somewhere around here because that poor excuse for a human being pinched me in the churchyard!"

Darlene dragged Susie out of the first pew and glanced over her shoulder. Using her body as a shield, she hurried her daughter out of the sanctuary. Taking that as a cue, everyone scrambled out of the pews closest to the casket and rushed down the center aisle toward the door.

"Oh, no!" My hands covered my mouth.

"What?" Mystery asked, clutching my arm in a bruise-producing grip.

"Victoria's going for Father Garrison."

She zoomed forward and rammed into him with both hands.

He flew through the air and landed with a muffled thump. Sprawled on the carpeted floor, he blinked, trying to get his bearings.

Those still in the church did another collective gasp that seemed to suck the oxygen from the church.

"Lordy, did she throw him?" Mystery whispered, tightening her grip.

"Pushed him."

"That was one heck of a shove."

The priest scrambled to his feet. He looked left, then right, with white-rimmed eyes. His white robes flapped like an egret about to take flight as he ran toward a rear door and disappeared behind it.

"Heck, I'd run, too." Mystery released her hold on my aching arm.

I shifted away from her. "Victoria's a fast learner. All her anger, combined with the emotions of the crowd, is giving her an enormous amount of power. I've never seen anything like it."

The well-defined ghost glowed brighter with each pulse of energy. Her face contorted into an expression that I could only call zealous rage. With little effort, Victoria turned the coffin.

Mystery's eyes widened. "Oh my!"

Most of the remaining people scrambled out of the pews and raced toward the church's front door, pushing and screaming like a frightened mob in a Godzilla movie.

Victoria fired the coffin down the central aisle like a polished wood torpedo, chasing the terrified parishioners. She stopped the coffin's momentum at the entrance and floated out the door into the churchyard, where I heard more screams.

"Ye gods and little fishes! She's powerful." Mystery reached for my arm again.

I moved out of reach. My heart felt like a hamster running on a wheel. "That casket is cherry. It must weigh three hundred pounds or more with a body in it. Nothing like terror to fuel a poltergeist."

"I'd call that a spooky temper tantrum," Mystery said. "I agree with you, I've never seen anything like it, either."

Katie tapped me on the shoulder. "That was quite a show." With a twinkle in her bright blue eyes, she said, "Can't wait to see what happens at the cemetery." She shuffled to the end of the pew and skulked away.

She probably doesn't want to get pinched again, or worse.

"Mystery, I'll be back in a second." I left the pew and crept down the side aisle toward the pulpit. After looking to make sure no one was watching, I slipped the envelope from the podium and hid it in my large purse. I returned down the center aisle at a leisurely pace with my best angelic expression pasted on my face.

Mystery stood and cocked a brow at me. I knew she was curious about the envelope because she's even nosier than I am. She shuffled out of the pew and joined me.

"What are you going to do with that letter?" she whispered.

"I'm curious," I said. "I want to know why the priest refused to read it to the congregation. It could lead to a motive for her death."

"When are you going to read it?" Mystery asked.

"Whenever I get a chance, which isn't now, if we plan to attend the funeral," I said.

The casket sat askew, almost blocking the threshold of the open front doors. We took turns squeezing between it and the door jamb.

The churchyard was empty except for the two funeral directors hiding behind the open church door and Victoria, who ghost-paced above the bushes. She'd expended so much energy with her malicious antics that she was fading in and out. She stopped and glared at us.

I avoided looking at her, but I kept her in my peripheral vision while we made our escape down the brick path and out the open gate.

Mystery turned and closed it with a clang.

I didn't release my breath until we were on the other side of the street.

"Sugar, that was intense." Mystery wiped the sweat off her upper lip with a finger.

"That's one angry and powerful spirit. I'm not sure what we're going to do about her," I said, shoving a wave of hair out of my face. "I hope she won't be able to power up like that again."

We watched the older funeral director inch his way to the casket. He reached out a trembling hand to touch it, as if it might explode. When nothing happened, he stepped closer and gestured for his partner to join him. They struggled to straighten the coffin in the tight space while casting wary glances around them.

I bet they've never experienced a funeral like this before.

"Shall we go to the cemetery?" Mystery asked, linking her arm in mine.

"Wouldn't miss it," I said, keeping a watchful eye on Victoria's ghost.

By the time we reached my car two blocks away, the undertakers had placed the casket into the hearse. I turned on my headlights, to signal that I was part of the funeral procession, before taking my place at the back of the line. Led by the police escort, the hearse tooled down Eustis and turned right onto Greene Street. Oncoming traffic pulled to the side and stopped as a sign of respect, a common practice in Alabama. After we'd passed the Weeden House, we turned left onto Williams Avenue.

I craned to see ahead. "I've never taken this route to Maple Hill." The procession soon turned onto California Street.

I admired the old headstones and tall monuments visible above the low stone wall surrounding the hundred acres of Maple Hill Cemetery. An array of mature green trees shaded the graves, creating a serene, park-like atmosphere.

I followed the procession onto McClung Avenue and through the open iron gates. When we approached a large bronze plaque on a post, I stopped so we could read it.

"MAPLE HILL CEMETERY
ESTABLISHED 1818
OLDEST AND LARGEST MUNICIPAL CEMETERY
IN CONTINUOUS OPERATION IN THE SOUTH."

Mystery said with a bit of wonder, "That explains why it has so many old tombstones."

"And so many earthbound spirits." I scanned the area, looking at the specters floating about. "Mystery, we need to tell Jasmine about this. She can ghost hunt up a storm. I've never understood why Eddie investigates smelly barns and dilapidated houses when he can come to the cemetery."

Mystery nodded. "Jasmine bought some of the basic equipment for her personal use during her RCPS outings. She'll probably come here on her next day off."

I shook my head and shot her a disapproving glance. "Not without me or Eddie. Some of these ghosts are old and wily. One may try to steal her body."

The horrified wide-eyed look on Mystery's face said it all. "Steal her body!"

I was about to explain when a female ghost zoomed toward the car and thrust her face through the windshield.

I jumped in my seat.

Sensing the specter, Mystery leaned back. "Ye gods and little fishes! It's like a freezer in here. Is it Victoria?"

"Who is Victoria?" the rude spirit asked.

"No, a different ghost showed up." I gathered some energy and pushed with one hand. "Out!"

To my relief, the specter glided away. I took some deep breaths to calm my sprinting heart.

"Mystery, you have to be firm with spirits," I said, using my instructor tone.

"I've only been doing paranormal investigations for less than two years," Mystery said. "I still have so much to learn. Did you mean that ghosts can possess people?"

"Yep. Fortunately, a spirit can't stay in a body for long because of the difference in vibrational levels, but it's quite disconcerting."

She looked at me with a terrified expression. "I don't like how cold it feels when a haint is close. I can't imagine how it would feel to be possessed. Yuck!"

"Quit worrying. It takes time to learn about the paranormal. I've been dealing with it my entire life, and I'm still learning."

"Did a ghost ever hijack you?"

"Once, when I was a kid."

"What happened?" she asked.

"Mom was with me. She expelled it. That's why I don't want Jasmine to ghost hunt alone."

"Don't you worry about her doing it with the RCPS group?" she asked sounding concerned.

"Not so much. Several years ago, I trained Eddie to expel unwelcome spirits. You don't have to be able to see ghosts to expel them. You just have to know what it looks like when they possess somebody."

We eased down narrow roads toward the back of the property, where cars were lined along the curb. I parked near a square stone post that had 34 carved on it.

I exited and glanced around to gain my bearings. An American flag on a nearby pole fluttered in the gentle breeze.

After considering our options, we chose a path that wove between gravestones and past two specters. A forest green tent with the funeral home's name in white covered the area in front of the casket, now resting on poles over the open grave.

I nudged Mystery. "Let's join the others."

We stepped onto the carpet of green artificial turf that the funeral home had placed under the tent to keep women's high heels from sinking into the moist soil. Two rows of metal chairs stood in front of the casket under the shade of the tent. No one occupied them except Darlene, her daughter, and Katie. Everyone else stood outside the tent. This struck me as unusual behavior on a warm sunny day. Most shifted from foot to foot as they looked around, giving the impression they were ready to flee at any hint of a disturbance.

I eyed the battered blanket of red roses and baby's breath atop the coffin. *They look the worse for wear after being hurled to the floor and run over by a speeding coffin.*

Mystery and I claimed seats in the second row. My chair wobbled on the uneven ground.

Mystery leaned close, sending the scent of her Chloe perfume drifting my way. "Where's the priest?"

I whispered back, "Don't know. I don't see Victoria, either."

Mystery sat her purse in the next seat. "If I were Father Garrison, I wouldn't show up. He deserves hazard pay."

I nodded. "It takes a while for a ghost to learn all the rules and tricks of ghostdom after death. I think Victoria is still attached to the confines of the churchyard. I hope it stays that way."

She nodded toward the front row. "Bless their hearts, Darlene and Susie must be terrified by now."

"And embarrassed. Good thing they left before the truly horrifying part began," I murmured, watching a squirrel scamper up a nearby tree.

The older funeral director stepped forward and cleared his throat. His complexion was baby-powder pale with bright pink cheeks. "Father Garrison is, um, unable to join us."

I thought, *more like unwilling and scared out of his wits. I don't blame him one little bit.*

"Would anyone like to say a few words?" The funeral director stepped back with a military bearing.

The mourners looked at each other, but no one spoke.

Darlene stood and turned. A flush of pink stained her neck. "I know my mother was a difficult woman and made many enemies in the community. Susie and I appreciate your support and need your prayers." She returned to her seat and hugged her daughter close.

A murmur ran through the small gathering.

"Would anyone else like to say a few words?" The director looked left, then right.

No one stepped forward.

"In that case, anyone who'd like to place a floral tribute on the coffin may do so at this time." He stepped back and folded his hands in front of him.

Darlene and Susie stepped forward. Each placed a white rose on top of the battered flowers.

When no one else stepped forward, the funeral director said, "Thank you for attending."

A few people ventured forward to offer condolences to Darlene and her daughter. They cast wary glances toward the coffin as they passed it.

I watched them with interest. *I wonder, are they relieved or disappointed that Victoria was a no-show at the gravesite?*

Mystery and I stood and waited outside the tent to give the family some privacy until Darlene was ready to join us.

"Any idea why she wants to talk to you?" Mystery cast a wary glance around the area.

"I asked to speak to her. I assume that is why."

She paused and squinted before nudging me with an elbow. "Isn't that Detective Ricci?"

"Yes." Remembering the plots of the many mystery books I've read, I said, "He wants to see if the murderer attends the funeral."

"Do you think he'll suspect us since we're here?

I shrugged. "Remember, Chris said they cleared us."

Ten minutes later, Darlene walked toward us, leaving Susie behind with Katie.

"I'm Darlene Hennessey." She offered a trembling hand. "Katie told me about you, Brianna."

I took it and said, "Sorry for your loss." I completed the introductions.

"I guess you're wondering why I asked to speak with you."

I thought I was the one who wanted to speak to you. "I understand this may not be the best time. We can talk tomorrow if you wish."

Darlene shivered and rubbed her arms. "No, I'd like to get it over with, if you don't mind." She glanced around. "Is there somewhere we can talk?"

Mystery handed her a card. "My business isn't far from here. We can meet there if you like."

She nodded while staring at the card. Her reddened eyes met mine. "I'll meet you there in an hour, if that's convenient. I need to get Susie settled. Katie has agreed to babysit for a short while. I hope you can help."

"See you then," I said, feeling cat-curious.

Darlene left to claim Susie.

I watched a procession of ghosts gliding toward the coffin. One stuck its head inside.

I sighed my disgust. "That's just poor manners."

Mystery glanced around. "What?"

I told her about the ghosts sticking their heads in the casket while having a discussion about Victoria's attire.

"That's awful."

"Told you they have boundary issues." I turned, preparing to leave.

Mystery grabbed my arm. "Can't you do something to stop them?"

"What do you want me to do, wave my arms and say shoo in front of everyone and Detective Ricci, who's skulking off in the distance?"

"Sorry, Bree, I hadn't thought about the circumstances."

I felt a sense of relief when we were back in the car. *Don't know why I'm feeling safer. Hot Stuff may be able to accelerate from zero to sixty in 3.1 seconds, but it isn't ghost-proof.* I buckled my seatbelt and said, "I want to drive through the historical section while we're here, if that's okay?"

"Fine by me."

"In my opinion, it's the prettiest part of Maple Hill." I drove to the front of the cemetery, which lay closer to California Street. I stopped at a large bronze plaque that named all the important people buried in the cemetery and got out. "Have you ever been on one of the Cemetery Walks?"

"No, but I've heard of them," Mystery said. "What are they like?"

"Members of the Huntsville Historical Society choose certain graves and research the people buried in them. Volunteers dress in clothes of the period, role-play the deceased, and tell you about that person's life. It's a big local event in the fall when the maple trees are in their full glory."

"We should go together this year, unless you go with Chris." Mystery gave me a bawdy wink.

My cheeks felt hot. *It's a good thing I'm not a poker player. I can't hide my feelings worth a darn.*

"Why did we stop here?" Mystery asked, looking around.

"I promised Mr. Craft I'd stop and take a photo of this plaque, remember? He's a member of the Huntsville Historical Society and does a good bit of research for them. I think they're working on a book."

"I'm not surprised. He loves anything that's old." She peered up at it. "I didn't realize we have five Alabama governors buried in Maple Hill."

"According to Mr. Craft, the first State Constitutional Convention assembled here in 1819." I took several photos with my phone and began walking down the narrow road.

"Are there many ghosts here?" Mystery asked.

"Some. I saw more at Bonaventure Cemetery near Savannah."

"Shouldn't they be haunting a house or something? That's where we do most of our clearing work."

"They're still attached to their bodies for some reason." I stopped in front of an eleven-foot-tall monument with a three-foot angel sculpture on top. "This was one of the tombstones featured at the last cemetery walk."

Mystery said, "Nice angel statue. The plaque indicates he was a fine person."

"What it doesn't say is he was a slave owner," I said.

Mystery frowned up at the angel before looking at her watch. "My ancestors were originally slaves in Georgia, until they were sold to a plantation in Huntsville. I guess you can't judge a person by his monument. As Mama would say, we need to skedaddle. I need to tidy the conference room before Darlene arrives."

CHAPTER 12

Mystery and I looked up when the bell on the front door of her shop jingled.

Darlene had changed into jeans and a loose shirt. She had Victoria's gray eyes, but her padded curves were nothing like her mother's thin, angular frame.

"Welcome to The Mystery Shop, Sugar. This is my assistant, Jasmine."

Darlene nodded to Jasmine while eyeing her hair.

Mystery gestured for Darlene to follow us to the rear of the building. "We'll be in the conference room, Jasmine."

"No worries. I'll lock up if you want to go home early," Jasmine said, her eyes alight with curiosity.

We sat at the oval conference table, Darlene at one end with Mystery and me on either side. No one spoke for several minutes.

"I appreciate you coming to answer some of our questions about your mother's death. I'm sure Katie told you about our conversation."

Darlene shifted back in her seat, looking confused. Narrowing her eyes, she said, "Katie only told me that y'all could help me claim my inheritance."

Now, Mystery and I exchanged confused looks.

I steadied my nerves with a breath before admitting, "I was the one who found Victoria. Well, technically, my dog did."

Darlene's eyes grew rounder as she rested her elbows on the table.

Pushing aside the silence, Mystery said, "I was there, too. In fact, I recognized her and ID'd her to the cops."

Mystery's a strong believer in *partial credit*. Her mother, Lucille Miller, once told me, "I swear, if that girl carries one spoon to the table, she wants acknowledgment for setting the entire table."

I offered a quick explanation of the events leading to this meeting. "We're confused as to why you think we can help with your inheritance?"

Darlene balled her hands into fists. "I need you to find out who murdered my mother for two reasons. First, I want her ghost to find peace and go away. I can't live with that woman haunting me." She sighed. "I know this must sound awful, but my mother wasn't a nice person." She looked at Mystery. "That's what you do, isn't it, make ghosts go to wherever? That's what the sign out front says."

Mystery's brows shot up, surprised, I think, at the vehemence of her words.

Hiding my own shock, I thought, *This is a new development. Our primary suspect is asking for help?*

"What's the second reason you want our help?" Mystery asked, her brows back to normal. "Detective Ricci is already doing an investigation."

"He's not investigating anyone but me!" she said, pounding her fist on the table. She took a deep breath, maybe to bleed off some anger. Her expression softened to a pleading one.

"As I see it, there are three problems." I held up one finger. "Who murdered your mother?" I held up a second finger. "After Victoria's performance today, it's no secret that your mom hasn't crossed over, so that needs to be addressed." The third finger rose. "There's no guarantee that solving the murder will make your mother leave this plane of existence."

"Then why bother?" Darlene asked.

"It's your best option," I said.

Darlene dropped her head into her hands and kneaded her temples. "That woman made my life miserable. I don't think I can survive her vindictive ghost. Is her murder the reason she went crazy at the church? And why didn't Father Garrison or Mother show up at the cemetery? Not that I missed her terrifying antics."

Remembering that Darlene had been one of the first to leave the sanctuary after Victoria hurled the flowers to the floor, I described her mother's maniacal performance after her departure. While a horrified-looking Darlene digested the information with a white-knuckled grip on the arms of her chair, Mystery stood, grabbed three bottles of water from the fridge, and placed them on the table.

"What's the second reason you want us to investigate?" I gave her my tell-the-truth look. Waves of desperation, not grief, emanated from Darlene.

"That awful detective won't tell me much of anything. Rumors are flying everywhere. It's so embarrassing. I don't even know for sure how Mother died. I believe he thinks I killed her. He kept asking me where I was between one and four on Monday morning."

"And...?" I said.

"Where any sane person would be, in bed asleep."

No alibi. "Why was your mother at the church at that hour?" I asked, settling into the chair.

Darlene uncapped a bottle with a trembling hand and gulped some water. "She was an insomniac and often joked that she was a creature of the night. She'd eat, watch television, and go for walks. I warned her it wasn't safe."

At least that part of the mystery is solved. I sat back in my seat. "Who would know about her nocturnal excursions?"

Darlene rubbed her forehead. "Almost anyone who knew her."

"Why would the police think you murdered her?" Mystery asked.

"Mom was well off. I'm her sole heir and inherit everything. Detective Ricci showed up yesterday asking me if I knew Mom had a one-million-dollar life insurance policy. Susie and I are the beneficiaries."

"Did you know about it?" I asked, my tone laced with suspicion.

Darlene shot me a disapproving glare before shaking her head. "There wasn't any policy in the house safe where I found Mom's burial information, and I haven't had a chance to go to the bank. I don't know how he found out about the policy."

"The rumor is y'all argued Sunday night, and your mother threatened to write you out of her will. Is that true?" I reached for my nearby bottle of water while waiting for the answer.

After a bitter chuckle, Darlene said, "My *loving* mother threatened to disinherit me anytime I refused to do her bidding. I'm not sure if she hated me or only wanted her way."

Or both, I thought. *It's clear she was vindictive and cruel during her life, and death hasn't mellowed her disposition.*

"I work as a librarian. My ex-husband, Tom, walked out on me and often doesn't pay his child support. Mother has been holding me as her financial hostage for a year." Tears sprang to her eyes. "Can you imagine what that's like?" she asked, her voice shrill. "If she wanted a shrub dug up, she'd call and ask me to do it. The woman had a professional gardener on retainer who came once a week, but she'd call me. If I refused, she'd remind me of the utility bill she'd paid the month before. Everything had strings with Mother."

Appalled, I thought, *Thank you, Lord, that I grew up with a loving mother.* Then I remembered, *Dad wasn't so great.*

Mystery leaned forward. "Sugar, why did she treat you that way?"

Blotting tears with a tissue she'd found in her purse, she said, "Because I look like my father, and she hates him for deserting us. I guess the poor man couldn't take it anymore."

Mystery and I exchanged questioning glances.

Darlene explained that her mother came from a wealthy family in Pittsburg. "My grandmother spoiled my mother and underdisciplined her. I was told that by the time she was a teenager, she was out of control. In defiance and to escape my grandfather's control, Mother married my father and moved to Huntsville. Mother told me I was two when he left."

That explains a lot. "I still don't understand why you want us to find your mother's killer?" I asked, sensing some subterfuge.

A slight flush crept up Darlene's neck. "According to the law, I can't inherit if I was responsible for her death. I can't probate the will as the executor, and the life insurance company won't pay the benefits until I'm cleared. Susie and I are at a complete financial standstill." She looked from Mystery to me. "That's why I need this case solved and soon."

The bubble of truth finally surfaces.

"Okay, we'll take the case to clear your mother's ghost," Mystery said.

Darlene's face brightened. With hopeful enthusiasm, she said, "I'm almost certain if you discover the killer, her ghost will go away, the police will know I'm innocent, and I'll be able to claim my inheritance."

"Do you have any theories about who murdered your mother?" I asked.

Darlene gave a vigorous nod. "Mom bragged just a month ago that she'd discovered Franklin Morrison had embezzled funds from his company. I don't know how she found out or what she wanted from him. Mom was delighted that she'd destroyed his life." She placed both hands flat on the table and leaned forward. "She told me he threatened her."

"How did she ruin his life?" I unscrewed the top off my bottle of water.

Darlene explained that Victoria had mailed whatever proof she had to the president of the company. The ensuing scandal had caused him to lose his job and reputation. "Franklin's wife divorced him and took the kids. Now he faces criminal charges and possible jail time."

Mystery reached over and patted Darlene's hand. "We'll start by talking to him. Jasmine will be coming back to help you with the contract and to gather any facts you can tell her. She'll also collect the *required* deposit. My business does more than ghost tours and equipment sales, it's also a ghost hunting and removal business."

Darlene gave a reluctant nod and clutched her water bottle as if it could keep her from sinking further into despair. "Unknown to me, Mom had my name on several of her accounts. This has allowed me to pay the few remaining funeral costs. I'm pretty sure there will be enough to handle the deposit if it's not too large."

After Mystery directed Jasmine to help Darlene, we moved to a far corner of the retail area and consulted in low tones.

"Do you think Darlene is innocent, since she's hiring your business to catch the killer, so her mother can cross over?" I asked.

"Probably, unless she thinks she's committed the perfect crime and this is a ruse. Can you check out Franklin Morrison tomorrow?" Mystery leaned against a counter and crossed her arms and ankles.

"Why me? You're the one who has the contract, not me," I said.

"Because you can read his vibes, and I can't. Besides, Jasmine is in class most of tomorrow."

"Okay, but only if Jasmine locates him for me before I leave. Kaya will be off part of tomorrow, and I have a shipment coming in. I can't run all over Huntsville looking for this guy."

"Deal." Mystery patted me on the arm. "I'm going to Nashville on Monday to work on Tiffany's case. Want to come help? It would be fun."

"What's happening in the Country Music Capital of the South?"

"Jason's attending a conference at the Omni Hotel next week for five days. I hope to set up the cameras, verify what's happening, and be back home by Tuesday, in plenty of time for us to inspect Tiffany's house for any paranormal activity."

"Sorry, I forgot. Too much happening at once." I frowned, feeling confused. "Why do you need me? I don't know anything about setting up spy equipment."

"It goes faster with two. All you have to do is hand me stuff. As Mama would say, it'll be a piece of cake. Besides, we can make it an exciting escape. When was the last time you stayed in a fancy hotel?"

"A long time, but I have a business to run, remember?"

"Kaya and Jasmine are out for Spring break starting Monday. They offered to cover the shops."

"You already asked them?"

"Of course," she said, fluffing her curls.

"What about Prissy?" I asked.

"Jasmine will be house sitting for me and dog sitting for you."

"You have it all worked out." I grinned and tapped my chin. "Sounds like fun. What could go wrong?"

CHAPTER 13

I parked in front of the superstore on Memorial Parkway, after fighting the Friday morning rush-hour traffic. I took a moment to reread the research that Jasmine had provided and shook my head with surprise. *Hard to believe the director of accounting for a large defense contractor now works as a cashier. I wondered if he fibbed on his resume as to why he was fired.* I closed the file. *On the bright side, he should know how to count back change.*

I exited the car and stared at the front of the enormous building. *How am I going to talk to Morrison if he's running a register?* I studied his photo, so I'd be able to spot him. Steely gray eyes stared from behind wire-rimmed glasses. *Haughty looking dude. Except for the glasses, he'd make an incredible Dracula for Halloween.*

I shoved the papers into my large purse and strode with determination toward the closest door. After acknowledging the greeter with a polite smile, I turned right to check out the cashiers. I passed a bin full of discounted Easter decorations and candy. The smell of chocolate called its siren song. *Goodness, that smells tasty. Maybe I should text Mystery and let her know it's on sale.* I was about to reach for my phone when a tall man wearing the store's trademark blue smock caught my eye.

That's him. My heart tap-danced in my chest, a combination of excitement and anxiety. *So far, so good, but how am I going to get him away from the register? I wonder what Vera would do?* Mystery's former boss was a licensed private investigator with years of experience. I lacked both a license and the experience.

Morrison was sacking the purchases of a stooped elderly lady who was digging through her wallet with gnarled fingers.

After he dropped the plastic bag into her cart, his frown seemed to relay, *Come on, hurry up!*

When the lady handed him a penny with an unsteady hand, he dropped it into the register drawer, slammed it shut, and ripped off the receipt to give her.

I was approaching the register, determined to question him then and there, when another employee walked up and said, "Time for your break."

Before the old lady had finished stuffing her receipt into her wallet, Morrison had turned off the checkout station light, locked his register, and walked away.

I hustled through a nearby closed register and followed him past the check-out counters and through the exit door.

He marched with a military bearing toward the side of the building and disappeared around the corner.

I rounded the corner in time to see him light a cigarette.

Huffing a bit, I said, "Mr. Morrison?"

He looked up and took a puff. His gaze worked its way over me, before he shoved his lighter into expensive looking blue trousers.

I introduced myself and offered my hand.

He took it in a grip that was beyond firm. His shark-like smile revealed teeth that would make any dentist proud. His energy was yucky, like cold, gritty muck.

I withdrew my hand and resisted the urge to rub it. Instead, I handed him a business card.

He read it and smirked. "Chocolates and Delights. Are you here to delight me, pretty lady?"

I ignored the implication. "I'm checking into Victoria Spellman's murder. Can I ask you some questions?"

"*May*, it should be *may* I ask you some questions," he said with a superior tone. "Who hired you?"

Great, he's one of those arrogant grammar folks. "That's confidential."

He frowned and exhaled a large plume of smoke "Why should I waste my break talking to you?"

I crossed my arms and cocked a hip, before giving him my don't-mess-with-this-redhead stare. "So that I'll go away. Of course, I could continue to hound you until my questions are answered." I shrugged one shoulder with an indifference I didn't feel. "Your choice."

He eyed me the way he might study a bug.

"Kudos to whoever took out that nosy blackmailer. I wish they'd done it before she ruined my life."

"It was my understanding that you were embezzling funds, got caught, and that ruined your life." My nose twitched as the acrid tobacco fumes drifted my way. My eyes began to water, and I resisted the urge to sneeze.

He waved away the comment, the cigarette creating a swirl of smoke. "The paper said someone bludgeoned the old busy-body to death." He shot me a razor-sharp smile that failed to reach his eyes. "Too bad they didn't torture her first."

His anger emanated like invisible waves of searing flames. I took an involuntary step back and raised my shields to avoid its force. "Where were you Monday between one and four in the morning?"

He took in a deep draw before throwing down his butt and grinding it with his shiny leather shoe. He exhaled the smoke in a slow, steady stream.

"Is that when it happened? What was she doing wandering around at that time of the morning?" He rubbed his prominent chin. "Probably digging up dirt on her latest victim." He eyed me from top to bottom and sneered. "Hard to believe a woman who owns a lingerie shop got to me before the cops."

What a misogynist! I planted a fist on each hip and stared him down. "Do you have an alibi or not?"

His laugh was bitter. "Ironclad. I was in the drunk tank for driving under the influence. That vicious old woman drove me to drink. Nearly lost my job here over that DUI."

I'm Southern, so I was raised to be polite in the direst of circumstances. "Thank you for your time." I whirled and strode toward Hot Stuff.

"If you get lonely, you know where to find me," he yelled.

My major in college had been business, but my minor in psychology gave me insight into Morrison's character. *What a sociopath. No acceptance of his wrong-doing. No remorse. No empathy for others.* I checked the time. *I'll have Mystery verify his alibi when I get back to my shop.*

CHAPTER 14

Sunday evening was so pleasant that I opened several of my windows to air the house while I packed. I was concentrating hard on what to take for the trip and didn't notice Pierre floating outside my bedroom window.

"Where are you going, ma chérie?"

I jumped, my undies flying from my grasp. My heart pounded like a drummer high on speed. I rounded on Pierre. "Are you trying to give me a heart attack?"

He held his palms up in supplication. "Why do you always accuse me of giving you a heart attack?" A slow smile spread like honey across his face. "If you were to die of one, we could be together, non?"

"No, because I will cross over and you will still be stuck here." I gritted my teeth and asked, "What do you want?"

He winked. In a seductive tone, he said, "I think you know."

"Besides that."

He shifted his position to achieve a lying-on-his-side levitation. "To know why you are packing?"

I explained the trip to Nashville while I retrieved my undies and packed them. I thought through each possible scenario and added bedroom slippers.

With a gleeful tone, Pierre said, "There are good things about being un fantôme."

"Like what?" I asked as I closed the suitcase.

"I don't have to think about what clothes to pack for Nashville."

He drifted closer to the window. "Since bathing or shaving is no longer necessary, I do not even have to worry about packing my travel kit." He did a flourish with his hand. "The joys of no longer being odorous."

I chuckled, amused by his enthusiasm. "Pierre, I'm glad you found something positive about your current state." I opened the suitcase again to add my phone and watch charging cables.

"Ah, there is more. I can float through things, which is impressionnant." Pierre grinned, looking quite pleased with himself.

"Indeed, impressive. I'll admit, I wish I could do that feat."

"What hotel are we staying in this time?" he asked.

I sighed with frustration. "I'm going to Nashville with Mystery. I don't know what you're doing."

"Going with you, bien sûr."

"No."

His brows rose. "Non?"

"You heard me. If you show up, I'll banish you from the hotel. It's ladies only."

Prissy chose that moment to jump onto the bed. She settled inside the suitcase on top of the clothes, wagged her tail, and offered me her most adorable doggie grin.

I shook my head. "Sorry, young lady. You can't go."

Prissy's perky ears drooped and her brown eyes took on a soulful expression.

"Don't look at me that way. The answer is still, no. Off the bed. You're getting tan fur all over my clothes." I placed her on the floor.

Pierre sidled closer to the window. "Think about it, ma chérie." He gave his best scoundrel grin. "You and me, alone, in a hotel room. We could order a bottle of wine and turn on some music." He produced a seductive wink and gave a sexy hip wiggle before puffing out his chest like a frigate bird.

Shivering from the cold coming through the window, I said, "First, you don't sleep." I rubbed my bare arms to warm them.

"I can watch you sleep, like I did in Paris, ma chérie."

"If you'll remember, that resulted in your banishment from my room. Second, you can't drink wine." I closed the suitcase.

He frowned. "That is unfortunate. However, it could help to stoke your internal fire." He waggled his brows at me.

"Third, you're dead, so there can be no intimacy." Before he could respond, I added, "Have you forgotten Mystery? We're sharing a room."

"Ah, oui." His grin widened. "The more the merrier, non?"

"No." I crossed my arms.

He frowned and drifted a few feet away. "You'll need protection." He flexed his biceps.

I smiled at his antics. "I can take care of myself. Besides, who will protect me from you?"

Frowning, Pierre ghost paced holding his hands behind his back. He stopped and faced me. "I can guard the door while you do your work."

I resisted the urge to throw something through the window, but only because I knew it would pass through him and land on the ground. "I appreciate your good intentions, but we have things covered."

He quirked his head to the side. "Covered with what?"

I exhaled my frustration. "It means we can handle it without your help. Instead, use the time while I'm gone to resolve your earthbound status."

Pierre crossed his arms. His jaw flexed like a lizard doing push-ups. "Is that why you are leaving me here, to punish me because I am not ready to leave this plane of existence?" He raised his chin and stared down his narrow nose.

"I'm not punishing you for anything. It's your choice to cross over. If you want to help me, you can protect my house.

This perked him up. He floated straight and clicked his ghostly heels. "I will guard ta maison with my life."

I thanked him, but didn't mention he had no life left to give. I told him goodnight and closed the window.

He blew me a kiss.

CHAPTER 15

Much too early for my taste, Mystery and I loaded our luggage into Hot Stuff, while Prissy looked at me with accusing brown eyes.

"Jasmine's going to take you to Mystery's house until I get home." I pointed a finger and gave her my sternest look. "Don't give her that starving look. No wheedling for extra treats. You hear?"

Prissy lay down and put her head on her paws while Jasmine loaded her bed, food and other needed items into the trunk of her 2012 Honda Civic.

I snuggled my furry kid and kissed the top of her head. "Be a good girl. I love you, Sweetie." I handed her to Jasmine. "Take care of my baby, and don't forget her squirrel fixation."

Jasmine rolled her eyes. "Believe me, I haven't forgotten the time I had to chase her for blocks thanks to one of those twitchy-tailed rodents. Prissy may be small, but she's fast."

I set the alarm and locked the door.

Prissy produced a disapproving yap.

That little dog always has to have the last word.

Jasmine placed Prissy into her car, joined her, and waved as she drove away.

I miss her already.

Icy cold ran down both arms causing my stomach to lurch. I whirled to find Pierre smiling at me.

"What's the matter with you?" Mystery asked.

I ignored her question. "Pierre, what are you doing here?"

He held his arms open. "I've come to wish you bon voyage and

to say au revoir. I will guard your home."
"Merci."
"De rien, ma chérie."
Mystery and I entered the car. I was ready to try my hand at some detective work that didn't involve angry spirits.
I waved goodbye to Pierre.
Mystery waved, too.
"He's on the other side of the car," I said.
"Oops." She shifted her wave.

We made a brief stop at the supercharger south of Nashville, which gave us a chance to grab a bottle of complimentary water, visit the spotless facilities, and call Jasmine.
"We're in Nashville. I'm putting you on conference call," Mystery said.
"Everything's cool here," said Jasmine. "Prissy's settled into my office. I talked with Kaya and everything is fine. Stop worrying!"
Like that will happen.
"Mystery, Tiffany brought in additional information that should help my computer search and filled out the form she forgot. She did it with *precision*."
Mystery grinned. "Is precision your word of the day?"
"Uh huh. That word helped me to sell our most expensive surveillance system."
"Good for you. Did you check Franklin Morrison's alibi?" Mystery asked.
"Yep. Morrison told the truth. He was in jail during the time of the murder."
We exchanged glances.
Mystery said, "As Mama would say, back to square one."
We heard the jingle of the front door bell.
"Gotta go," said Jasmine. "It's a customer."
Fifteen minutes later, we approached downtown Nashville. It was only one-thirty, yet the traffic was robust. Feeling anxious, I checked the large touchscreen as the navigation mode announced the upcoming exit. My hands tightened on the wheel when I exited from Interstate 65 to merge onto the congested Interstate 40. I maneuvered through bumper-to-bumper traffic in an active construction zone to reach my next exit. Once I was on Second

Avenue, I sighed with relief. Three turns later, I was on Korean Veterans Boulevard.

I spotted the glass façade of the Omni and pulled Hot Stuff to a halt at the entrance.

Mystery unbuckled her seatbelt. "My research shows the hotel is hosting not one but two conferences this week—lawyers and proctologists."

I chuckled. "Both professions stick it to you with a high bill."

A smiling team of handsome young men surrounded Hot Stuff, ready to unload our luggage and with hopes of valet parking my baby. One of the attendants stood close to my door, holding an ID tag and a pen.

The hotel's website said the valet parking fee was over twenty dollars a day. "Are we charging the valet fee to Tiffany's account?"

Mystery grinned. "Why not? It's an investigation-related expense."

I set the Tesla to valet mode and handed the credit card-sized key to the charming young man. "Do you know how to use this key card?"

"Yes, ma'am." He smiled and leaned closer. "We love Teslas."

"Y'all be careful with it, you hear?" Mystery said.

"Yes, ma'am."

"Good." I leaned inside and grabbed my phone and purse. I gave the valet my name and mobile phone number. After noting it on his pad, he pulled off a receipt and a tag with a number. "You'll need to present this tag to claim your car, ma'am." He handed them to me.

I kept the tag but passed the receipt to Mystery while walking toward the hotel door.

We entered the massive lobby. The primary decorative scheme included lots of gleaming wood, shiny cream-colored stone floors, and seating areas arranged artistically atop crimson area rugs.

"I'm going to text Mama and Jasmine that we've arrived safely," Mystery said.

"Good idea. I'll text Kaya." I pulled my phone from my purse.

When we finished, Mystery pushed her phone into her huge purse. "We need to find a discarded room keycard. Vera always found one to switch for a universal key."

"Where in the world will we find one of those?"

She shrugged. "Walk around, someone may have dropped one."

After fifteen minutes, all I'd found was a gum wrapper. Mystery found me and shook her head.

"Let's try the pool or gym," I suggested.

We entered the pool area and walked around as if we were checking the facilities. We passed a woman reading a romance novel in a lounge chair near the shallow end of the pool, while two kids splashed around in the nearby water.

A rotund man rose from his lounge chair near the deep end and waddled toward the pool. His key card was on a small table next to his drink.

I took a step forward, but Mystery caught my arm.

The man paused, came back, downed the rest of his drink, and headed back toward the pool.

Mystery strolled by and picked up the room keycard on the table, while the man's back was to her. She was sliding it into her pocket when he jumped into the pool, creating a splash that was sure to be the envy of the young boys. He came up sputtering and rolled onto his back to float, his stomach creating a fleshy island amid the lapping water.

With an urgent whisper, she said, "Let's go."

We walked back to the lobby.

A wall clock at the registration desk showed the time to be two p.m. We had arrived early because Mystery knew from her conference experience that the closer it came to the four o'clock official check-in time, the longer the queue. She also wanted to make sure the request she'd made for a room next to Jason's would be honored.

Three clerks stood behind the wide check-in desk. A younger male and female clerk huddled to the right, chatting. A middle-aged woman with dark hair occupied the other side, intent on some task that I couldn't see.

"Which one should we choose?" Mystery asked.

I edged closer to pick up their vibrations. I chose the middle-aged woman with dark hair, whose white blouse was tight across her torso.

The lady greeted us with a tired smile. She had the look of someone who wanted to go home and soak her feet.

"You look like you've had a long shift," I confided with an understanding smile.

"You're right. It's been a long day." She managed another weary smile.

I glanced at her name tag. "Well, Marion, when I wince that way, it means my shoes are uncomfortable."

Marion glanced down the counter toward the younger clerks, who were now laughing. She eased closer. "The hotel insists we wear black high heels, but they aren't the ones standing in them all day."

I gave her an empathetic nod. *Bless her heart, she's suffering.*

"It's not like anyone can see your feet behind this counter. That's a silly rule." Mystery crossed her arms.

"That's what I told them."

I thought a moment and donned a wily smile. "I can tell you how to get around that painful dress code."

Marion straightened. A gleam of hope twinkled in her blue eyes. "How? I'm desperate."

"Make an appointment with a podiatrist and tell the doctor about your foot problems. Ask him to write you a prescription stating that you have to wear a certain type of shoes if you're required to stand over thirty minutes."

Marion's eyes widened. "Do you think it'll work?"

"It worked for one of my friends," I said.

Marion glanced down the counter again. "If there's anything I can do to assist y'all while you're staying here, please let me know."

"I have a reservation." Mystery leaned closer and lowered her voice. "There is one little thing. I requested a room next to Jason Blake. Could you make sure that happens?"

"Are you friends?" Marion asked, already typing.

I saw Mystery's crossed fingers behind her back. "Yes. Please don't mention it to Jason." She gave a conspiratorial wink. "It would spoil the surprise. He doesn't know we're coming."

Marion continued to type on the computer while squinting through the bifocals perched on her nose. "There are interconnected suites on the fifteenth floor. I can reserve the one next to yours in his name."

"Sugar, that would be perfect." Mystery smiled and handed the clerk her business credit card.

Marion lowered her voice, so the man and woman approaching the desk wouldn't hear. "Check-in isn't for another two hours, but your room is ready, so I'll let you go up."

"Thank you, Marion," we said in unison and walked to the center of the room.

The large man from the pool waddled barefoot toward the front desk, clutching a towel around his middle and leaving a trail of wet footprints behind him.

Mystery nudged me and smirked. "Wanna bet he lost his room key?"

The valet arrived with our luggage, looking eager to escort us to the suite. While on the way, I remembered Mystery telling me that her former boss, Vera, always located the cameras in the hotel's lobby and hallways. I made a mental note of each one and suspected Mystery did the same.

When we reached the elevators, the valet said, "Second floor is the conference area. You'll need to use your room cards to go past it." Once inside, he touched my keycard to a sensor and pushed the button for the fifteenth floor.

After we were in the room, Mystery tipped the valet and closed the door behind him while I looked around.

The room featured a soothing color scheme of beige and gray with punches of red accents. The two queen-sized beds looked tempting. The floor to ceiling window overlooked the Music City. We stepped closer to enjoy the view.

The AT&T skyscraper rose tall against the robin's-egg blue sky. I could understand from its shape how it acquired the nickname, "Batman building."

When we entered the bathroom, Mystery said, "This is quite nice. Much better than the cheap dumps Vera described that cheaters flock to for a quickie."

I admired the dark natural-stone counter of the vanity while brushing my teeth.

When I came out, Mystery was looking through the installation toolkit.

She held up a one-hole punch and with a tone of triumph, said, "Found it."

"What are you going to do with it?" I asked.

"I called Vera last night. She's in Colorado now. She gave me an earful of tips on how to handle this." She told me her plan.

My stomach sank like an anchor. *We're going to get caught and go to jail. The closest people to bail us out are two hours away.*

Before we left the room, we discussed the locations of the cameras we'd spotted.

"Follow me," Mystery said.

We headed down the stairs in search of a maid's cart. While in the stairwell, she pulled out two hats and a dark jacket that she'd stuffed inside her large purse. She donned the jacket and one hat, and handed me the other.

I stuffed my red hair under it and pulled it down to shield my face. *Jeez, I hope this works. What am I gonna say when the police show up?* Vera had always loved to tell tales of her escapades while running investigations. I wished now I'd listened closer.

Mystery opened the stairwell door to the floor below ours. A cart sat parked by an open door halfway down the hall. A passkey card lay on top of the nearest stack of clean towels.

It took everything in me to get my feet moving. My heart tap danced against my ribs while I walked down the hall. *What would Vera do if the maid comes out?* I pondered while trying not to hyperventilate. *Knowing Vera, she'd talk her way out of it. Can we do the same?*

Mystery managed to squeeze between the cart and the wall.

Feeling like an idiot, I mimed talking to the maid that was nowhere in sight inside the room.

Mystery whispered, "Just as Vera said, the passkey looks just like the room cards."

Using her body to block her actions from the hall cameras, she hole-punched the correct corner of the room card she had swiped at the pool. With trembling fingers, she fumbled the maid's master card from the wrist key holder and replaced it with the palmed card. She pocketed the universal card.

I checked our escape options. *The elevator's closer than the stairwell.* I nodded in that direction.

Careful to act casual, we strolled toward the elevator as if we had no concerns.

Mystery poked the button.

We waited and waited and waited.

I pushed the button again. *Come on. I don't want this maid to spot us.* Sweat formed on my upper lip. I swiped it away with a sleeve.

A dark-haired maid wearing earphones and a blue uniform

appeared in the hall, bobbing her head. She dumped a load of sheets onto the floor beside the cart and went back inside without looking up.

I slumped with relief. *Phew, that was close.*

Mystery pushed the button a third time.

The elevator dinged and the doors crept open. We rushed inside as the maid walked out, carrying a load of soiled towels.

Thankful to be out of view, I punched the lobby button. The elevator doors didn't move. *For chrissake!* I pushed the button harder to close the door. The metal doors glided together. I took a deep breath, pulled the hat from my head, and handed it to Mystery. She stuffed it back in the bag while I fluffed my hair.

By the time we reached the lobby, Mystery had shrugged off her jacket and returned it and her hat to her bag. We meandered through the seating area, doing our best to appear casual, before choosing chairs that provided a clear view of the entrance, the check-in desk, and the hallway to the elevators.

The whole experience felt surreal, like a scene in a movie. This was nothing like investigating a haunting where we would set up cameras and recorders, take readings with Mystery's ghost hunting equipment, and wait for me to talk with the ghost.

I could tell from Mystery's bouncing leg that she was tense, too.

"Bree, I think Vera must have nerves of steel."

"I agree."

"I remember a story Vera once told me. She set up a room with cameras before the guy she was investigating checked in. At the last minute, the mark decided to upgrade his room. She lost a day on the investigation because she had to sneak the equipment out of the room after a family of four had settled in, and then reinstall it in the correct room. At least I know to wait and install the spy equipment after Jason checks in, thanks to her."

I nodded. "I certainly don't want to install it twice."

I settled down and read some more of my novel, *Big Four*. Mystery read on her tablet while we waited for Jason and his assistant, Sierra. Like so many things in life, it was a rush to wait situation. Thirty minutes later, I decided to check my email, so I put away my book and grabbed my iPad from my bag.

I was deleting the junk mail when our marks came through the door, all smiles and holding hands. I nudged Mystery with my elbow. She looked up and stiffened.

Jason had a medium athletic build and wore a blue polo shirt with jeans. His short dark hair looked neat. Sierra's jeans molded to her every curve, and her low-cut tee shirt advertised her wares. Her long blonde hair was pulled up into a high ponytail that swished with every step.

Mystery recorded their bliss on her tablet while pretending to read it. When they left the check-in counter to go to their room, we followed.

Jason and Sierra didn't even wait to get on an elevator. He pulled her into a nearby alcove, where they engaged in a passionate lip-lock like a couple of hormone-driven teenagers.

I glanced over at Mystery.

She was already recording them.

Good grief, can't they wait until they get to the room?

CHAPTER 16

Mystery handed me the maid's universal card to try on our door, while she took another look at the copy of the conference schedule that she'd found abandoned at the bar.

I sighed with relief when it worked.

"It says the hospitality room will open in an hour, followed by a 'welcome' dinner."

"Good." I smiled. "I have time for a catnap."

She put down the brochure. "An excellent idea. I was so excited about this little adventure that I had a hard time falling asleep last night."

The sound of voices and a closing door jerked me awake.

Mystery sat up and yawned. "Sounds like they're leaving."

Triggered by hers, I yawned, too. "Thank you, Marion, for the adjoining rooms."

"Amen to that," Mystery said while unlocking the door on our side.

We sat for a few minutes to discuss our strategy.

While Mystery finished preparing her equipment, I left the room and caught an elevator to the second floor. My first task was to confirm that Jason and Sierra were in the hospitality suite.

They were. Each had a drink and were conversing with two other couples. The room was filling as more folks arrived and the line at the bar formed a snake across the room.

"You folks stay in there and drink it up for a while," I mumbled.

Spotting a public restroom, I popped inside and entered the handicapped-accessible stall, where I hung Mystery's large conceal-carry purse on a hook. I tried to channel Vera while I transformed myself. Ten minutes later, I exited the stall sporting a long blonde wig, a different jacket, and another wide-brimmed hat to shield my face. I didn't want to be recognized by the hotel's security camera while I broke into Jason's room.

I peeked out the restroom door. *Good, all is clear.* Using a sexier, hip-rolling gait, I strolled past the hospitality room to confirm the two lovers were still boozing it up.

I rode the elevator to the fifteenth floor, where I sexy-walked to Jason's door. Looking both ways for any witnesses, I took a deep breath before using the universal card. When the light turned green, I slipped inside.

I pulled on gloves while deep breathing to slow my escalating heart rate. *Calm down.* I unlocked Jason and Sierra's connecting door so Mystery could bring in her tools and devices.

Moving with speed and precision, Mystery wasted no time in planting recording devices and video cameras. It was clear that her years of experience helped in the choice of hiding places. I acted as her assistant, which meant I followed directions and handed her tools.

Everything was going well, until I lost my footing while climbing down from a chair. I toppled to the floor with a bang. "Drat!" Pain sizzled from my hip down my leg.

Mystery rushed over. "You okay? I should've adjusted that camera myself instead of asking you to do it."

I heard laughter in the hall.

Stiffening with alarm, I scrambled to my feet. I rubbed my hip and listened.

The voices stopped outside the door.

My heart lodged in my throat like a pulsating golf ball.

The wild-eyed expression on Mystery's face showed a state of complete panic. What happened next felt like a frantic comedy routine on fast forward. She grabbed the tool kit and stepstool, ran into our room, and shut the door.

The lock clicked.

With my escape option gone, I grabbed the hat and bag off the bed and shoved them underneath it.

The door to the suite swung open. I dove behind the heavy drapes and held them still.

"I'll only be a moment. I left my favorite lip color in the bathroom. I'll want to freshen my lipstick after dinner," Sierra said with a flirty tone.

"Your lips look luscious enough to me," Jason said, his voice husky.

I was sure they could hear the pounding of my heart. Then I remembered the chair. I'd moved it over a few feet to help Mystery install a camera. *What if they notice? Here I am in another state with no PI license. If we get caught, Mystery's mama will never let us hear the end of it.* I took a breath and thought about my mom. *She'll think it's a hoot.*

After some giggling, Sierra said, "Later, Stud. Not now, you'll mess up my hair."

"We can skip the rest of the meet-and-greet and play now. You know, work up an appetite for dinner," Jason said, his tone dripping inuendo.

Sweat gathered on my brow. *No playing now, Jason. We haven't turned on the equipment yet!* I licked my dry lips and tried to think of what I would say if they discovered my hiding place. Nothing plausible came to mind.

A movement to the left caught my eye. Afraid to move my head, I tried to focus on the black thing crawling toward my face.

A spider!

I cringed. *Don't move. Don't scream.*

The spider inched closer. I could see the spiky hairs on its long, jointed legs.

Jason, stop pawing that woman and leave. Now!

My eye twitched. The eight-legged beast from hell kept advancing. The closer it came, the larger the hairy monster loomed.

"Stop." Sierra giggled. "I don't want to miss a thing. It's my first real convention."

The creature had moved so near it was now a black blur. I squeezed my eyes shut and sucked in a breath. *Go away. Go away. Go away.* It touched my face. A spasm of fear raced down my body. *God, help me!*

The door closed with a muffled click.

I shot from behind the curtains in full terror, rubbing my hands over my face. I yanked off the wig and beat it without mercy on the carpet.

Mystery opened the door and stuck in her head. "Good Lord, what are you doing to that wig?"

"Spider!" I gasped. The horrid creature dropped to the floor. I chased after it, trying to stomp it, but the arachnid scrambled back under the curtains. Shuddering with disgust, I willed my thundering heart to stay in my chest. "That's all I needed, a ninja spider. I'm not made for this crap. Give me a ghost any day of the week. Geez, I don't know how Vera had the nerves for this type of work."

"Me, either. Sugar, I almost wet my pants."

I shot her a glare. "Was that before or after you locked me out of our room?"

Mystery had the decency to look embarrassed. "I panicked."

I rubbed my aching hip and limped across the floor. Grunting, I moved the heavy chair back in place. It was only then I noticed the screwdriver I'd been holding when I fell, lying beside the leg of the chair. I slumped against the wall. "That was close."

We wasted no time collecting the rest of our stuff. Hoping no one would notice, we left Jason's side of the adjoining doors unlocked.

After Mystery closed our door behind her, I hurried into the bathroom to replace the bedraggled wig and straighten it.

Good grief, how many beauty products did Sierra bring on this trip? I counted seven lipsticks lined up on the counter.

We had decided the hotel camera should record my false persona leaving Jason's room in case something went wrong. I crammed the hat on my head, retrieved the bag, eased out into the hall, and sashayed to the elevator despite my protesting hip. The elevator doors glided open.

There stood Jason and Sierra, holding hands.

My heart hammered in my chest while I held my breath. *Stay calm. This is not the time for a fall-apart.* I lowered my eyes and stepped to the side, so they could exit.

Neither of them even looked at me as they stepped out. Sierra said, "I'm sorry, Honey, but I picked up the wrong lipstick. I need the darker pink one."

I eased past them into the elevator.

"No matter how many times I tell you how great you look, you always have to tweak something, don't you?" Jason said as he ran his hand up and down her back. "You're such a vixen."

Sierra giggled as the doors closed, cutting off the rest of the conversation.

For a grown woman, she sure giggles a lot. I leaned against the side of the elevator and released my pent-up breath. "As Lucille would say, that was too close for comfort."

I walked through the lobby and returned to the same public restroom, mumbling, "Stupid terrorist spider. I'm lucky I didn't have an accident." I entered the handicapped stall, took care of business, and changed back into the outfit I'd worn earlier. Satisfied with the results, I left the restroom, walked down the hall, and slipped into an open elevator.

After I entered our room, I dropped Mystery's oversized purse on the bed and asked, "Are we eating out?"

Mystery shook her head. "Vera advised that the less we're seen from this point on, the better. Let's order room service.

Mystery ordered a steak and I decided on the salmon.

While we waited, Mystery made sure all the equipment was working. "I hope ole Jason doesn't drink too much, so he can provide a stellar performance."

I chuckled. "Wasn't stellar one of Jasmine's words of the day last week?"

"Yep. That girl's vocabulary has improved since I gave her that word-of-the-day calendar for her twenty-first birthday."

"I think all our vocabularies have improved." I sprawled on the bed, looking forward to dinner. We had both ordered a glass of wine and chocolate cake with dinner.

Mystery stretched. "Tonight, we'll let the cameras do their thing while we get a good night's sleep in our comfy beds. According to Vera, the performance they put on for us in the alcove by the elevators is all we need to prove an affair. What I hope to film tonight will provide the needed backup proof that should ensure Jason won't fight Tiffany's request for a divorce."

I jolted awake from a nightmare where a giant spider picked me up with its hairy legs. I glanced around, taking in the splash of light shining through a slit of the hotel's blackout drapes. "Calm down, girl, you're in Nashville."

Mystery sat up. "What? Is something happening?"

"I don't think so." I crawled from the bed and grabbed the conference schedule, which showed breakfast at eight o'clock and the first session at nine.

I yawned. "I'm taking a shower. By the way, you snore."

"Do not!"

"Do so."

Mystery raised her chin and crossed her arms. "If that's true, you wouldn't hear me if you'd gone to sleep first."

I shook my head in disbelief and headed for the shower.

Once I'd finished showering and dressing, we phoned for room service and took a moment to check the camera feeds.

"Goodness! They're at it again," Mystery said.

Not interested in being a voyeur, I sat at the desk with a mirror to apply makeup while Mystery headed to the shower. I'd just finished when there was a knock on the door.

"Room service."

I threw a spare blanket over the equipment before opening the door.

A pimply-faced youngster who looked too frail to carry the laden tray smiled at me.

I considered taking the tray, but it looked heavy. "Please put it on the table over there."

The young man huffed over to a round table and with some effort placed the tray where indicated.

I handed him a tip and escorted him out the door, walking between him and the covered equipment.

Mystery came out of the bathroom followed by a cloud of steam. "Oh, good."

After pulling over the high-backed desk chair, we dug into the scrambled eggs, crisp bacon, and croissants. We were enjoying a second cup of coffee when the door to Jason's room closed with a bang.

Mystery dabbed her lips with a napkin, stood, and checked the monitor before turning it off. She looked at me and sighed. "I admit, I'm excited about what we accomplished, but I still don't want to spend my life chasing down people having affairs. I know Vera wanted me to get my PI license, but it's all so sordid."

"I agree. It's time to clear the room, pack up, and go home. My fur baby is waiting.

CHAPTER 17

On Wednesday, I raised my hand to block the eastern rays while digging in my purse for my sunglasses. Mystery, Jasmine, and I then piled into the Mystery Shop's van to go to Tiffany Blake's home in Huntsville's oldest historic district. Mystery and Jasmine sat in the two front bucket seats, while I squatted on a small pull-down seat that the previous owner had jury-rigged in the cargo space behind the passenger seat. Unbeknownst to Mystery and Jasmine, Pierre was tagging along.

"Watch those corners!" I yelled, while holding on to the bottom of my seat with a life-or-death grip.

Pierre chuckled while levitating nearby.

I stuck my tongue out at him while struggling not to land on the floor. Childish, I know.

Mystery eased the van to a stop in front of our destination. The nondescript white cargo van was perfect for these occasions, except for the suicide seat in the back.

Jasmine peered through the windshield. "Wow, this place is nice." She shivered. "Does it seem kinda cool in here to you?"

Mystery set the parking brake. "A tad." She shot me a do-we-have-a stowaway-haint look.

I nodded. "Heck, we don't need air conditioning when my ghost friend, Pierre, is in the van." I frowned at him. "Too bad he has no temperature control."

Pierre lifted his chin with a look of disdain. "I am unappreciated."

Jasmine looked at us with unease in her eyes. "I need to talk, y'all. I've made a decision. I've applied to grad school at UAH, so I'm changing my plans and staying in town after I graduate in May." She gave Mystery a pleading look. "Are you still willing to work around my class schedule?"

I could tell by Mystery's smile how relieved she was to not lose her.

Patting her shoulder, Mystery said, "That's wonderful news, Sugar. You bet I will."

Jasmine smiled and sat straighter.

We exited the van and looked around.

Jasmine pointed to a residence several houses down. "Ain't that the house we did a ghost investigation on last year?"

Mystery huffed before whispering, "Stop pointing! Remember our confidentiality policy?"

People are funny about their neighbors knowing their house is haunted. The nicer the neighborhood, the more paranoid customers are about their privacy.

"Sorry." Jasmine lowered her arm.

Mystery frowned at her and wagged a finger. "Sugar, you owe the bad habit jar a dollar for saying ain't."

Determined to help Jasmine sound like the intellectual powerhouse she is, Mystery has instituted several improvement programs. Besides the word of the day calendar, Jasmine has to place a dollar in the charity jar every time she mispronounces a word, uses poor grammar, or says a bad word. Ain't is on the poor grammar list. Mystery also agreed to participate in this self-improvement exercise. They both consider it to be a win-win. If I mess up while visiting the shop, I also donate. Jasmine has picked the local homeless shelter as the charity for this year. Despite the agreement, she insists on playing oh-pitiful-me every time she has to pay up.

Jasmine grumbled under her breath as she fumbled in the pockets of her jeans. "I'll put it in the jar when we get back to the office." She looked up and squinted in the bright sunlight. "I like all that fancy gingerbread looking stuff on Tiffany's house."

I followed her gaze and saw Pierre drifting up to take a closer look. "It is nothing compared to the belle architecture of Paris."

Mystery glanced up. "It's pretty, as long as I'm not the one painting it." She slid open the van's side door and patted a large black case. "Let's start with the basic kit first. We'll come back for the infrared cameras and tripods later."

Jasmine mumbled under her breath while she pulled the case out of the van.

Ignoring her theatrics, Mystery and I strolled down the brick walk.

Mystery looked over her shoulder. "Jasmine, did you know this area is called Twickenham after a city with the same name in England?"

"Nope," Jasmine said.

"It has the largest number of antebellum homes in Alabama," I said, enjoying the warm sun on my face.

"I think Mr. Craft has hoodooed you both. Got you interested in ancient furniture, moldy old houses, and history," Jasmine said, as she trudged up the steps to the porch with the unwieldy case.

"Smart people continue to learn, Jasmine. What's your word of the day?" I asked.

"Ancient."

Mystery gestured toward the beautiful homes. "I'm serious, we live in a famous place."

Jasmine shifted the case to the other hand and gave us a disbelieving look. "What's so famous about Huntsville?"

"Sugar, it was dubbed the Rocket City more than fifty years ago during the space race, when Wernher von Braun's rockets sent men to the moon."

"Huh. I watched a fiftieth anniversary special on TV about the moonwalk. It's amazing they did anything with the computers they had back then."

"That's true," I replied as I climbed the stairs to the porch.

Pierre sniffed. "Those rosbifs aren't worthy of having this area named after them."

I paused and asked, "Why do the French call the English, roastbeef's?"

"Because they are always cooking roast beef, bien sûr." He waved his hand in a dismissive gesture. "They truly have no taste when it comes to fine cuisine."

Jasmine huffed. "Brianna, what are y'all talking about?"

I explained as I stepped up onto the porch.

Pierre drifted behind me.

Tiffany had painted the wood-planked house blue-grey with cream accents. Beveled-glass sidelights surrounded the Williamsburg blue door. Mystery rang the doorbell. Beethoven's Fifth chimed.

Tiffany answered, looking a bit breathless. "Oh, good. You're here." She craned her neck to look at the van. "Thanks for not showing up in a van that said 'Ghost Busters.'"

I would have thought the remark humorous if I hadn't heard it so often.

We walked into a moderate-sized square foyer. An oriental runner continued to the stairs that led to the second floor.

Pierre zipped up and down the stairs, grinning in delight, before he floated near the ceiling in the dining room to study the crown molding.

Why is he so interested in crown molding?

A triple-mirrored antique mahogany hall tree stood against the wall. I examined the intricately carved piece. "This is lovely. You've kept it in good condition."

Tiffany ran a finger over one of the face carvings. "It belonged to my grandmother. It's gorgeous, but it sure is a pain to dust."

To the left was the formal living room, which contained an eclectic mix of antiques and modern sofas and chairs. The color scheme of blue and beige with brown accents created a soothing atmosphere. To the right was the formal dining room.

"So," I said, "this is the floor the ghost likes best?"

"Yes." Tiffany shrugged her shoulders. "I don't know why. I've never heard my parents speak of anything bad that happened on the first floor."

Jasmine looked up at the dining room chandelier and whistled. "Nice."

Pierre floated toward the chandelier and touched one of the crystal pendants. "I will wager she purchased this in Italy. Even the French go to Murano for their chandeliers."

Unaware of the interplay, Tiffany walked farther into the dining room. "Thank you, Jasmine. This amber crystal chandelier came from Murano, Italy. They do amazing glass blowing there." She waved her hand like a game show model. "My first husband and I picked it up on one of our vacations to Venice."

Pierre shot me an I-told-you-so smile.

Jasmine sidled closer to me and whispered, "Did you see that pendant move?"

I gave Pierre *the look.*

Jasmine becomes over-excited at the mere mention of ghosts. I almost didn't invite Pierre. I feared she'd be distracted by knowing he's here. If she could see him doing a loop the loop, while offering a devil-made-me-do-it smile, she'd be agog.

I whispered back, "Pierre. But don't tell Tiffany." Looking for anything to distract Tiffany, I said, "This looks like a 19th century Regency dining set. Is it mahogany?"

Tiffany touched her throat. "Why, yes. I see you know your antiques. It seats twelve when fully extended. My grandparents often hosted large affairs. They adored mahogany. I'm quite lucky to have all the original chairs and matching pieces."

Pierre zoomed down and hovered an inch over the table in a sitting position, one leg crossed over the other.

I moved closer to him and said under my breath, "Look around for any ghosts."

He nodded and skyrocketed up the stairs.

Wish I could move that fast, only I'm not willing to become a spook to do it. A concern bounded into my mind. *If he encounters another ghost, will it welcome him or become territorial? Ghosts do get territorial and can steal energy from each other.*

Tiffany spoke up, capturing my attention. "Did you hear about what happened at Victoria's funeral?"

I nodded. "Mystery and I were there, but we didn't see you."

"I didn't know her all that well. I only saw her at board meetings. Besides, I had a dental appointment. According to the Camellia Express, some people in the community are terrified that she'll haunt them."

A prickle ran over my skin like stinging nettles. "Anyone in particular?"

"Amos Hunt, for one. He was Victoria's attorney. I know his secretary, Jessica. She told me he never charged Victoria a fee for any of her legal work. Jessica thinks he was afraid of Victoria when she was alive."

Interesting. I wonder what dirt she had on him?

Jasmine pulled out her phone and typed in the attorney's name. She looked at Mystery and said, "Want me to check him out?"

"Yes." Ready to get down to the business at hand, Mystery said, "Tiffany, we'll probably be here all night. If it makes you feel better, we'll unload, set up our equipment, and leave. We'll come back in one of our cars after dark, so your neighbors will be none the wiser."

Tiffany's cheeks flushed. "That might be best. I don't want this to leak to the Camellia Express. You can park in the back. In fact, it might be best if you move your van there before you unload the rest of your equipment." She scrunched her nose. "The lady across the street is my nosiest neighbor."

"No problem, Sugar. Where can we unpack our case?"

"I keep a card table set up in the den. Follow me."

We followed Tiffany through a narrow butler's pantry lined with glass-fronted cabinets and drawers that led to a large kitchen.

Jasmine ran her hand over a countertop. "Love this granite. I'll have a countertop like this in my house someday."

Tiffany smiled at her. "I'm sure you'll enjoy it when you do."

We turned left into a den dominated by a large fireplace with a giant flat screen television over it. A row of home-cinema style leather seats faced it. A card table with two folding chairs stood near a pair of French doors, which led out to a covered porch and garden.

"Will this do? I like to do puzzles on this table because the light is good." Tiffany gestured toward the garden. "I plan to install a fountain out there. Since Victoria's, um, murder, the Historic Preservation Board called an emergency meeting to elect a new president. Jason and I were able to push through our request toward the end of the meeting. Jason has his heart set on a patio so he can grill out. I'll admit it will be nice to look out and see splashing water."

"This will do fine. Right now, Jasmine and I are going to record some initial EMF and temperature readings in the house," Mystery said.

Tiffany looked at me with a what-will-you-be-doing cock of her tapered brow.

I shrugged and grinned. "I'll do my psychic thing."

We joined Jasmine at the card table. Mystery flipped on The Ghost Meter to make sure the batteries were working. The EMF signal flew to five milligauss. I looked up into the amorous eyes of Pierre, who I'd thought was still upstairs.

He announced with authority, "Il n'y a pas de fantômes."

I nodded. "Y'all, I need to run out to the van for a moment." Once I was outside, I turned to face Pierre, who drifted through the door. "Thank you for your help, but you're throwing the meters into a frenzy. We can't get an accurate reading while you're in the area."

"It must be my sex appeal and charm that are affecting your silly machines." He winked. "I will see you later."

When I returned, Jasmine picked up the thermometer, vibrating with excitement to use her new toy on her first official paranormal investigation. Mystery picked up The Ghost Meter and flipped it on.

I peeked over her shoulder. *Good. No reading.* I pointed toward the kitchen. "Lead the way, Tiffany."

We walked through the kitchen and breakfast nook.

"Find anything?" asked Jasmine, her gaze glued to the thermometer.

"Just the usual spikes around the fridge and appliances." Mystery moved the meter back and forth. "You?"

"Nope. Let's try the dining room next," Jasmine said.

No responses on either instrument.

"I'm seeing no disembodied spirits," I said, admiring the antiques.

We climbed the stairs, which led to two bedrooms, a fancy home office, and two baths. We didn't find any unexplained EMFs or temperature variations. Pierre was right, no specters up here.

When we were back downstairs, Mystery handed Jasmine the device to put back in the case. "Tiffany, we're not picking up anything so far."

"I swear, I hear doors slamming down here, and things aren't in the right places," Tiffany said, giving us a please-believe-me look.

"We don't doubt you. We'll know more after tonight." Mystery patted one of the recliners. "While Jasmine brings in the rest of the equipment, let's sit down so I can give you a report about Jason."

Jasmine huffed and walked out the door, mumbling, "I'm not a Sherpa."

Tiffany paled. She eased down to the edge of a seat, her posture rigid. "It's bad, isn't it?"

Her emotions spiked, forcing me to raise my shields. *Poor woman. She looks like she's bracing to get hit by an eighteen-wheeler.*

Mystery pursed her lips before saying, "Sugar, your suspicions are correct."

Tiffany's shoulders drooped. She slid back into the seat and crossed her arms.

"Jason and Sierra showed up at the hotel holding hands, and they got into a hot kissing session close to the elevators." Mystery gave her a bless-your-heart look.

"Dear God." Tiffany rubbed her temples. "How bad was it?"

Mystery pulled out a DVD. "Pretty bad. I have it recorded, but I suggest you not watch it. It'll only upset you."

Even I didn't want to watch it. I suggested to Tiffany, "Why don't you let Mystery mail it straight to your attorney?"

"I'd prefer he not know where it came from, since I'm a ghost hunter and not a licensed PI," Mystery said.

Tiffany reached for the disc. "I might as well get past the denial stage. I have an appointment with Dr. Stone tomorrow. It'll give me something to vent about."

Mystery's brow furrowed with disapproval. "Are you sure?"

Tiffany swallowed, then squared her shoulders and nodded.

With a resigned look, Mystery handed her the DVD. "We'll finish setting up the rest of our equipment and come back at seven."

"If y'all will remember to come in the back way, it would be better. I don't want the neighbors to tip Jason off that I'm up to something."

Promptly at seven that evening, Mystery eased her car into the meager space behind Tiffany Blake's house. She frowned. "This is tight. I'd rather have a new house where I could have a two-car garage."

"Folks will give up a lot to live in the historic district. Some of the larger homes do have multi-car garages," I said.

"I wouldn't mind living here," said Jasmine. "I love all the fancy woodwork and crown molding."

We exited the car, and Mystery led the way to the back door. Tiffany had failed to turn on the porch light, making the narrow, uneven brick path even more treacherous.

A cloud slipped in front of the moon. Mystery grabbed the iron railing and felt her way up the two steps to a small concrete porch.

She raised a hand to knock. Before she could, Tiffany flung the screen door open.

Mystery hopped back into me to avoid the door.

I fell against Jasmine.

Jasmine, with flailing arms, tumbled into a hedge of holly bushes. "Ow! Get me out of here."

Mystery and I rushed to her aid and managed to pull the cursing, thrashing Jasmine free from the barbed leaves before helping her to stand.

Jasmine snatched her arms from our grasps. She griped under her breath, "Make us sneak in the back door in the dark, and then fling open the door like that."

Mystery grabbed her arm and gave it a little shake before whispering, "Cool it, we're on the job. You owe the bad habit jar big time, Sugar."

"S-Sorry," Tiffany stammered. "I-I was so upset that I wasn't thinking straight."

Once we were inside, I could see Tiffany had been crying. Mussed hair framed her blotchy face.

Is this the same well-groomed woman we saw this morning?

Mystery clucked her tongue. "You watched the video, didn't you, Sugar?"

Tiffany covered her face and sobbed, her shoulders heaving.

Spikes of grief from Tiffany zinged along my nerves, forcing me to raise my shields.

Mystery wrapped Tiffany in her arms like a comforting blanket. They stood like that for a few moments.

"He-he did things with her that made me blush. What's wrong with me?" she wailed.

Jasmine harrumphed, picking spiky leaves from her hair. "You mean, what's wrong with *him*. Girl, you're just fine."

When Tiffany had calmed down, I asked, "Do you want us to clear your bedroom first, so you can go to bed?"

Tiffany shook her head. "I want to hear what you say first."

Mystery said, "Let's start." Everyone followed her to the den. "Here's what we're gonna do. I'll work the EMF meter, Jasmine will work the thermometer, and Brianna will do her psychic thing. Tiffany, you're welcome to come along and hold the recording device. I'm going to ask you not to talk unless we ask you something. Any questions?"

"How do I work the recorder?" Tiffany asked, sniffling into a tissue.

"We'll turn it on. You just need to hold it," Jasmine said.

"Let's start in the foyer." I led the way with Mystery, Jasmine, and Tiffany following behind me like a flock of imprinted ducklings. Once we'd gathered, we formed a circle. Tiffany's gaze darted about as if a specter might appear at any second.

I stretched my arms above my head, brought them down to my side, and wiggled my shoulders to loosen them. Closing my eyes, I took a deep breath, and exhaled with slow deliberation.

My shields were fully lowered. I glanced at the EMF meter in Mystery's hand. *Nothing, at least so far.*

"I'm ready." I recited the date, time, location, and the reason for the investigation for the recorder's benefit. I keep detailed records of all our cases, hoping to learn more about the detection and clearing of earthbound spirits. Who knows, I may write a book someday under a nom de plume.

Mystery led the way into the living room.

I looked around the room, top to bottom, and touched several objects. "There's nothing here beyond the expected."

"No significant EMF signals," Mystery said, as she moved the monitor around, reminding me of the character Egon Spengler in the movie *Ghost Busters*.

"Temperature is a steady 76 degrees," Jasmine said.

I tucked a strand of hair behind my ear. "Let's wait a minute and see if something manifests."

Tiffany looked wide-eyed at each of us in turn.

Since none of our instruments registered anything, we moved back across the foyer to the dining room.

I walked around the table until I'd covered the entire room. I placed my hands on the table. A cheerful warmth spread from my hands to my arms, filling my body. I smiled.

"Got anything?" Mystery asked looking hopeful.

"No apparitions, but this table exudes happy energy," I said, still enjoying the sensation.

This brought a gratified smile to Tiffany's face. "Many pleasant dinners have been eaten at that table."

Mystery brought an index finger to her lips to remind Tiffany to be quiet. "I've got nothing. What about you, Jasmine?"

"The temperature has dropped to 75 degrees, but it's holding steady."

We covered the entire house and the back garden.

I gestured to include the yard and house. "Sorry, Tiffany. I've seen no spirits on *your* property." I didn't mention the spirit dressed in a top hat peeking over the fence. He looked like the ghost I drove through the day Mystery and I discovered Victoria's body.

"Tiffany, what time of day or night do these noises occur?"

"Only at night."

I stepped closer. "Have you seen any apparitions or felt cold spots?"

"No. Well, that's not quite true. I did once this morning while I was standing near you."

Pierre.

"Things are rearranged in the house," said Tiffany. "I'm a bit, um…organized. I like for things to be in certain spots. After I've heard noises, I've come downstairs the next morning and found things in the wrong places."

I leaned against a black wrought iron table. "Give me an example."

"Come inside and I'll show you."

We followed her back inside.

"The weirdest one involved my Swarovski crystal animals." Tiffany led us into the living room to a lighted display case nestled into a corner. "One morning, I found all these animals on the middle shelf in a line on the coffee table. It really upset me because my mother gave me one for every major occasion until she died." Her eyes widened into a hopeful look. "Do you think it's Mom?"

"Where did your mother die?" I asked.

"In the hospital."

I rubbed my chin and tuned in to the house. "My intuition tells me it's not her."

Jasmine joined the group. "Has anything happened since your lying, cheating, no good, sorry excuse of a husband left for the conference?"

Tiffany's eyes first rounded and then narrowed. "Now that you mention it, no. It's been quiet as a cemetery since the weasel left."

I laughed. "Believe me, cemeteries are anything but quiet." *At least for a psychic.*

We stood in silent contemplation for a moment. The grandfather clock in the living room chimed the half-hour.

Mystery and I looked at each other and said in unison, "Gaslight?"

Both Tiffany and Jasmine looked confused.

I suggested, "Let's sit in the den and discuss this." When we had selected seats, I said, "*Gaslight* is a classic 1944 black-and-white mystery film, about a woman whose husband slowly manipulates her into believing she's going insane."

"That snake!" Tiffany shot to her feet. "How is he doing it? He's in bed with me, claiming he's heard nothing." She paced up and down the room.

"I suspect he's had some help from Sierra," Mystery said.

Tiffany stopped and fisted her hands on her hips. "But I watch Jason set the alarm every night. How is he managing this ruse?"

We sat for a few more moments and thought. The steady ticking of the clock seemed loud in the quiet room.

I rubbed my face. "It may be as simple as his accomplice has the security code and a key to the house."

"Sugar, we can stay here tonight, but I honestly don't think it's necessary. We'll leave the equipment set up and come back to check the results in the morning. If you want us to stay, we will, but it'll inflate your bill," Mystery said.

"I'm not worried about the bill." She waved a hand in the air. "But I trust your judgment if you think it's not necessary."

"Good," I said, happy to avoid an all-nighter.

"I want to install some hidden surveillance cameras on the first floor tomorrow. Is that okay with you?" Mystery asked.

"Whatever it takes to solve this mystery. I want my quiet house back and for things to stay where they belong."

We stood, ready to leave.

Mystery winked. "Let's see if we can catch a sneak."

CHAPTER 18

Thirty minutes before my normal wake up time, I received a call from Mystery. Yawning wide enough to make my jaw crack, I asked, "What?"

"When I got to Tiffany's this morning, she looked rough. Girl, she had dark circles and her eyes looked all bloodshot. I bet she didn't sleep a wink. And her hair, it looked like she was wearing a dirty string mop on her head. You know how picky she is about her appearance."

"Did she stay up all night again watching that fool's antics on DVD?" I asked.

"Yep. When I asked her why, she said 'The cheating, moaning weasel comes home tomorrow. I need to get my game face on.' I told her she needed a session with Dr. Stone."

I yawned again and asked, "Any ghosties or bumps in the night?"

"Not a one."

"There is one remote possibility," I said sitting up. "She may have a poltergeist that's attached to her husband. It's rare, since usually a poltergeist is attracted to teenaged girls." I ran fingers through my hair hoping it didn't look as bad as the description of Tiffany's. "I still suspect Jason has someone helping him."

"She wants to know one way or another. We're fixing to set up spy cameras, so we can catch this so-called haint in action."

"Sounds like a plan, since we can't be there when Jason comes home."

It was close to noon by the time Jasmine and Mystery returned from Tiffany's house. Clay had handled the place in their absence without any problems.

Lucille Miller had invited us for a home-cooked meal that she was bringing to Mystery's shop, so Kaya and I closed a bit early for lunch. We were waiting when Mystery and Jasmine arrived.

"Mystery, your *madre* called. She's bringing lunch today." Kaya stood taller and flashed an excited smile. "She asked me, and Brianna to come eat."

Mystery grinned. "That's great, Kaya. Do you like soul food?"

She twisted her mouth to the side. "I guess. I'll eat just about anything."

Prissy greeted Mystery and Jasmine with yipping, tail-wagging delight. They petted and sweet-talked my little dog.

I stepped forward with her leash. "Hold still, girl, so I can hook you up. Can I take her out your back door?"

"Sure, Sugar. You know Miss Prissy has the run of my place, including christening the weeds in the back."

After a brief relief mission, Prissy and I returned in time to watch Kaya and Jasmine place a floral plastic tablecloth on the conference table along with paper plates, napkins, and flatware.

The bell on the door jingled. Before we could check to see if a customer had wandered into the shop, Lucille bellowed, "Baby Girl! Come take this platter."

When I entered the front, the delightful aroma of hot fried chicken hit me.

Lucille is a former literature professor at Alabama A&M University. She stands proud at five-foot-eight. The leopard print top she was wearing matched her purse, which matched her shoes, which matched her jewelry.

Count on Lucille to always be perfectly color-coordinated, I thought.

"Sure, Mama." Mystery kissed her cheek and took the large foil-covered platter. "How many chickens did you cook? This thing is heavy."

"That's why you're carrying it instead of me. I had to make sure there would be enough for everyone. Your grandmother always said, 'Better safe than sorry.'"

Jasmine poked her head out of the back room. "Is that fried

chicken I smell?"

Mystery gave Lucille a watch-this wink. "Jasmine, this golden, crispy chicken won't pass your lips if you and Kaya don't get the rest of the food out of Mama's car."

Jasmine and Kaya sped past us, nearly colliding with me as they rushed toward the door.

Lucille produced a deep chuckle. She smiled at me. "I'm glad you and Prissy could come."

I stepped forward and hugged Lucille. That woman hugs like she means it. I flipped my hair and gave Mystery a she-likes-me-better-than-you look. "I appreciate it, Lucille."

It was then that Lucille noticed Clay. "My, my, who is this handsome young man?"

Mystery made the introductions and explained that he was her new part-time help.

Jasmine and Kaya headed back toward the shop carrying large covered casserole dishes. Mr. Craft must have spotted the parade of food, because he stopped guarding his parking spaces and met the two young women at the door.

Lucille pointed at him. "Now, I didn't think to call and invite Adam, but he's always welcome. Bless his heart, I'm sure he's tired of his own cooking."

Mr. Craft held the door open for Jasmine and Kaya, who thanked him.

Lucille waved, gesturing for him to enter. "Adam! Get yourself in here. We're about to have a bite of lunch. My Mama always said, 'The more, the merrier.'"

He inclined his head. "I'd be a fool to resist an opportunity for a gourmet Southern meal with five beautiful ladies." He placed his hand over his heart. "Thank you, Lucille, for taking pity on an old man."

Lucille glided toward the back room, her back straight and her head high. "Come on, y'all. Let's eat before it gets cold." She pointed at Clay, who looked unsure what to do. "You too, young man. Don't stand there with your mouth open ready to catch flies. You're invited, too."

Mystery rushed to put up the Closed for Lunch sign.

After everyone was seated around the conference table, Lucille patted Mr. Craft's hand. "Adam, would you say grace?"

His cheeks reddened. "I'm honored, Lucille. Lord, bless this food before us. Bless our talented and lovely cook, and please keep our businesses profitable."

"Amen!" everyone intoned.

We each reached to uncover the dish closest to us. Steaming mounds of collard greens and macaroni and cheese scented the air along with cornbread and butter.

Kaya's large brown eyes narrowed as she sniffed at the mound of greens on her plate. "What's this green stuff?"

"It's collards," Mystery said. "Nobody makes them better than Mama. Hers are never bitter." She frowned at Lucille. "Can you believe she won't tell me, her daughter, her only child, the secret ingredient?"

"Now, Baby Girl, you know that someday you'll inherit my secret cookbook."

Jasmine handed Kaya some hot pepper sauce. "I like them with this on top."

Kaya accepted the bottle. "Now, I understand hot sauce." She smiled while shaking a liberal amount over her greens.

Mystery watched with growing amazement. "Sugar, you're going to burn your tongue right out of your mouth."

Kaya's smile widened. "I'm Latina. I like things hot." She shot a saucy wink at Clay that elicited a frown from Jasmine. "You should meet my papá. He even puts hot sauce on his ice cream."

Both Kaya and Jasmine giggled before returning their attention to the food.

Lucille wiped her hands and asked, "Kaya, how many in your immediate family, Darlin'?"

"I have two brothers and one sister. I'm the youngest."

"That's a big family. What does your father do?"

"My papá owns a landscaping business."

Lucille nodded. "I'll keep him in mind. Yard work bothers my back. I may have to give in and get help this year." She looked over at Mystery and cocked a brow.

I watched the exchange while biting into a drumstick. *Mystery pays someone to care for her lawn, so I don't see her working on her mother's. With her back, she'd be seeing a chiropractor every week.*

Mystery ignored her mother's silent hint. "Mama, this chicken is perfection. It's crispy outside and tender on the inside."

"Glad you like it, Baby Girl."

Clay said, "Mrs. Miller, this mac and cheese doesn't taste anything like what they make in the cafeteria at UAH. What's in it?"

"Call me Lucille. It's a combination of three different kinds of cheese. That's all I'm revealing. My Mama always said, 'A wise lady always keeps a few secrets.'" She glanced at Mystery. "The recipe for the mac and cheese is in the secret cookbook, too."

"This was delicious, Lucille," Mr. Craft said, wiping his hands with a paper napkin.

Mama reached over and patted his blue-veined hand again. "Thank you, Adam."

Jasmine looked at Kaya with an excited twinkle in her eyes. "Has Brianna told you we have a new suspect in Victoria's murder?"

Clay's head shot up. "What murder are you talking about?"

I told him about the murder and Amos Hunt.

Lucille looked up, her eyes bulging with alarm. "Y'all are investigating a *murder*? You're not police detectives! Besides, that attorney has a reputation for representing some shady characters in town."

Mystery tried to explain what we were doing, but I could tell by Lucille's pursed lips and stiff posture that she didn't like it one little bit.

"Baby Girl, I feel for Darlene's situation, but it's not safe. There's a heartless murderer out there. If the killer thinks y'all are close to solving the crime, your lives may be in danger." Lucille's expression changed from disapproval to worry.

Mystery didn't respond, and neither did I. We all focused on eating the dwindling food on our plates for several minutes, ignoring the hot topic of murder that was probably flaming in each of our minds.

Lucille looked around the table. "Did anyone bring in the pecan pies?"

"Pies!" Jasmine lunged from her seat and headed out the door.

We all laughed.

Lucille primly dabbed her mouth before wiping her hands on a fresh napkin. "That child does love my pecan pies."

"Señora, I mean Lucille, how did you come up with Mystery's name?" Kaya asked.

Lucille threw back her head and laughed.

"My husband, Courtland, and I married right out of high school. We wanted children, but no matter how hard we tried," she produced a wicked wink, "we had no luck."

Clay shifted in his seat, and his ears turned pink.

"Dr. Hadley told Courtland, God rest his soul, that he had lazy sperm. Those little guys got all tuckered out before they reached my eggs. Back then, they didn't have all the fancy procedures to help couples conceive, like they do nowadays. We accepted our childless fate and threw ourselves into our studies."

"Then how did you have Mystery?" Kaya asked.

"When I was in graduate school, I woke up sick as a drunken sailor on shore leave. I remained unwell for several mornings. I went to the doctor, fearing the worst. You know—the C-word. Dr. Hadley's new partner didn't know about my husband's lazy sperm, so he included a pregnancy test along with the other ones.

Several days later, Dr. Hadley called me at home. He told me to come in the next morning and to bring Courtland."

Jasmine came in, holding aloft not one, but two pecan pies. She placed them on the table and started slicing the first one.

Lucille had a faraway look in her eyes. "There we were, fidgeting in our seats in Doc's private office. The last time we'd been there, he'd told us we couldn't have children. My mind raced through every fatal disease I could remember." Her gaze focused on Mystery. "Your daddy told me he was doing the same thing."

Jasmine started scooping slices of the pie onto smaller paper plates and passing them around. She looked up and said, "This is the part of the story I like best."

"The Doc told me I was pregnant. Courtland and I looked at each other and then back at him. Courtland asked, 'Doc, how could this happen?'

He smiled so wide it wrinkled his face and said, 'It's a mystery.'

So, I named my baby girl Mystery."

"I've always wondered about her name but was too polite to ask," said Mr. Craft, before placing the last of his cornbread in his mouth. "That's a wonderful story. How long have you been widowed?"

"Almost ten years." She patted Mr. Craft's hand once more. "I still miss him."

He gave a knowing nod. "My Mary passed almost fifteen years

ago. Not a day goes by that I don't think about her."

Everyone focused on eating their pie. Time seemed to stretch like pantyhose.

I looked up first. "This is fantastic. I like the way you always put extra pecans inside, so there's not so much gooey stuff."

"Thank you, Darlin'." Lucille looked at Mystery. "My pecan pie recipe is also in my secret cookbook."

Mr. Craft peered at me from under his brows. "Tiffany Blake came into my store yesterday and bought a Wedgwood vase. I'm an old friend of her parents. She was telling me all about your investigation of her home. Do you really think it's haunted?"

Lucille's eyes widened. "What's this about a haunted house?"

Darn, he shouldn't have mentioned that in front of Lucille.

Shifting under Lucille's penetrating gaze, Mystery said, "I don't think it's really haunted."

Lucille wasn't happy when Mystery decided to do ghost tours, but calmed down when she described it as primarily about historical events. After the last window breakage, Mystery's signage clued Lucille into our ghost-clearing work. She's been worried ever since.

Now her eyes looked ready to explode from her sockets. "So, you're not sure if the house is haunted? What if there is a haint? They're dangerous."

What could Mystery say? Ghosts can be treacherous.

"Now, Mama—"

"Don't you, now mama, me. Do your little ghost tours if you must, but you need to stop these investigations!"

My anger grew while I listened to Lucille talk to Mystery like she was ten in front of her staff and friends.

Mystery's bosom rose as she tilted her chin up. "Mama, you know I love and respect you. I don't tell you how to live your life. Please don't make demands on mine."

I wanted to clap my hands and say, "Go Mystery," but wisely resisted.

Lucille's eyes widened. "Well, I never!"

"Please don't start in on your, how many hours of labor you endured to have me and this is the thanks you get, routine." Mystery crossed her arms.

Lucille closed her mouth, looked down, and stabbed at her pie with her fork.

No one said another word until our plates were empty.

After pie, Clay, Kaya, and Jasmine volunteered to clean up.

Mystery and I carried the empty serving containers to Lucille's car. She was settling the empty dishes in her mother's backseat when Lucille said with a stiff tone, "I found something I know your granny would want you to have." She handed Mystery a large canvas bag. "This contains her watercolors, brushes, and paper."

"Oh, my!" Smiling wide, Mystery said to me, "She was an accomplished artist. Remember the landscape you like so much? Granny painted it."

She hugged Lucille, who looked surprised. "Thanks, I'll put these to good use. I haven't painted since she died."

When we went back inside, Mystery unpacked the bag onto the cleared conference table. There were lots of brushes: fat, skinny, round, flat, and some weird specialty ones. She opened a metal case that held dabs of watercolors waiting to be resurrected with a little water. Individual tubes of Windsor Newton watercolors were there to replenish the wells. There were three different sized pads of watercolor paper, one Strafford 140 and two different sizes of Arches 300.

She picked up the tubes. "I remember my confusion as a child about the color names. Nothing was a simple red or blue or yellow or green or brown." She read the names on some of the tubes: Alizarin Crimson, Burnt Sienna, Burnt Umber, Raw Umber, Lamp Black, Cobalt Blue, Winsor Lemon, Viridian, Winsor Blue, Scarlet Lake, Winsor Yellow, Yellow Ochre, and Payne's Grey.

She repacked the supplies in the bag. "Now I just need to find the time."

I nodded. "Time is elusive like the wind. We need to get together to paint sometime. My mother taught me to paint, too."

"Maybe some Sunday?"

"Sounds good," I said, "as long as we don't find anymore dead bodies."

Mystery looked up. "From your lips to God's ears."

CHAPTER 19

After rearranging some of my displayed items, I fished my phone from a pocket and called Mystery. "Have you heard from Tiffany this morning? Any screaming phantoms or misplaced objects?" I cradled the phone between my ear and shoulder while leaning to slide open the door on a glass case. I straightened a selection of bridal garters before closing the door.

"As a matter of fact, yes." Mystery said, sounding excited. "I was about to call you. Jason arrived home yesterday afternoon, and she found her menagerie of glass animals lined up on the dining table this morning. She's here at the store. Can you come over?"

"Kaya should be here in ten minutes. Can she wait until then?"

The muffled sound of voices led me to believe Mystery had covered the mouth piece of her phone.

"Tiffany said she's not in a hurry. Come when Kaya gets there." Mystery disconnected the call.

When I arrived, Mystery and Tiffany were sitting on stools and talking across a display case of spy cameras while sipping steaming cups of java. The smell triggered my mouth to water.

I grabbed a stool and joined them.

Mystery tapped her acrylic nails on the glass top. "I was telling Tiffany that I'll send Jasmine by after she gets out of class to download the images from the hidden cameras. She's due here in an hour."

"What did Jason have to say about the glass animal migration?" I asked.

"The weasel suggested I might want to move out for *my safety*." Her voice oozed sarcasm. "Can you believe it?"

"*Your* safety? Shouldn't he have concern about *his* safety, too?"

"No, apparently not," said Tiffany. "He can't seem to make up his mind about what's happening. First, he says I'm hallucinating and crazy, then he accuses me of sneaking around in the night and moving things, and now he thinks the ghost is haunting only me."

"There's something hinky going on. Maybe the footage from the cameras will give us the answer as to who is helping Jason," I said.

"That's not all." Her voice rose an octave. "He even suggested I sell the house to a lady who has expressed interest."

I shifted on the stool to get more comfortable. "How convenient. Do you know the identity of the prospective buyer?"

"Yes. Just a minute. I wrote down her name somewhere."

Paper rattled inside her large purse.

"Here it is! It's Mrs. Gladys Johnstone." Tiffany held up the wrinkled slip of paper.

Mystery wrote down the name on a nearby pad.

I glanced over at the paper. "Can Jasmine find out more about this woman?"

"I'll get her on it when she clocks in."

"You're not going to sell, are you?" I asked.

"Heck, no! It's my family home. The only way I'll leave there is in a body bag," Tiffany said.

I shuddered when the image formed in my mind's eye.

"Lordy, I hope it doesn't come to that," Mystery said looking concerned.

Indignant anger flooded through me. "We can't let that scoundrel get away with this."

Mystery patted my hand. "Calm down, Bree. We'll figure out what's going on."

Tiffany stood and ran her hands over the front of her slacks. "Gotta go pick up Jason's shirts from the cleaners before my maid arrives. I swear that man orders so much starch that the material crackles."

She left with squealing tires as if the demons of Hades were chasing her.

I was preparing to leave when an acquaintance, Ron Jeffery, entered the store. He's the widowed, well-groomed, and successful owner of a mid-level accounting firm in the area. He and Tyree had been acquaintances. His furrowed brow warned me this wasn't a casual visit to Mystery's store.

After an exchange of greetings, he said, "Mystery, I need your help. Burglars stole several laptops from my office over the weekend. I'm fit to be tied because there's client information on those laptops. They had passwords and encryption, but I'm still concerned."

"Sugar, I don't blame you," she said.

"Have you called the police?" I asked.

"They sent out an officer who took a report. I doubt they'll find the thieves or the laptops, but at least the report will help me file an insurance claim."

"Are you looking to improve your surveillance?" Mystery asked.

Jasmine pushed through the front door. This surprised me, since she typically parks behind the store like the rest of us.

Mystery slipped her the note she'd written to investigate Gladys Johnstone.

Jasmine read it and nodded before disappearing into the computer room.

"Yes." Ron ran a hand down his face. "I feel so violated. I have locked doors, and I do everything I can to protect my equipment and my clients' confidentiality. Apparently, it wasn't enough."

"You can only do your best." Mystery gave his hand on the counter an understanding pat.

He smiled down at her the way Eddie looks at me—enamored. I couldn't help but feel the tingle of sexual energy between him and Mystery. Sometimes my gift makes me feel like an energy voyeur.

"Thieves are a wily bunch, but Mama always told me, 'You steal from someone, you'll lose it twice over.' I believe she's right. In the meantime, let me show you the system I think will work for you."

I wished Ron luck on finding his thief and left.

Twenty minutes later, Mystery called.

"Ron asked me out to dinner!"

"That's great. He's a nice guy and a widower," I said, hoping she'd met her special match.

"I didn't know that. When did his wife die?"

"She died of breast cancer about nine months ago. Did you say yes?"

"I'm not ready yet."

I exhaled my disappointment that Ron might be the one for her.

"I know, I should have accepted, but the time's not right. I told him to ask again in a few months."

I chuckled. "At least you didn't say a few years."

Jasmine's voice carried over the phone. "Are you talking to Brianna?"

"Yeah. Why?"

"I have something you both need to see," Jasmine said with an incredulous tone.

I yelled to Kaya, "Be back in a minute."

I rushed out of my shop and pushed through Mystery's door, sending the bell into a tizzy. I followed her and Jasmine to the computer room.

The chair squeaked when Jasmine sat. She grimaced. "I need to oil it." She reached for the mouse and brought up a file.

"Sugar, what did you find?" Mystery interlaced her hands above her head and stretched. I counted five audible pops of her spine.

Jasmine glanced up, excitement sparking in her eyes. "I started researching this woman who offered to buy Tiffany's house and found something fishy."

I leaned closer to see the monitor.

"Yeah? What?" Mystery asked.

Jasmine pointed at the screen. "Mrs. Gladys Johnstone is Jason's eighty-year-old aunt."

"Really?" I pulled over the other office chair and sat. "Tell us more."

"She's living in that nice retirement community on the southside of town."

"Well, if she's living in an assisted living facility and is eighty, why does she want to buy Tiffany's home?" I asked.

Jasmine gave me a knowing smile. "I used our search engines and a little ingenuity to discover that Jason has power of attorney over her affairs. I bet he'll purchase the house with his aunt's funds and then inherit all her possessions when she dies, including Tiffany's home, if he can pull this off."

I narrowed my eyes. "He is the worst kind of a sneaky and conniving husband. I bet Tiffany doesn't know this Johnstone woman is Jason's relative. That polecat!"

"Weasel," corrected Jasmine.

Mystery pointed at Jasmine, "Sugar, find out everything you can about Jason. I want to know what other dirty tricks he's involved in around this town."

"Will do, but first I need to finish some background checks that are due tomorrow." Jasmine glanced at the time displayed on the top of the screen. "Brianna, are you still checking out Amos Hunt today?"

"I have an appointment with him in thirty minutes. Guess I need to get a move on." I hurried back to my shop and grabbed my purse from the drawer. "Kaya, I'm off to question that attorney about the murder. I hope to be gone an hour at most."

"No worries." She picked up my dog and hugged her. "Prissy and I will sell lots of lingerie. Be safe."

I headed for the back door, not sure what I'd encounter while interviewing this attorney that Lucille described as infamous.

CHAPTER 20

Amos Hunt's office, located on the corner of Madison and Gates, was an old two-story house. A plaque out front indicated it had once been an attorney's office in 1900. I eyed the dark red metal roof designed to look like shingles. The stonework had been painted to match the roof. Beige vinyl siding covered the rest.
Amos Hunt must have done all those renovations before Victoria became president of the Historical Preservation Board.
I walked up the stairs and entered the lobby. The faint smell of mold caused my nose to twitch. *I wonder why so many old houses smell moldy. I wouldn't be able to work here.* I dug through my purse and managed to find a tissue in time to catch a sneeze.
"Bless you," a young woman with purple hair said before answering the phone that perched on the edge of her large desk. She raised an index finger and finished connecting the call.
When she hung up, I stepped forward, stated my name, and added, "I have an appointment with Mr. Hunt."
Purple Hair eyed me with apparent interest before saying, "Please have a seat." She pointed toward a line of chairs across one wall, before phoning someone to report that I'd arrived.
Within minutes, a petite woman with honey blonde hair and merry blue eyes came down the staircase to greet me. "I'm Jessica Warren, Mr. Hunt's assistant. Please follow me."
We turned right at the top of the creaking carpeted stairs. I followed Jessica into an office that contained several file cabinets and two red leather chairs that sat in front of an L-shaped desk. I

perched on the edge of one chair and looked out the window to see another historic home, also now a lawyer's office. "Nice view."

"Yes, I enjoy it. Mr. Hunt is on a call with an important client at the moment. He'll be with you soon."

I nodded. *Does that mean I'm not important?* There was something about her energy field that reminded me of a combo of sour, smelly socks and barbed wire. I was tempted to raise my shields, but needed to read her. I tried to think of a way to start a conversation. "I believe I know a friend of yours."

Jessica cocked her head to one side, reminding me of the way Prissy does the same gesture. "Yeah? Who?"

"Tiffany Blake."

She offered a genuine smile that crinkled her eyes. "She's the nicest lady, not snooty like some folks who live in the historic district." She scrunched her nose. "I can't believe she married such a skunk."

"Oh?" I raised my brows, feigning surprise. "Why do you say Jason's a skunk?"

Jessica leaned over her desk and lowered her voice. "He's a player. Made a pass at me once."

Interesting. I leaned closer. "Really? What did you do?"

"Told him, no way. Don't date married men. Besides, I like Tiffany. She drives like a maniac, but she's sweet."

"Sounds like he's a true scoundrel," I said, hoping she'd offer some helpful tidbits.

Jessica nodded and continued speaking in a low tone. "My boss told me Jason's been in trouble with the Alabama State Bar. He didn't say why. Don't think Tiffany knows he's on probation."

"Why haven't you told her?" I whispered back.

Jessica leaned back and held up her hands. "Not me, let someone else tell her. Ever heard of 'kill the messenger'? Besides, I don't want to become involved in a divorce proceeding or lose my job."

I kept her talking about several local rumors, hoping to gain rapport and trust while eyeing the passing time on the large clock to her left.

Jessica paused and narrowed her eyes at me. "I'm curious, what business do you have with my boss? You're not his typical client."

What's his typical client? I thought fast about how to handle the question and decided on part of the truth. "Tiffany told me he was afraid of being haunted by Victoria Spellman." I handed Jessica one of Mystery's business cards. "I consult with this company. We do paranormal investigations and help troublesome ghosts move on."

Jessica's eyes shifted back and forth while reading it. When she looked up, I saw fear in her widening eyes.

"He's scared all right. When she was alive, that hateful woman controlled him like she owned him." Her neck reddening with sudden anger, she added, "She treated me like I was gum on the bottom of her shoe!" She glanced at the closed door before saying in a hoarse whisper, "Did you know he never charged her for all the legal work he did? He told me to hide it from the other partners."

I again matched her whisper. "Do you think your boss murdered her?"

Jessica leaned back and produced a forced chuckle. "I'm sure he wanted to wring her neck many times, but he was in Chicago, on vacation with his wife. Just got home yesterday." She glanced at the closed door again. "At first, he was ecstatic to hear she was dead. Ever since I told him about the funeral, he's been as edgy as a cat in a ring full of snarling pit bulls. Tried to catch footage of her casket on my phone, but I was running, so it was a useless jumble."

"If you disliked Victoria so much, why did you attend?" I asked, sitting back in my chair.

"The partners insisted I represent the firm." The color drained from her face. "Never seen anything so frightening. That coffin nearly ran me down!"

I empathized. It had been a frightening scene, even for me.

I glanced at my watch, hoping to send a nonverbal message. It'd been thirty minutes, and Hunt remained behind the closed door. Feeling guilty for leaving Kaya in charge most of the day, I asked, "Do you think it will be much longer?"

She shrugged before studying the chipped nail polish on her thumbnail. "Who knows?"

I stood. "I need to leave. Please tell Mr. Hunt why I was here, and call me if you can think of any other information regarding Victoria's death."

I thought over what Jessica had told me while walking down the creaking stairs. The smell of mildew seemed worse on the first floor. Purple Hair was on the phone but waved as I left.

While slipping into Hot Stuff, I realized I had neither the

authority nor the resources to verify Hunt's alibi because I wasn't a licensed PI. I also wanted to find out something about the state of the murder investigation, so I fished Detective Ricci's card out of my wallet and phoned him. To my surprise, he agreed to see me in thirty minutes. I called Kaya to let her know I'd been delayed.

I settled into the seat across from Ricci's cluttered desk. The knot of his Tabasco sauce and chili pepper tie was loose.

"This worked out well," he said with a pleased smile. "I was about to phone you. We're questioning a suspect and want you to look at a lineup."

I sat back in my seat. *He didn't say anything about a lineup!* "You don't understand." I tapped the edge of his desk and fixed him with my gaze. "I'm here to give you some information about the case."

It was his turn to lean back. "The Victoria Spellman case?"

I explained that Darlene had hired Mystery's business to clear her mother's ghost, and I was helping.

Ricci went pale and shifted in his seat.

"We think the only way to get her ghost to cross over is to solve her murder case." Ignoring his thinned-lipped look of disapproval, I told him about the suspects I'd interviewed and the path the investigation had taken. By the time I'd finished, his jaw muscle pulsed a steady rhythm.

"I just left Amos Hunt's office. Can you please check his alibi?"

Ricci's brow furrowed. He looked even less happy about my request. "Ma'am, we're well aware of the victim's connection to Hunt. HPD and the FBI have been investigating him for months."

My jaw dropped. *The FBI!* Feeling somewhat foolish, I closed it, and asked, "Why?"

"For providing questionable legal services to loan sharks. Hunt is eyeball-deep with gambling debt. He's been setting up phony corporations in the Caymans to launder money." Ricci crossed his arms. "So you see, we know exactly where he was when someone murdered Victoria Spellman. I'm only sharing this information so you'll keep your nose out of things before you blow months of the FBI's work."

"I had no idea. I hope I didn't mess up anything."

He gave me a stern, get-out-of-my-murder-investigation look while tapping his index finger on a case file. "You need to leave the

Spellman murder to the professionals. You could be placing yourself in danger."

I grimaced. *He sounds just like Lucille. He's probably right.*

He stood. "Follow me."

I tried to make sense of what I'd heard while Ricci led me into a small dark room lit by the light coming through a one-way mirror.

Ricci held his finger to his lips and picked up a microphone. He switched it on as five red-headed men lined up to face us. He asked them to face left, then right.

He turned off the mike. "Recognize anyone?"

I whispered, "Can you have them face the wall? I only saw the back of the guy."

Ricci turned the mike on again and said, "Face the wall," before turning it off.

I stared hard at each one. Number three had the right shade of red hair, and there was something about the way his ears stuck out. *He's also the right height and build.* "I know this sounds crazy, but can I see them jog away from me?"

Ricci rubbed the back of his neck and huffed as if annoyed. With a sour expression, he opened the door and had a quick whispered conversation with someone. In a few minutes, the room on the other side of the mirror emptied. Someone knocked on the door.

Ricci placed a hand on the doorframe and the other on his hip. His jacket gaped, exposing his shoulder holster. "We're going to step outside the door. The potential suspects will have their backs to you. I'll ask each one to jog down the hallway."

I nodded and followed him out the door.

Number one took off. Each shoulder rose alternately with every step. The person I saw had a smoother stride.

Number two wasn't the guy either.

The minute number three jogged down the hall I was sure it was him. I leaned closer to Ricci. He smelled like garlic and spaghetti sauce. I whispered, "I'm ninety-nine percent sure it's number three."

He nodded.

"Do you think he's the killer?"

Ricci shook his head. "Seems to have been coincidental. People who work in the local law offices reported that he jogs in that area most mornings. We asked you to identify him to be sure it was the same guy you saw."

I nodded, thinking about some of the cop shows I'd seen. "I didn't see him at the funeral."

"He wasn't there. Thanks for coming in." He looked at me like a father talking to a wayward teen. "Stay out of my case. You hear?"

I crossed my fingers behind my back. "Yes, Sir."

CHAPTER 21

When I returned from talking with Ricci, my eyes scanned the shop. The displays had been straightened, and the glass cases gleamed. "Things look good in here. Thank you."

Kaya's welcoming smile brightened. Maybe because of the hardships in her past, she seems to absorb those positive moments like a humming bird does nectar. "No problem. I've finished unpacking and displaying all the new arrivals. What took you so long? I was worried. Did Mr. Hunt give you any good information?"

I caught Kaya up on the events of my afternoon.

"A police lineup! Are you going to do what Detective Ricci says and drop the case?"

I gave her a wicked smile. "What the good detective doesn't know won't worry him. He's right about one thing."

"What's that?"

"We do need to be careful. Whoever killed Victoria is still out there and dangerous. I've been so caught up chasing clues, I'd forgotten that important fact." What I couldn't tell her was the feeling of impending doom I've felt whenever I thought about Victoria's ghost. A sense of urgency weighed on me. If Victoria grew stronger, I wasn't sure I could stop her. I could empathize with the seismologists studying the San Andreas fault. I sensed something would happen, but had no idea when and how bad it would be.

She nodded. "Mystery called. Jasmine downloaded the data from the cameras at Tiffany's house and linked it all into a steady stream.

She wants you to come over."

I sighed. "I feel like I've been gone all day. Sorry."

Kaya shrugged. "Hey, you're the boss. This is no different than when you had to be gone for jury duty. Besides, this sounded important."

I strolled to the secure drawer and stowed my purse. "I still hate to be gone so much."

Kaya smiled. "That's why I'm here."

I turned and came to an abrupt stop. Pierre floated in front of me with crossed arms. He winked and asked, "Did you miss me, ma chérie?"

"Is everything okay? Did you forget something?" Kaya asked with a peculiar tone.

"No, I mean, yes. I'm fine. I think I'll take Prissy with me." I looked around. "Where is Prissy?"

"Next door. Jasmine said she was going to take her hostage and spoil her rotten with dog treats until you came to see what they found."

I chuckled. "I guess I better go rescue her, but first, why don't you take a break?"

"Sounds good." She headed toward the restroom.

I whispered to Pierre, "What are you doing here?"

"Checking on you." He flipped a hand. "Although, I'm not sure why I'm taking the pain. If the killer murders you, we can be together."

I crossed my arms. "Thanks for your concern."

He pouted and waved a finger. "Ma chérie, so sarcastic. No wonder I cherish you."

I huffed. "You need to get over your infatuation, go back to Paris, settle things with your murderer, and cross over."

"Why are you fixated on this crossing over business?"

Before I could answer, Kaya returned. "Thanks for the break. Do we have a customer?" She looked around.

"No."

She frowned. "I thought I heard you talking to someone."

I did my best to smile. "Just myself. I hope to be back soon."

Pierre followed me to Mystery's shop and ghosted through the plate glass window.

Wish I could do that. I wonder how it feels?

Prissy charged toward me with a doggie smile and wagging tail. I picked her up and hugged her.

Pierre floated closer.

Prissy's lip curled, revealing her canines, while she produced a rumbling snarl.

Eyes widening, Mystery and Jasmine looked at me.

"It's Pierre," I said, my voice full of exasperation.

"Awesome." Jasmine grabbed a nearby meter and turned it on. "Five milligauss!"

Wide-eyed, Pierre backed away from the device that she'd unknowingly almost rammed into his gut.

"Mon Dieu!"

I bit my lower lip to suppress a giggle.

Mystery rolled her eyes. "The girl is ghost crazy. What did you find out?"

I told them what I'd learned from Hunt's secretary, about the lineup at the police station, and what Ricci had told me about Hunt.

Mystery harrumphed. "Sounds like another suspect bites the dust."

Looking at Mystery with confusion, Pierre asked, "What does this 'bites the dust' mean?"

I took a moment to explain the expression.

"J'en reviens pas. Such strange American expressions."

I followed Mystery and Jasmine into the computer room.

Jasmine winked and pointed at her monitor. "You're going to *love* this."

We settled into our seats, and then Jasmine pulled up the correct file. "Watch closely." She hit play on the video.

I squinted at the screen and shook my head with disbelief. "Just when I think I've seen it all."

Jasmine rolled her eyes with clear disdain. "Rank amateur."

Pierre drew himself up and crossed his arms. "Imposteur!"

"I'm calling Tiffany to come see this," Mystery said.

We were discussing Victoria's ghost in the retail area when squealing tires alerted us to Tiffany's arrival.

Without exchanging a word, we all hurried to the back of the store in case she jumped the curb and drove through the window.

Watching this, Pierre asked, "What is happening?"

Tiffany's Volvo screeched to a stop in front of Chocolates and Delights.

He glanced over at me. "Does she always drive like the French during l'heure de pointe?"

I nodded. "That woman's a terror on brakes."

"I'm sure her tires don't last long either," Jasmine said.

We migrated to the front counter.

Tiffany shot through the door, jingling the bell and filling the room with her flowery scent. "Hey, y'all." She slung her Louis Vuitton purse over her shoulder. "What do you have to show me?"

Mystery crooked her index finger. "Follow us."

Once Jasmine and Tiffany took their seats at the computer, Mystery and I stood behind them to once again watch the video.

Pierre stuck his head and shoulders through the wall next to me.

I jumped, hand to my heart, and sucked in a breath. My heart felt like it would jump from my chest at any second. I shot him a scathing look. *As I live and breathe! I wish he'd warn me when he plans to pop in that way.*

Unaware of the drama behind her, Jasmine played the footage.

Something white came in the back door of Tiffany's house. Each camera picked up the sheet-covered figure as it went through the kitchen and dining area, across the foyer, and into the living room. Wearing surgical gloves and using extreme care, the ghost wannabe transferred the menagerie of glass animals from the display case to the coffee table. The shrouded figure closed the cabinet door, retraced his or her steps, reset the alarm, and left through the kitchen exit.

Tiffany leaned forward. "What the heck! Who's under the sheet?"

"We don't know. We were hoping you could help us with that information," Mystery said, leaning against the wall.

Tiffany rolled her finger in a circle. "Play it again."

I leaned in closer.

We watched the film three more times.

During the fourth play, I shouted, "Stop! Back it up a tad."

Jasmine complied.

"See there." I pointed at the screen. "Our fake ghost is wearing a watch."

We all leaned closer to the monitor, including Pierre.

Tiffany shivered from the drop in temperature and squinted. "Well, what do you know? We have a time-conscious spook." She rubbed her arms. "Is it cold in here to y'all?"

"Maybe a bit." I cocked my head toward the door.

Pierre moved to the doorway and hovered there with crossed arms, looking put out.

He almost turns us into ice pops and he's offended? Frenchmen!

Jasmine used a software program she'd written to move in and enlarge the watch. "Looks like a Fossil to me, and the hand looks small and feminine."

Tiffany huffed. "That bimbo Sierra wears a Fossil watch."

"We need more proof than a brand of watch to implicate her in this little charade," I said.

Mystery tapped her nose with her index finger. "What surprises me is the sheet. I can see hiding her identity, but why not wear dark clothes and a stocking mask instead? It's so hokey."

"Maybe she thought if I came downstairs to investigate, I'd see something white moving in the dark and have a come-apart," Tiffany replied. "I wear contact lenses and remove them at night. Without them, my vision is blurry at best."

"Can you sneak out of bed tonight and help us?" Mystery asked.

"Oh, yeah. Once the Weasel is asleep, an F4 tornado could hit the house and he'd sleep through it."

"Bree, can you come?" Mystery asked.

"If you need me. I suggest we take your car. A blue Prius will attract less attention than a red Tesla."

"True." Mystery grinned and leaned closer. "Here's what we need to do."

CHAPTER 22

It was five until eleven when Mystery dropped Jasmine, Pierre, and me, along with a small bag of supplies, a half-block from Tiffany's home. We didn't want to chance closing car doors alerting nearby neighbors or Jason. In this type of neighborhood, insomniac neighbors would phone the police and report a suspicious vehicle in the area in a heartbeat. I watched Mystery drive away. *I hope she finds a good place to park.*

Jasmine shivered and rubbed her arms. "It felt like she had the air conditioner on full blast in her car."

I gave Pierre the stink-eye. "I asked Pierre not to come, but he insisted I needed his protection."

He held up his hands and drifted farther away from Jasmine.

Excitement flashed in her eyes. "He's here? Now!"

"Yep."

"Brilliant."

Pierre looked smug.

Dressed like cat burglars, we walked down the tree-shadowed street toward Tiffany's back entrance. The gibbous moon created pools of silvery light where it shone between the patches of leaves.

I glanced around at the darkened windows of the neighboring houses, relieved to see no lights. "Here we are, wearing dark clothes and carrying a bag. I hope the police don't pick us up thinking we're burglars. It's a classic movie setup."

Jasmine stuffed her hands into the pockets of her hoodie. "All I need is to be arrested. Would I have to put an arrest on future job applications?"

I nodded. "But only if it's a felony."

We turned right and walked down the driveway. Jasmine led the way up the narrow walk, which was still crowded by untrimmed bushes. When she reached the steps to Tiffany's back porch, she glared at the holly bush.

I smiled to myself. *The girl sure does hold a grudge.*

I'd told Pierre about the holly incident earlier. With a look of mischievous glee, he reached to jiggle some leaves on the bush.

I glared and shook my head. *Don't do it.*

He paused, and then grinned manically before jiggling them anyway.

Jasmine's eyes popped. She backed against the stairs and sat down hard.

Pierre grimaced. He rushed forward to help, but then stopped short of touching her.

I huffed and whispered, "Look what you caused with your shenanigans. Jasmine, it's only Pierre." I shooed him away and reached down a helping hand.

Pierre assumed his injured look.

"I didn't know what to think at first," Jasmine said with a quavering whisper.

Before I could answer, Mystery came up the drive just as Tiffany eased open the door and gestured us inside.

We crept through the doorway and stood in the kitchen. The only light was moonbeams slanting across the floor from the window.

I sniffed with longing. The kitchen held the lingering aroma of chocolate chip cookies. I could tell by the twitch of her nose that Mystery had also smelled the cookies. I swear the woman has built-in chocolate radar.

Tiffany closed the door, locked it, and reset the alarm. Putting a finger to her lips, she led the way using a penlight. We settled onto the furniture in the darkened living room to wait.

Pierre hovered around the chandelier, poking one crystal, then another. "The smell of the cookies is driving me insane."

I shook my head with dismay. *He's worse than a kid. I wonder if he was like this when he was alive, or did death release his inner child?*

Light from the moon sliced through a crack in the draperies. It created light and dark moving patterns on the carpet as the leaves of the tree on the front lawn danced in the breeze. The grandfather clock ticked a steady, calming rhythm.

My mouth watered. *I sure could use one of those cookies right now.*

Jasmine unzipped the bag. The sound echoed in the silence. Each of us froze to listen but heard nothing. Tiffany's gaze met Jasmine's, causing them to erupt into giggles.

Pierre rolled his eyes with the superior air of a true Frenchman.

This disdain from a man who was poking chandelier crystals and whining about cookies only a moment ago. I made lowering motions with my hand while shushing them.

"Where do you want me to be?" Tiffany whispered, sounding both anxious and excited.

"In the foyer." Mystery stood and walked to the spot where she wanted Tiffany to hide. Light slanted through the glass panels surrounding the door. "Stand behind this little section of the wall. Our visitor will come in the back and turn off the alarm, and will then walk straight through the kitchen and butler's pantry before turning right into the dining room. When the fake ghost walks into the foyer and heads toward the living room to reach those glass animals, you'll be here to uncloak the intruder."

"And I'll kick Sierra's hiney." Tiffany assumed a satisfied grin while making a kicking motion.

I held up a warning hand. "I know it's tempting. Remember, Sierra works for a bunch of lawyers and Mystery's filming everything. You don't want assault charges or a lawsuit. Besides, we're not sure it's her."

Tiffany huffed and crossed her arms across her pink fluffy robe. "Oh, it's her, all right."

"Don't forget to hit the alarm panic button in your pocket. I'll hold the spotlight while Jasmine calls 911," I said.

"What do we do when the alarm company calls?" asked Tiffany.

Jasmine spoke up. "I'll answer the phone and tell them we have a burglar. I'm calling the police on my cell in case Jason answers your house phone before I can get to it." Jasmine pushed the button on the handheld recorder, established the date, location, time, purpose of the mission, and hit pause. "It's set up, and we're ready for our fake ghost. I'll turn it back on when the time comes."

We all returned to our seats. The clock chimed midnight, causing everyone but Pierre to jump. We settled back into our previous positions and waited.

Pierre performed aerial maneuvers in the dining room to entertain me. He paused before swooping up the stairs.

I craned my neck to see the stairway. *Where's he going now?*

A few minutes later he returned. "Jason is sound asleep."

I nodded before nudging Jasmine, who had started snoring. Forty minutes had passed, and my backside was beginning to feel numb, reminding me of the sensation I had experienced in the church pews at Victoria's funeral.

I stood and was about to stretch when a noise at the back door broke the silence, causing me to freeze in place.

"It's her," whispered Tiffany. She rose and crept to her position in the foyer behind the wall by the staircase.

I picked up the spotlight and knelt behind the end of the sofa in the living room. My heart raced with anticipation. *This is it.*

Jasmine activated the recorder that sat on the hall tree in the foyer and joined me and Mystery behind the sofa.

The back door creaked open.

The sound sent an icy dribble down my spine. I held my breath to better hear. *What if our fake ghost has a gun? Why didn't we think of this sooner?*

The alarm chirped. *It's been disabled*, I thought. *Time to uncloak a ghost wannabe.*

After a quick peek into the butler's pantry, Pierre floated back across the dining room into a corner near the front door. "Our faux fantôme has arrived."

A sheet-draped figure entered the dining room. It paused beside the table and looked around.

I stiffened with alarm. *Did she hear us? Did we make too much noise?*

The figure took a few more steps and stopped again, looking toward the foyer where Pierre floated.

Can she see him? I inhaled and then held it. I could feel her building panic hitting me like a wave. *She's going to cut and run.*

The draped figure turned and raced back through the butler's pantry, sheet flying. The door closed.

Jasmine cursed and stood. "I know. I owe the bad habit jar a dollar."

Tiffany rushed over to us. "What happened?

I sprinted across the house toward the back door, with Mystery close behind. We ran down the stairs in time to see taillights disappear around the corner. *Well heck, she got away.* By now my heart pounded like a drum in a rock and roll band. I exhaled my frustration with a huff.

Mystery was breathing hard with her hands on her hips. "Well, shoot."

We walked back into the house. When I entered the dining room, Tiffany rushed toward me.

"Did she get away?"

I shrugged. "All I saw was taillights."

Jasmine walked over and turned off the recorder.

"I don't understand what happened," Tiffany said. "We were quiet."

"Me either," Jasmine said.

Mystery led Tiffany to the sofa in the living room to brief her, since she couldn't see what happened from where she stood. "She walked as far as the dining room, stopped, and then ran for it."

"But why?" Tiffany asked.

Pierre zoomed down and pointed at the recorder that Jasmine had moved to the end of the sofa. "The light."

"Pierre thinks it has something to do with the recorder. She may have seen the light." I said, "Jasmine, turn on the recorder for a moment."

When she did, a bright blue light lit up.

Tiffany said, "Well, diddly squat, what do we do now?"

"Don't panic, I have another idea," Mystery said.

CHAPTER 23

Yawning, I filed last week's invoices away so Kaya could enter them into QuickBooks when she came to work.

I looked up and jerked when Pierre floated through the wall. I placed a hand over my heart. "Geez, I wish you'd stop doing that."

He looked down as if repentant. "I do it so often, I forget it frightens you."

My jaw stiffened. "It startles me. There's a difference."

"Ah, English is my second language. I can be forgiven a few language mistakes. Oui?" He offered a look that was both doleful and sexy.

"Since you're here, perhaps you can help me understand a few things. If the fake ghost is indeed Sierra, why did she involve herself in this scam with Jason? If he'd fool around on Tiffany, he'd do the same to her someday. To me that's just plain crazy."

He shrugged one shoulder. "I am a man. I do not understand women." He cocked a rakish brow. "Except," he smiled, "what makes them moan with pleasure. Perhaps she likes bad boys?"

"Maybe so. You do understand men. Why is Jason doing all this? He's an attorney, which makes him an officer of the court."

Pierre's lips formed a crooked smile. "I am an artiste. I know nothing about being an officer of the court." He ran a translucent finger along the desk. "I do know men do stupid things and sometimes make decisions from their—how do you Americans say it—south pole."

I laughed. "Ain't that the truth?"

Pierre pointed at me. "If you were at Mystery's shop, you would owe the bad habit jar a dollar."

True.

I heard the back door open. "It's me," Kaya yelled.

"I'm in my office."

Kaya popped her head in. "You want me to turn on the open sign and unlock the door?"

I glanced at my watch. "I never noticed that it's almost ten. Yes, please."

Kaya smiled and left.

Pierre smiled. "You will be busy soon. I will go."

Poof! He disappeared.

My cell phone chimed the Aretha Franklin tune, *Respect.*

"Is Kaya there?" Mystery's voice sounded high and breathless.

"Yes, why?"

"Come to the churchyard right away. I think Victoria's out of control. You need to see this."

When I arrived, a man with dark brown hair sat with his back to me on the tailgate of a paramedic's vehicle. One of the medics dabbed something onto his bloody shoulder wound. He flinched and turned his head to avoid looking at the process.

I rushed over to Mystery. "What's going on?"

"Bree, you're not going to believe it. That's Jason Blake."

I glanced back, recognizing him now that he'd turned our way. "I can see that, but what happened?"

"I think Victoria lit into him like a rabid raccoon."

"Couldn't happen to a nicer guy. Why was he here? He doesn't strike me as the church type."

"Father Garrison told me the Historical Preservation Board is meeting in the church and Jason wanted to put another request before the board. Father called me after Jason was attacked. Darlene told him about my services."

I glanced back over at Jason, who was having his wound bandaged. *I have to admit, he's a nice-looking guy and in good shape. I can see how he won Tiffany over.* "What did Victoria do to cause him to bleed?"

"That wicked haint bit him." She cocked a hip and rested a fist on it. "Don't folks get past that behavior after toddlerhood?"

I chuckled. "You would think so." The seriousness of this trend hit me. "So, she's graduated from pinching to biting. This isn't good."

Mystery shot wary glances toward the churchyard. "According to Father Garrison, she started chomping on folks a couple of days ago. He's concerned because Victoria's level of violence is increasing. She's bitten him several times and pushed him down a set of stairs causing him to sprain his right ankle. That's why I'm here. He asked if I could help. The problem is, I can't see her to evaluate the situation, but you can."

"Makes sense. Victoria's probably still fuming about the funeral. Who else has gotten hurt?" I asked, watching as Victoria glared at her latest victim.

"Katie Abernathy."

Katie? "Was she hurt bad?"

"Not as much as Jason," Mystery said.

Upset that my newfound dog-walking buddy had been attacked, I said, "Let's go talk to Victoria."

Mystery nodded. "And tell her to mind her manners." Fired up by indignation, she strode to the gate, yanked it open, and walked inside the fenced area. She looked ready to lecture the ghost on proper Southern behavior.

Mystery's a formidable foe with live folks who aren't her mother. She's no match for an angry poltergeist. She doesn't always think things through when her temper is in full flame.

I followed her, my stomach tumbling. "Come back on this side of the fence!"

Mystery planted both fists on her hips. "Listen here, Victoria. You need to mind your manners and quit biting people. You hear?"

Victoria's feral eyes fastened onto us like Velcro. The poltergeist screeched and zoomed toward us with her maw open.

Mystery had no idea that a supernatural buzzsaw was heading her way.

I grabbed her arm and yanked her back through the gate. Panting from the effort, I slammed it shut with a metallic clang. I continued to pull Mystery away to avoid the grasping, claw-like fingers that reached for us.

"Stop it!" I commanded.

Victoria backed away from the fence. Her angry expression

shifted to shock.

The paramedic stopped bandaging. He and Jason turned to look our way.

The ghost and I locked gazes. "Why are you behaving this way?" I asked with a concerned tone.

The ghost touched her head before pointing at Jason. "He hit me. He'll pay. I'll find him, and he'll pay."

"You won't like the consequences if you do. Let me help you cross over."

She glared at Jason. "I don't want your help. He must pay."

"I want to help you."

Her face contorted into a mask of malice. "I don't want your help. I want him!"

I shrugged.

Gesturing for to Mystery to follow, we walked across the street for privacy.

I glanced over at Jason, who was staring at us. "If she learns to leave the confines of that fenced area, there will be trouble. Let's go. We need to think this through without Jason watching us."

We sat in Mystery's conference room, trying to decide what to do, while Jasmine worked the front.

"I guess there's no way to bind a ghost, right?" Mystery asked. "No magical ropes or other bindings?"

"I wish. Remember, I'm a psychic, not a witch. If there is such a contraption, I know nothing about it." I scraped my fingers through my hair. "I wish Mom lived closer so she could help. I'm beginning to think I need more training. All I can think is the sooner we solve the murder, the faster Victoria can cross over."

"What if she's stubborn and doesn't want to cross over?"

"Saints preserve us, don't even think it. I have a date with Chris tonight, but what can I do? I can't say, oh, by-the-way, Victoria's spirit told me Jason Blake may have killed her."

"Does he know you're psychic?"

I shook my head. "I don't bring up that topic until after the third date."

"Why not?"

"Don't want the hassle if we're both not interested in a possible relationship."

Jasmine tapped the doorframe to get our attention. "Tiffany's holding on line one. She sounds excited."

Mystery hit speaker on the phone. "Tiffany, Bree and Jasmine are listening. What happened?"

"I found all the dining chairs in the living room this morning. What's the plan?"

Mystery looked into Jasmine's eager face. "Are you free tonight?"

She nodded. "I need the extra cash."

Mystery asked me, "Can you come again?"

"I wouldn't miss it. I'll reschedule my date with Chris."

"Won't he be mad?" Jasmine asked.

"He had to cancel our date two days ago because of work. I think he'll understand."

"Okay, Tiffany. It's a go. Same as last time," Mystery said, penciling it into her black appointment book.

"I can't wait," Tiffany replied.

Mystery disconnected the call. "This should be interesting. I hope we don't spook our 'fake haint' this time."

"Me, too. When are you going to give up and get an automated scheduling system?" I asked.

She slammed the book shut. "When I get good and ready."

I held up both hands in surrender.

"Um, do y'all remember the report on Jason that Mystery asked me to run?" Jasmine asked. "Some interesting things came to light."

We leaned closer.

Mystery arched a brow. "Such as…?"

"Jason married a woman named Sophie Bianchi. She *allegedly* committed suicide nine months before he met Tiffany. It seems the medical examiner declared the cause of death to be an overdose, yet the manner of death was listed as undetermined."

"What does manner of death, mean?" Mystery asked.

"I looked it up, there's natural, accident, suicide, homicide, and undetermined. So, that means they're not sure how she overdosed," Jasmine said.

Mystery asked, "What did she OD on?"

"Sleeping pills. From what I could find out from some of Sophie's neighbors, she thought her house was haunted." Jasmine did her neck thing. "I don't think Tiffany knows about Sophie."

"Why do you say that?" I asked, winding my hair into a ball and holding it in place with a clip from my purse.

"She never mentioned that he had a previous marriage when she gave me all the background information about him," Jasmine said.

"Not good," I said. The more we dove into what seemed like a simple haunting, the more it resembled a twisted maze. "I'll see if Pierre will come. We may need some ghostly assistance."

Jasmine's smile widened. "Awesome."

That girl is ghost crazy for sure.

The grandfather clock chimed midnight. A noise at the door alerted us that our fake ghost had arrived.

Mystery, Jasmine, Tiffany, and I stood and moved into our positions to catch the person who was fake-haunting this home.

Tiffany closed the gap in the drapes to further darken the living room before taking her position behind the wall in the foyer.

Jasmine started the recorder, whose light was now taped over, and placed it in a less noticeable location. She joined Mystery and me behind the sofa with her phone in hand. She whispered, "All the cameras are operational."

I whispered directions to Pierre and watched him zip into the dining room to wait for our intruder. Then, I knelt behind the sofa and gripped the powerful flashlight with sweat-slick hands. I strained to hear over my heart pounding in my ears.

The back door creaked open. The alarm beeped once before it was turned off.

Mystery, Jasmine, and I peeked over the edge of the sofa.

A white-sheeted figure came into the dining room and paused. The black eyeholes looked around. The figure moved forward a bit more and stopped again to listen.

I held my breath, afraid that any sound would alert the person under the sheet.

The fake ghost stepped into the foyer and stopped in front of the staircase.

Before it could notice Tiffany, I turned on the high-powered light, aiming for the eye holes cut into the sheet.

The shrouded figure threw up both hands to block the glare and froze like a papier-mache statue.

"Gotcha!" Tiffany yelled, ripping the sheet away.

Sierra screamed and swung away from the light. She stepped back on the sheet, slipped, and fell, banging her head on the floor. The sound was loud in the quiet house.

Tiffany dropped the sheet, held up both hands, and backed away. "I didn't touch her. Honest." She reached into her pocket and pushed the panic button.

The alarm wailed.

I rushed forward and leaned over Sierra, who appeared to be unconscious. Dropping to my knees, I felt for a pulse, fearing she was dead. A steady throb reassured me that at least she was still alive. "She's been knocked out."

Jasmine was on her cell with a 911 operator, reporting the break-in.

I stood. "Tell the operator someone fell and hit her head. We need paramedics and an ambulance."

Jasmine did as I directed, and then declined to stay on the line.

We formed a circle around Sierra while I pointed the spotlight on her.

"I hope we got all this on camera," Tiffany said, bending over to look at her quarry.

"I'll check right now," Jasmine said.

Mystery stopped her by placing a hand on her arm. "Wait. Did you hear that?"

I doused the flashlight after a floorboard creaked.

We skulked back out of sight into the living room. Moonlight streamed through the beveled glass surrounding the door, lighting Sierra with a pale silvery glow.

The sconces over the stairs clicked on, flooding the scene with golden light.

Jason bellowed, "Tiffany! Where are you? Why the heck is the alarm going off?"

Dressed only in pajama bottoms, he pounded barefooted down the steps to the landing. There he stopped and gawked at Sierra, who still lay sprawled at the base of the stairs with her long blonde hair fanned around her head like a halo.

"Sierra! My God, what happened?" He hesitated, hand on the rail. "Get up before Tiffany finds you."

Silence.

"Hurry up or you'll ruin everything!" Jason said.

The front door flew open, slamming against the wall so hard that it bounced back a few feet.

Alarmed, I locked gazes with Pierre. His rounded eyes looked as startled as I felt. He zipped over to join me in the shadows of the living room.

The atmosphere changed, becoming heavy. Sudden dread filled me.

Jasmine cowered between Mystery and me. Mystery snaked an arm around her pulling her closer.

Tiffany joined us, her face pale as fresh snow. "What's going on?"

"I'm not sure, but it's not good. Stay close," I said. My stomach clenched with alarm while I tried to determine what we would face.

Tiffany crowded against my other side.

A chill wind tore inside, blowing some envelopes off the shelves of the ornate hall tree. They whirled once in a circle before scattering across the foyer floor. Frost formed on the insides of the windows and mirrors.

"This would be a good time to pray," I said, wondering if I was up to handle the situation. My skill sets lie toward helping disembodied spirits on their journey, not subduing out-of-control poltergeists.

Shivering, we all backed further into the shadows, puffing clouds of condensation with each breath.

Victoria raged through the doorway like a killer blizzard and rocketed straight toward Jason.

Pierre placed himself in front of us and spread his arms.

I wasn't sure what good it would do, but I appreciated it. I looked around him for a clearer view.

"Stay behind me," he ordered.

Victoria clawed Jason's face and naked chest like a rabid cougar.

He screeched in agony as gouges that bled tiny streams of bright red blood appeared on his skin.

"God help us," Mystery whispered while crowding closer.

He screamed and screamed and screamed, flailing his arms in an attempt to beat her off. While wrestling with his unseen foe, he begged for help.

Tiffany grabbed my arm. "What's happening? What should we do?"

I'd never seen a poltergeist with this kind of rage or power. *How do I stop her?* I wished desperately for my mother, but she was in Savannah, and I wasn't sure even she would know what to do. My mind raced for possible solutions but none seemed adequate.

It all happened so fast. Before I could devise a coherent strategy to save Jason, Victoria flung his bleeding body down the stairs. He landed with the resounding thud of a thousand-pound pine, cracking his head against the floor. His neck was twisted at an odd angle.

Victoria hovered over his body; her visage contorted with angry triumph before spitting on him. The ectoplasm dripped down his cheek.

She paused and focused her malicious grin on me.

Christ Almighty!

She pointed a Tiffany. "Tell that one he would've killed her next, like he did Sophie." The poltergeist flew out the front door in a fury of wind and ice.

I slid to the floor and my friends went down with me.

After a few minutes, the room began to warm.

Pierre dropped his arms and said, "Je ne voudrais pas qu'elle se fâche contre moi."

"I wouldn't want her angry at me, either," I said. "When she looked at me, I thought we were goners."

I stood and took a shaky step forward, intending to check Jason's pulse.

His spirit floated up from his body.

I scrambled back, breaking into a cold sweat. I've seen ghosts all my life, but this was the first time I'd seen one rise from their body.

Jason looked down at his physical shell with a confused expression. He attempted to touch different areas of his corporeal spirit.

A cold gust of wind, more powerful than the last, whistled around the room. The inside of the windows instantly recoated with ice. My breath fogged when I exhaled, creating tiny ice particles. I yelled over the wind, "Help me move Sierra."

Tiffany stood frozen, her terror-filled eyes as round as saucers.

Mystery and I grabbed an arm each and dragged the unconscious woman into the living room. I placed an arm around Tiffany, who couldn't take her eyes off Jason's body, and led her, Mystery, and Jasmine to a far corner, where we stood huddled together.

"I don't know what's happening, but it's not going to be good. Brace yourselves," I said.

"Cher Dieu, sauve-nous!"

I could tell by Pierre's lapse into French and his expression that he was scared. Despite this, he once again took a defensive position in front of us.

I could see what was happening. I wasn't sure who was better off, me...or the others who couldn't see Jason's confused ghost. I whispered, "Pierre, do you know what's happening?"

"Ma chérie, I do not know, but I am concerned."

The gusting wind wailed like the screams of tortured souls. Bolts of lightning struck outside the house, flashing through the windows like electrified spears. Crashes of thunder rattled the windows in their frames.

Mystery cringed and held Jasmine's trembling body tight against her, while she whispered prayers.

I tried to pull a shocked-stiff Tiffany further into the corner.

Shrieks and moans filled the room. A crack split the foyer floor, and red-tinted smoke that smelled of brimstone billowed out.

Tiffany screamed. She pointed a shaking finger at the crack before collapsing to the carpet with a muffled thud.

Indistinct shadows swirled in a vortex from the opening and flew around the foyer.

I dropped to the floor, pulling a terrified Jasmine with me. Mystery joined us, eyes bulging.

Pierre once more provided a blockade while muttering, "Notre Père qui es aux cieux: que ton nom soit sanctifié;que ton règne vienne..."

Mystery whispered, "Is he saying an incantation?"

"He's praying in French," I said, unable to control the waver in my voice.

Jasmine leaned closer, "Are those demons?"

"Shhh!" I placed my index finger in front of my lips.

Jason's spirit backed away toward the stairs, holding up his hands to stop them.

The sinister shapes reached for him with long bony fingers.

He struggled against them. "Nooo!"

They pulled him screaming into the vortex. It sucked back through the floor and out of sight. The gap in the hardwood floor closed with a loud snap.

The storm stopped.

Silence fell.

I stared at the space where the crack had been. Nothing was left but a wispy swirl of smoke that stank of ozone and brimstone.

Chest heaving, Mystery asked, "Dear Lord, what just happened?"

Jasmine sank the rest of the way to the floor. "Holy crap! I'm straightening up my life."

Good idea. Me too, I thought. I couldn't seem to stop shaking.

Tiffany propped herself up on one elbow and rubbed her head. "Did I faint?"

"Lucky you," Jasmine said.

Jasmine and I helped her to stand. She swayed a bit until she regained her balance.

A moment later, blue lights flashed across the foyer and reflected in the mirrors. A police officer approached the porch, gun drawn. He stepped through the open door and looked from Jason's dead body to Sierra's unconscious form.

When he spotted Mystery, Jasmine, Tiffany, and me in the living room, he said, "Everybody put your hands on your heads."

Pierre raised his palms. "I cannot protect you from the police."

The officer wasn't taking any chances. He had us cuffed and face down on the floor by the time his backup arrived.

After what I'd just experienced, this was nothing.

CHAPTER 24

Tiffany drew herself up to her full five-foot-four inches. Only her pink robe, fluffy slippers and the handcuffs softened her regal air. "Officer. I'm Tiffany Blake, and I own this house." She nudged Sierra with the toe of her pink slipper. "This woman broke into my home." Her indignant tone was difficult to hear over the blaring alarm.

Officer Manitomb's gaze roamed over Mystery, Jasmine, and me, where we sat handcuffed on the sofa, and then returned to Tiffany. "Ma'am, can you turn off the alarm?"

"Yes, of course."

Manitomb jerked his head at a younger officer.

The officer switched Tiffany's cuffs to the front and led her by the arm through the dining room.

Manitomb walked over to me.

Pierre slipped between us like an unseen shield.

Manitomb shuddered and looked confused before taking a step back. He redirected his attention to Mystery. "What's going on here?"

"I'm Mystery Jones. I own the Mystery Shop in Five Points. Mrs. Blake hired our firm to determine if her house was haunted. Paranormal investigations are our specialty."

The alarm stopped bleating, leaving a ringing silence.

He stuck a finger in one ear and rotated it. "Did you say paranormal investigations?"

"Yes, sir. We're the local haint hunters."

Tiffany returned, clutching a purse to her chest with her cuffed hands. The policeman trailed behind her.

"I checked her ID," the officer said. He leaned against the doorframe and crossed his arms.

Manitomb gestured for Tiffany to join us in the living room. "Okay, folks, what happened to her?" He squatted and touched Sierra's neck with two fingers.

"She slipped on her sheet, fell, and hit her head," Jasmine said. "I requested an ambulance when I called 911."

Manitomb stood and adjusted the wide black belt around his ample waistline. His gaze worked its way up to the top of Jasmine's clown red hair. "Who're you again?"

I spoke up. "This is Mystery's technical assistant, Jasmine Williams."

He looked at me with steely gray eyes. "What's she doing here?"

"She set up the cameras and operated the recorder," Mystery said through clenched teeth.

Manitomb's gaze focused back on Sierra. "Okay, but who's the woman tangled up with a sheet with eyeholes cut into it? Did y'all have an out-of-season Halloween party?"

"No," Tiffany said, pulling the collar of her robe tight around her throat.

He looped his thumbs in his belt. "Is she a house guest?"

"She's not a guest," said Tiffany. "She's my husband's mistress and his partner in crime. She broke into my house and was pretending to be a ghost."

Manitomb rubbed his chin and looked down at the sheet before doing a just-when-you thought-you'd-seen-it-all shake of his head. "Everybody, take a seat until the detectives arrive."

The house phone rang.

"That's the alarm company calling," Tiffany said, starting to rise.

Manitomb gestured for her to sit and answered the phone. After listening, he grunted and handed Tiffany the receiver.

"Hi. It took y'all long enough to call. The police are already here." She turned her back to everyone and whispered the password into the phone before hanging up.

I never knew how uncomfortable handcuffs could be. They were hard and seemed to pinch everywhere. *At the very least, they could cuff our hands in front, the way they did with Tiffany.*

Sirens wailed in the background.

Moaning, Sierra braced herself on one elbow. She shielded her eyes from the light with the other hand. "What happened?"

The sirens stopped. The officer leaning in the dining room doorway walked over and opened the door. Within minutes, two uniformed paramedics came in carrying cases. One knelt by Sierra and began asking questions while fitting her with a blood pressure cuff.

The taller paramedic checked Jason's neck for a pulse. He looked at his partner and shook his head. After examining Jason's face and chest, he said, "Good Lord, did a cougar get in the house?"

Manitomb pointed at Jason. "Good question. What happened to him?"

How do we explain this to the police? They won't believe us.

Sierra screamed. "Jason!" She crawled toward him. "Honey, are you okay?" She rose to her hands and knees and shook him. "Jason, what happened to you?" Tears flooded her eyes and dripped onto his body.

Manitomb stepped forward, "Ma'am, this is a crime scene. Don't touch the body. Back away."

The paramedic who had been taking her blood pressure pulled her back.

Tiffany stood and stared wild-eyed at Sierra before collapsing unconscious onto the couch.

"Good Lord, what next?" Mystery said. "I never figured her for the faintin' type."

Now the older paramedic was leaning over Tiffany.

The only thing that could make this situation worse is if Chris showed up.

Twenty minutes later, Detectives Ricci and Haddington walked in and took in the scene with one quick glance. When Ricci's gaze settled on me, he asked, "What the heck are y'all doing here?"

Chris's jaw dropped, before he reined-in his shock and assumed his neutral cop expression.

I'd told him I was working tonight but I'm sure he didn't expect to find me at a murder scene.

After twenty minutes of explanation, Ricci told the young officer to remove our cuffs so we could show him the camera footage.

Jasmine hooked the video camera that covered the foyer to the large television in the den and ran the footage.

Ricci's tan face paled while he watched the events unfold.

Manitomb cursed under his breath.

Chris's jaw once again dropped. He glanced over at me before stepping closer to the screen.

Tiffany, who had been carried to the sofa, stirred. I gathered her close and patted her cheek. "Can she have some water, please?"

The young policeman headed toward the kitchen.

We could hear Sierra wailing in the foyer.

Tiffany closed her eyes and bowed her head, tears streaking her pale cheeks.

When the video ended, I followed Chris and Manitomb into the foyer where Sierra rocked, holding her head in her hands.

Chris pointed at Sierra. "Cuff her."

The older paramedic stood. "We need to take her to the ER. She may have a concussion. The ambulance is here."

Chris nodded to the officer standing by with cuffs. "She's under arrest. Read her rights to her, and go to the ER. Book her after she's been released by the doctor." He turned to Manitomb. "Call it in."

Manitomb keyed his mike. "We have a 1056. Call the coroner."

CHAPTER 25

Mystery and I discussed the previous night's horrors while we waited for our breakfast orders at Another Broken Egg located in Jones Valley. Though it had too many chicken decorations for my taste, the cozy ambiance did provide a calming influence on my shredded nerves. Our pleasant waitress brought us coffee and left to take an order from an older couple who were seated nearby. I gazed out the window. The large tree-covered hill between us and Tiffany's home provided a buffer that offered an illusion of safety.

Mystery sipped her coffee and returned the mug to the table with an unsteady hand. "Bree, what were those wraith-like creatures?"

"You saw those?" It hadn't occurred to me at the time that the rest of my companions could see the crack in the floor and what came out of it, since they couldn't see Jason's and Victoria's ghosts. Everything happened so fast.

Mystery lifted a hand to her chest. "I'll never forget them. Scared the living daylights out of me!"

I nodded before settling deeper into my chair. The very memory of the demons sent ice slicing down my spine. "Me, too. I've never seen them before. I called Mom this morning and she told me about them. I hope you don't have nightmares.

"Too late! I woke up screaming at four-thirty." She leaned closer. "You didn't answer my question. What were they?"

"Emissaries from Hell, there to claim Jason's soul. Mom told me that murder marks the soul of the perpetrator."

Mystery shivered, pulling her sweater around her shoulders. "I wondered if that was the case."

I regretted not thinking of a sweater myself. The climate control was set on frigid. If I didn't know better, I'd have thought we were surrounded by a legion of spirits. Rubbing my goose-pimpled arms, I said, "I thought Detective Ricci would never finish interrogating me. He kept asking me the same questions over and over. Did Chris do the same to you?"

"Yep. If we hadn't had the cameras recording the whole time, we'd probably be in jail or the hospital's psychiatric unit by now."

"I'm beginning to believe that Ricci's phasmophobic. He twitched every time I mentioned the word 'ghost.'"

She nodded. "Did you notice he broke into a sweat and looked ready to flee while watching the video?"

"Yep." I spread my hair across my shoulders for warmth before grabbing my hot coffee mug. "It's not easy to explain that we watched a vengeful ghost kill someone. I'm glad y'all left those cameras in place."

"Me, too. Mama would say we'd be up the creek without a paddle if we hadn't." She cocked her head and gave me an assessing look. "Did you tell Ricci you saw the haints?"

I shook my head. "I reported what I saw as if I couldn't see the ghost. I didn't want him or Chris to think I was over the edge and wandering in the weeds. Maybe that's why Ricci kept questioning me. Do you think he suspects I was leaving out information?"

Mystery shrugged before taking a sip from her mug.

"I sometimes think the best cops have psychic gifts they refuse to acknowledge." I pulled the warm mug of coffee closer to my body.

The waitress delivered our steaming food with a warm smile. "I'll be back in a jiff with more coffee."

Before she left, I said, "Could you make it warmer in here? I'm freezing."

The older couple two tables over looked our way. The tiny bent woman said, "So are we. Us old folks have thin blood."

Mystery and I exchanged a we-need-to-lower-our-voices look.

The aromas of bacon and fried breakfast potatoes made my stomach growl. I rubbed it, willing it to calm down. *I'm going to feed you. Hold on.*

Mystery picked up a fork and speared a fried potato. "I don't know how we're going to prove Jason murdered Victoria, now that he's dead. I don't think that vicious haint will move on until Jason is proven to be her killer. Even worse, we may never know his motive. You know how much I hate unanswered questions."

I cut my fried eggs into small bites. The yoke oozed like sunshine across the plate. "You're not the only one." I rubbed the back of my neck, trying to relieve some of the tightness. "I didn't get home until three-thirty this morning. I'm beat."

"Why did it take so long?" Mystery asked. "Jasmine and I left at two."

I picked up my knife. "I managed to get Chris outside alone and tried to wheedle some information out of him."

Mystery stopped chewing and leaned closer. "Did he spill?"

"Some tidbits, but it wasn't easy. I could tell he was still trying to process all the paranormal stuff."

"What did he say?"

"According to him, Jason couldn't have murdered Victoria," I said, waiting for Mystery's reaction.

She was swallowing a bite of egg and nearly choked. When she could speak without coughing, she croaked, "You said Victoria pointed at her head and accused Jason of hitting her."

"That may be true, but the blow to the head wasn't the cause of death."

Looking even more confused, she asked a bit too loudly, "Did she have a heart attack? Maybe a stroke?"

I shot a meaningful glance at the couple leaning closer to overhear.

"Nope." I whispered before picking up a crisp slice of bacon.

She scowled at me. "I hate it when you drag things out."

With defiance, I lifted my chin. "I hate it when you call me and pretend to be someone else."

She huffed and sat back, crossing her arms.

"Oh, all right." I put down the bacon and wiped my hands, "Victoria was poisoned."

"Poisoned!" Glancing at the nosy twosome, she leaned closer and whispered, "With what?"

I leaned in, too. "They're not sure yet. So far, they've ruled out arsenic."

CHAPTER 26

At eleven, Kaya came in, all smiles. She took one look at me, and her brown eyes softened. "What happened? Did someone die?"

I paused. I didn't want to lie about such a serious event, but I feared losing her as both an employee and friend. My tribe is small. Because of my abilities, I don't have many friends. I'm an only child. My father continues to reject me, and Mom lives three hundred sixty-five miles away. It can get lonely sometimes.

I took a deep centering breath the way Mom taught me, and said, "We need to talk."

Kaya stopped what she was doing and froze. Her mouth thinned and fear flooded her energy field moving in fast waves toward me.

I held up a hand. "Calm down, I'm not firing you."

She did a long exhale, her shoulders drooping. "Gracias a Dios."

I told her *everything*.

With widening eyes, she pulled over a stool and sat to listen. She never said a word until I finished. I gave her credit for not running screaming from the building.

The fear dissipated from her energy field. "Well, this explains a lot. I was afraid you were hallucinating or something. I'd walk in and you'd be talking to nothing."

"I was speaking to Pierre Garnier." I explained how I met him and how he migrated to America by attaching himself to his painting that I'd bought.

"That's so romantic."

I managed to not roll my eyes. "Contrary to what certain

Hollywood movies would have us believe, a love affair between someone alive and someone dead wouldn't work."

She sighed. "Too bad. Is he guapo?"

I cocked a brow. "Guapo?"

She chuckled. "Sorry. Hot."

"Yep." I described him to her. I leaned against the counter and crossed my ankles and arms. "I'm surprised this isn't freaking you out."

She shrugged. "I'm Catholic, and my ancestors were Aztec. Did you know the Aztecs celebrated the Days of the Dead before the Church brought Christianity to Mexico? We still celebrate All Saints Day and All Souls Day as the Days of the Dead, with parades and parties and cemetery picnics with food for our ancestors. My family is quite aware of the spirits of our ancestors, even if we can't see or talk to them the way you do."

I sighed. "I feel better, now that you know."

"Me, too," she said. "It's not fun wondering if your boss is loca."

My face must have relayed my confusion.

"You know, crazy."

"Oh, I thought it was loco."

"Not if you're female."

I nodded. "Let's close for lunch. I ordered two large pizzas to be delivered to Mystery's shop."

She stood taller and grinned. "I like pizza."

Mystery, Kaya, and I were awaiting the pizzas' arrival when Jasmine tromped into the store with her head down.

Mystery crossed her arms. "Sugar, you look like a thunderstorm ready to unleash its fury."

Ignoring her remark, Jasmine stomped over to the purse drawer. After unlocking it, she yanked it open, stuffed her purse inside, and slammed it shut hard enough to make it bounce open again.

I felt my ire rise.

Mystery stepped forward. "Whoa! You want to talk about whatever's stuck in your craw before you break that drawer?"

Jasmine looked at her feet before closing it again. "Sorry." She paced and flung her arms in the air. "Why can't men be faithful!"

"That's been a mystery since time began. I don't think anyone in this room will solve it." I came around the counter and placed my hand on her shoulder. She buzzed with a combination of energies. I picked up traces of anger, fear, and confusion. "Is this about Jason?"

Jasmine shrugged off my hand and resumed her pacing.

We waited, giving her time to walk off some of her frustration.

Minutes later, she stopped in front of Mystery and broke into sobs.

Kaya rushed forward and placed an arm around her friend's heaving shoulders.

I handed Jasmine some tissues. I'd expected some kind of emotional reaction. We hadn't talked about what had happened at Tiffany's after we left the police station in the wee hours. *She looks the way I feel, exhausted. I'm running on caffeine and sheer determination.*

Jasmine looked at Kaya and then me.

"It's all right. Kaya knows everything," I said, pleased to see the relieved look on Jasmine's face. I hadn't thought about the burden Jasmine felt while trying to guard my secrets from her good friend.

Jasmine looked at me with tear-reddened eyes. "Did we do something to cause Jason's death?"

Shocked by the question, I stepped back. I'd never considered that she'd assume any responsibility for what had happened.

Jasmine wiped her eyes before honking into a tissue. "I feel bad, like it was my fault. If we hadn't investigated Tiffany's case, then none of this would have happened."

"Sugar, Jason's own actions caused his death." Mystery stepped forward and rubbed circles on Jasmine's back, the way I had soothed her when we'd found Victoria's body.

I understood all too well that guilt related to death wasn't always logical. "What would've happened if we hadn't investigated?"

Jasmine sniffled and thought for a moment. "Tiffany would have been gaslighted and lost her house and who knows what else."

I suffered an involuntary shiver as I remembered Victoria's revelation. I took a moment to gather my thoughts before explaining what I'd seen and heard the night before.

Jasmine's eyes grew rounder with alarm. "So, Jason really did kill his first wife?"

"I don't know," I said. "Ghosts, like people, can lie."

The pizza delivery guy arrived.

"Lunch is here, ladies. My treat." I knew we needed this time together to process what we'd witnessed.

Mystery perked up. "Thank the Lord. As Mama would say, 'I could eat a horse.'"

Kaya looked at Jasmine. "Do you still have some of that hot sauce left?"

Jasmine winked. "Sure do."

I paid the driver and carried the warm boxes to the conference room. When Jasmine lifted the lids, the room filled with the aroma of delicious spicy goodness. We dug in like the hungry, traumatized people that we were. Food is the great soother.

Kaya was finishing the last bite when a screech of tires drew our attention to the parking area.

"There's Tiffany. She may be able to answer some of your questions about Jason," Mystery said.

Pale and red-eyed, Tiffany slouched as she came into the shop. Even the jingle of the bell sounded subdued. Without a word, she trudged over to a stool and perched. Her energy felt dull and sad.

I introduced Kaya, who offered a sympathetic smile.

Mystery patted Tiffany's shoulder. "Hey, Sugar. You hanging in there?"

Tiffany pushed her blonde hair out of her face. "Last night was the most horrible thing that's ever happened to me." She wiped her eyes with a crumpled tissue in her hand. "Thanks for turning over the footage from the cameras to the police. Without that proof to back up our story, we'd be sitting in jail right now, or worse."

"What could be worse?" Kaya asked, looking from Tiffany to me.

"The psychiatric unit," I said. I've always had a fear of being committed and medicated because my gifts were thought to be hallucinations.

Mystery sat on a stool across the counter. "Sugar, that was your footage. You paid for it."

Tiffany rested her elbow on the counter and cupped her chin. "I heard they arrested Sierra and hauled her off to jail after she was released by the emergency room. They're charging her with breaking and entering and attempting to commit fraud."

"At least something good came out of all this mess," Jasmine said, wiping away the last of her tears.

"My house is a crime scene, complete with yellow tape. I'm

staying at a hotel for a few days. I shudder to think what rumors the Camellia Express is spreading." Tiffany looked at Jasmine, who had moved to stand beside her. "I didn't get to bed until five o'clock this morning. You don't look too perky yourself."

Jasmine quirked a shoulder. "I was too upset to sleep, and I had an early class this morning. I wasn't at my brightest."

Tiffany rubbed her temples. "I slept until ten, but I still feel like a road paver has squashed me flatter than a fritter. Jason's secretary woke me. The firm wanted to know if he was sick. He had a court case scheduled at two o'clock."

"I bet the news of his death shocked her," I said.

"Oh, yeah. I went to Jason's office to clean out his desk. Sierra got out on bail and came to the law firm ten minutes after I arrived. By then, everyone in the firm knew the entire story. They fired her on the spot. I doubt she'll be able to get another paralegal position in town." Her hand formed a fist. "It took everything I had to control myself. I wanted to snatch her bald."

Mystery nodded. "Sounds reasonable."

Jasmine pumped a fist in the air. "I'm so glad they fired her. She deserved it."

"I spoke with both his secretary and his boss." Tiffany tucked a lock of hair behind her right ear. "His boss wasn't a bit surprised that he was in trouble. Jason was on probation with both the firm and the licensing board for various infractions. He was one mistake away from being fired and possibly disbarred. He said the only reason he hadn't already fired Jason was because he was a documenting fiend. He kept notes about everything." She rubbed her neck and moved her head around until there was an audible pop. "I had no idea anything like this was going on in his professional life."

I knew some of it, but hadn't found the right time to tell her. "Did you know about his late wife, Sophie?"

Tiffany stared at me like I'd fallen over the cliff of reality. She gripped the counter to steady herself. "What are you talking about?"

I started my explanation with Jasmine's research and ended with what I'd seen and heard last night.

Tiffany's hand covered her throat. "Oh my, I could've been his next victim. Jason was the one that suggested that I ask my doctor for sleeping pills."

"It's a disturbing thought," I said.

Tiffany nodded and ran her hand over her face. "So, the whole fake haunting and discrediting me in front of his friends was a setup to kill me and inherit my estate?"

"Looks that way," Jasmine said.

Tiffany massaged her temples. "That's not the half of it. Bonnie, Jason's secretary, is delighted about Sierra's arrest. She filled in a good bit of information about what was happening at work." Tiffany leaned in and lowered her voice. "She walked in once and caught them in his office."

"That weasel!" Jasmine said, slamming one fist into her other hand.

Kaya looked like she was watching a soccer match, her head tracking from one of us to the other.

"Why didn't Bonnie let you know?" I asked.

"She has a kid with muscular dystrophy and couldn't afford to lose her job and insurance," Tiffany said. "I can't hold it against her. She was in a no-win situation."

Jasmine leaned against a counter and crossed her arms. "I bet Sierra's having the worst day of her life." She counted the points off on her fingers. "She got caught in a crappy ghost costume while breaking and entering, banged her head, ended up in the ER with a concussion, was arrested, her partner in crime died, and now she's lost her job."

Tiffany pulled a tissue from her purse. "You can call it a 'bad day,' I call it Karma. I have no pity for her." After wiping under her lashes, she reached back into her purse and pulled out her wallet. "I came to pay for the remainder of my bill. I don't know what I would've done without you ladies and Dr. Stone."

"Glad we could help, Sugar." Mystery went to her office and returned with a printed, itemized bill for Tiffany's approval.

After squinting at the page, Tiffany wrestled her Visa from a slot in her wallet. "It's new. The slots haven't loosened up yet."

Mystery accepted the card with a relieved-looking smile and completed the transaction.

Tiffany scribbled her signature on the pad, took the card, and put it back in her wallet.

Mystery eyed her haggard face with a concerned look. "Sugar, are you going to continue to see Dr. Stone?"

"Oh, yes. I still have so much to work through. It's disconcerting to discover your husband isn't the type of person you thought you married. I'm going to take a copy of the video, so she won't think I'm crazy when I start talking about a ghost attacking Jason."

I don't think you'll have any trouble convincing her. "If anyone can get you on track, it's Dr. Stone." I gave her hand a reassuring squeeze.

"If we can help you in the future, don't hesitate to pop in," Mystery said.

"I suspect I may be back. I'm finding out more every hour about how cunning and secretive Jason could be. I suspect Jasmine may have to research some of his accounts. From what I can tell so far, some of our joint assets seem to be missing. There's no telling what else I may find when I go through his papers. If it hadn't been for y'all, I'd never have known he had an aunt at Redstone Village. I'm still not sure how things will work out for the poor lady with him gone." She looked at her watch. "Oh!" She snatched her purse. "If I don't hurry, I'll be late for an appointment with my attorney. At least Jason hadn't changed his will." Tiffany bustled out the door and into her Volvo.

I cringed as Tiffany backed out without even looking and sped down the street.

Jasmine shook her head. "Of all the mysteries we've investigated over the years, the one that baffles me the most is how Tiffany passed her driver's test."

I rubbed my chin. "If what Tiffany said about her finances is true, y'all might not be through with her case yet."

CHAPTER 27

I was working in my office when my front door alarmed pinged. I found Ricci standing with his back to me, hands jiggling the change in his pockets, while his sharp gaze covered every part of the retail area.

Prissy joined me, yawning.

He turned when I walked up to the counter. It was only then that I noticed his Tinker Bell tie.

Prissy placed herself between the detective and me.

He smiled and reached down to allow her to sniff his hand. "Remember me?"

After a brief sniff, Prissy wagged her tail.

He grinned and rubbed the dog's head. "You're so adorable I keep forgetting you're a lethal weapon."

"It's a great disguise," I said.

He chuckled. "Can I have a few moments of your time?"

Curious, I said, "Let's talk in the conference room."

Ricci followed me to the back of the store. I'd had Mystery install a camera, so I could watch the retail area of the shop from screens in my office, the conference room, and the small warehouse area while Kaya was in class.

We were seated at the table with two cups of coffee when he got straight to the point. "During your investigation for Mrs. Blake, did you discover any fraud or missing funds?"

I remembered Tiffany mentioning missing funds and deduced she'd reported it to Ricci. "We were trying to verify if her house was haunted," I said. "All I know is Jasmine discovered Jason planned to use his elderly aunt's funds to buy Tiffany's home. If you need more information, you'll need to talk to Jasmine, because she's the one who does the computer searches."

The detective made a note in a small black notebook. "I've heard about the aunt's situation from Mrs. Blake. I may need to check that he wasn't also stealing her money." After a few more questions, he put away his notebook. "Thanks for your cooperation. I'll follow-up with Jasmine."

Back in the retail section of the store, he glanced around again. "My wife's birthday is in a month. If I come back, will you help me pick out something nice."

"I'll be glad to assist you. I can't help but admire a guy who wears a Tinker Bell tie."

His olive complexion reddened as he smoothed the tie. "A birthday present from my youngest granddaughter." He waved and headed toward the door.

I yelled after him, "Be sure to check your wife's clothes for sizes before you come back. Since you're a top-notch detective, I'm sure you can handle it."

He stopped and grinned. "I see why Chris likes you so much." He pushed through the door and turned left toward Mystery's shop.

A warm thrill flowed over me. "So, Chris talks about me to his partner. Interesting."

Several hours later, I was talking with Pierre while unpacking merchandise in the stockroom when my cell phone rang the song *Respect*. I shoved hair out of my face and picked it up.

"Help!"

The call ended.

I rushed out of my warehouse door with Prissy behind me. Sprinting, I and pulled open Mystery's back door and slid into the dimness.

Pierre ghosted through the wall to join me. "What is the matter?"

"I don't know," I whispered. "All she said was, help."

Prissy gave a low growl in her throat.

I picked her up.

Loud voices caught my attention. *What in the world is going on?*

A deep male voice said, "Don't you be lying to me, girl. I know you've got money, and I mean to have it."

Jasmine's voice trembled. "I told you, I don't get paid every week."

Mystery yelled, "Get out of here. I've called the police."

Ready for action, I raced down the hall and rounded the corner into the retail area. *Nobody messes with my friends if I'm around.*

A tall, broad-shouldered man with a half-moon shaped scar on his ebony cheek had Jasmine by both arms and was shaking her.

Jasmine kicked and clawed like an angry cat.

No, you don't, you brute! I put Prissy down. "Get him, girl!"

The dog sped, barking and snarling, toward the intruder.

Moon Scar paused, looking for the threat.

Prissy sank her teeth into his ankle, shook it, and held on.

Bellowing with pain, he yelled, "Get off me!" He tried to shake Prissy loose.

I grabbed my stun gun from my pocket before wading into the fray.

Mystery was already circling him clutching hers. She almost had him until he swatted the stun gun from her grasp. Her forward momentum pushed her into him. She raked her long acrylic nails down his face.

He screamed like a rabbit.

Jasmine broke free of his grip.

He staggered, covering his face with both hands.

Prissy continued to growl and shake his foot, keeping him somewhat off balance.

I grabbed the back of Jasmine's shirt and pulled her to a safer distance.

Pierre moved in and pushed the intruder.

Moon Scar staggered back into a display case.

Prissy hung on, shaking his foot. Blood trickled to the floor.

Moon Scar lowered his hands. I saw bloody gouges on his face. A wicked look gleamed in his eyes. The malevolence of his energy slammed into me, almost sending me to my knees.

He glared down at Prissy.

"Don't touch my dog!" I tagged him with my stun gun.

Mystery pulled Jasmine behind a display case and stepped in front of her.

The gun didn't have the desired effect. He was still standing.

Confused, I took a step back.

Shaking his head, he turned toward me. He puffed with rage and looked ready to charge.

I glanced down at my stun gun that was now out of juice. *Why didn't he go down? Is he high on something?*

He looked down at my dog gnawing on his ankle with destruction in his eyes.

Fear blazed fiery ice through my veins. I commanded, "Prissy, come!" I prayed the dog would obey.

Prissy ran to my side and sat. She continued to growl and show her now bloody teeth.

"Get out and don't come back!" I yelled, pointing at the door. I only hoped I sounded braver than I felt.

"Don't tell me what to do, you—"

Pierre shoved Moon Scar toward the door.

Moon Scar looked confused, but then his eyes widened. His energy field changed from rage to fear. He took a few steps closer to the door and pointed at Jasmine. With a tone wrapped in malice, he said, "I'll deal with you tonight."

Pierre's face contorted with anger. He rammed into Moon Scar with both hands.

Moon Scar fell to the floor. Looking around for his invisible foe, he scrambled to his feet and stumbled toward the door. He opened the door, staggered out, and ran.

Mystery ran to the door and locked it before rushing back to Jasmine. She gathered the shaking young woman into her arms.

"Who was that maniac?" I asked.

Between sobs, she said, "That's Damien, Mom's latest loser. He was trying to shake me down for money."

Mystery hugged her tighter. "Your safe now, Sugar.

"No wonder you're frightened by him. I'd want to move out, too." I picked up Prissy to check her for injuries. "Good girl."

"Are you all right, ma chérie?" Pierre's gaze flowed over me, looking for wounds. "Did he hurt you?"

"Nope. Thanks to you and Prissy, we're okay." I noticed that Pierre's defensive measures had drained him. He was almost transparent wavering in and out like a faulty circuit.

"Do what you can to recharge." I wanted to hug him, but I knew that would only drain him more.

"Bree, thanks for coming so fast." Mystery reached over and petted Prissy. "You are so brave." She looked around. "Pierre, I don't know where you're floating, but thanks. You're my haint hero."

"Mine, too," Jasmine said.

Pierre looked pleased as he attempted a gallant bow.

"Pierre just gave y'all a weak, yet elegant, French bow," I said.

Jasmine nodded. "Excuse me. I need a moment. I'm going to get Prissy a treat." She walked unsteadily toward the conference room.

I put Prissy down. She followed, doing her tail-wagging swishy walk. I suspected as soon as Jasmine was out of sight, she'd be hugging the little dog. I would.

Pierre pointed out the window. "I'm going to follow him and make sure he does no further mischief."

"Are you sure you're up to it?"

He smiled. "It is good to know you have concern for me."

"Of course, I worry about you." I waved. "Thanks again."

He returned the gesture and floated out the window.

Mystery ran her hands through her short curls. "Thank goodness Damien's gone. Mama is on her way with a cake. No telling what would have happened if Mama had been here."

The vision of Lucille, chasing Damien with a long cake knife while decked out in one of her pretty outfits, made me smile.

Jasmine came back into the retail area. Her cheeks were stained with tears, and she was hugging Prissy like she was a teddy bear.

Two uniformed police officers knocked on the door and peered inside.

Mystery huffed. "It's about dang time."

I took Prissy out the back and over to my shop. She needed some food and water. I locked up before returning to talk to the officers.

Ten minutes after the police left, Lucille started banging on the glass with her fist.

Mystery rushed over, opened the door to let her in, and relocked it.

"What in Sam Hill is going on?" Her gaze went from Mystery, to me, to the drops of blood on the floor, and settled on Jasmine's face. "What are you crying about, Darlin'?"

"Mama, I walked in to find Chantel's latest boyfriend attacking her in an attempt to get money. She's afraid to go home." Mystery went back to cleaning the blood off the floor.

Lucille placed the Tupperware container on the counter and wrapped Jasmine in a crushing hug.

Jasmine sniffled and clung to her.

"Darlin', it's going to be all right. You need some chocolate. It fixes most things."

A bolt of insight hit me. *No wonder Mystery is a stress eater. Lucille always gave her chocolate to make her feel better when she was growing up.*

Jasmine blew her nose again. "Chocolate can't fix all my problems, Ms. Lucille."

"Maybe not, but it can make this moment a bit better. Come to the back and sit down. Let's talk."

"I'll be back. I need to walk Prissy," I said, sprinting out the door.

When I returned ten minutes later with Prissy, Mystery was hanging the out-to-lunch sign.

Lucille picked up Prissy and rubbed her ears. "I heard you were brave." She smiled at me. "Thank you for helping. I don't know what I'd do if I lost Mystery." Tears welled in her eyes.

"You're welcome. I love her, too."

She nodded, swiping at her tears.

I followed Lucille to the conference room with the cake. I placed it on the table while Mystery poured coffee into four sturdy white mugs. Jasmine sat, still trying to regain her composure.

Lucille sliced the multilayer chocolate cake into generous portions and placed them on paper plates. The smell of cocoa and butter permeated the room.

That is the smell of comfort.

Mystery replaced the pot and grabbed four forks from a drawer before joining us at the table.

Jasmine took a bite of the cake. Her glum expression changed to a wide-open smile. "This is the best chocolate cake I've ever had."

Lucille patted her shoulder. "Like I said, chocolate makes everything better."

Jasmine paused with a large bite on her fork. "I guess that's why the students at Hogwarts got chocolate bars after a dementor attack."

Lucille's eyes widened. "A what attack?"

"Dementor, you know, like in Harry Potter."

Lucille looked over at Mystery. "What is a Dementor and who's

Harry Potter?"

I giggled, then coughed, trying not to choke on my cake. *Can't wait to hear this explanation.*

Mystery rolled her eyes.

"Don't you be rolling your eyes at me. You may be a grown woman but I can still take you."

"Mama, it's not real. Jasmine's talking about a series of fantasy books written by J.K. Rowling."

Lucille cocked her head. "Oh, I see, I think. Let's get back on track. Tell me your problem, Jasmine."

Jasmine swallowed and reached for her coffee to wash down the cake. "Ms. Lucille, everything's not bad."

"That's good." Lucille rolled her hand, indicating she should proceed.

"Thanks to a school counselor and Mystery, I've gotten scholarships to pay for college."

Lucille nodded, giving her daughter an approving smile.

"I love working for Mystery, but I can't make enough money here to rent my own place. The only thing I could come close to affording is an apartment in the government housing area. I don't want to live surrounded by drugs and crime."

Lucille's well-groomed brows inched up her forehead. This time she turned an accusatory gaze toward Mystery.

Great, Lucille thinks it's Mystery's fault.

"Mama, I'm paying her as much as I can afford. You folks need to remember, I'm a new business and struggling to make payroll right now. Besides, Jasmine can only work part-time because she's in college. Despite that, I've put her on my insurance, since Chantel doesn't have any coverage."

Lucille's shoulders lowered. Her frown softened into a gentle smile when she looked at Jasmine. "Darlin', you know you're like family to us."

Tears welled in Jasmine's eyes, polishing them to a high sheen.

She patted Jasmine's hand. "I'd adopt you, but you're already a legal adult."

"Adopt me?" Jasmine wiped her nose with a tissue. "Ms. Lucille, I love Mom, but I would've given anything to have been adopted by y'all." She shot a pleased grin at Mystery. "We could've been sisters."

Mystery responded by shoving cake into her mouth and chewing. I wondered, *Where's Lucille going with this?*

Lucille picked up her coffee, closed her eyes while inhaling the heady aroma, and took a sip. "I'm here today to celebrate my surprise. Mystery doesn't know about my current project because she hasn't been by the house in a coon's age." She peered over her cup, giving Mystery a disapproving scowl that looked like it could deliver a thousand papercuts.

Mystery slumped. "Mama, I've been swamped."

"She really has been," I said.

Lucille ignored us. "I've cleaned out all the junk from my detached garage and had it renovated into a one-bedroom apartment. Nothing much, but it comes furnished. I'm getting older, so I need some help from time to time." She nudged Jasmine. "Besides, I get lonely living in that big ole house by myself."

"That's great, Mama."

"I was hoping y'all would help me set up a lease and tell me how to do background checks on potential renters. I've heard some horror stories from some of my friends." She shot a playful wink to Jasmine. "This sounds like an ideal opportunity for both of us. I'll rent the apartment at a reasonable rate, if you're willing to do all my lawn care and help out around the house when I need you." She smiled like a real estate agent pushing a fixer-upper. "I want to rent to someone I know and can trust."

Jasmine stared at Lucille with her mouth open, exposing cake mush.

Lucille threw her head back and laughed. "Close your mouth, Darlin', or you're gonna catch flies."

Jasmine placed her hand over her mouth and chewed, before swallowing. "Oh, Ms. Lucille!" She stood, leaned over, and hugged the older woman.

She patted Jasmine's arm. "That's enough."

"Knowing my mother," Mystery said, "you better hear the rest before you get too excited."

Lucille glowered at her daughter. "Mystery's right. There will be rules and other requirements. You'll have to sign a legally-binding lease and keep the place neat and clean."

"I can do that, honest." Jasmine crossed her heart with her right hand.

"No drugs, booze, or men. I'm not having you throw your talent and life away."

Jasmine's eyes went round. She said with a shocked tone, "No guys?"

"Oh, you can date, Darlin', but I'm not having men staying overnight on *my* property. I'm not running a den of iniquity!"

"How much is the rent?" Jasmine's eyes shifted back and forth like she was afraid to hear the answer.

"Can you handle two hundred dollars a month plus utilities with your part-time salary?"

Jasmine beamed. "Yes, ma'am."

"Oh, I nearly forgot. It would be nice if you could attend church with me on Sundays."

"No problem. After seeing those shadow things that took Jason, I'll do anything to avoid them."

Lucille sat back in her chair like she'd been struck by lightning. "Who's Jason? What things are you talking about?"

Mystery's hand flew to her mouth while she tried to not choke on her cake.

I inwardly cringed. *Here we go again.*

With dramatic gestures, Jasmine told Lucille about Jason and the dark shadows that had claimed him.

After aiming a brief disapproving look at Mystery, Lucille turned in her chair and took both of Jasmine's hands in hers. "Darlin', listen to me with your heart and that fine mind of yours. Don't ever make fear of something be your motivation for lasting change."

"Why not?"

"If you do, when the threat is gone and you feel safe, you'll return to self-defeating habits."

"But I don't want to go to Hell," Jasmine whined.

"Always focus on what you want, not what you don't want," Lucille said, giving Jasmine's hands a little shake.

"I don't understand." Jasmine said.

I said, "Whatever we give our attention and focus to, will grow in power in our lives. Our thoughts and desires are a form of energy. Positive attracts positive, negative attracts negative."

Jasmine's brow scrunched. "So, Mom's focus on the wrong things may be attracting the wrong kinda guys?"

Lucille nodded. "That's right. She needs to focus on what she wants in life and how to get it in a positive way. The same applies to you."

Jasmine looked at Lucille with an earnest expression in her doe-like brown eyes. "I guess this means Mom needs to fix her own problems." She frowned. "My efforts haven't helped."

Lucille looked sad. "No. You see, only she can save herself. She has to want it."

Jasmine rolled her eyes. "This could take forever."

Lucille nodded. "Mystery's grandmother used to say, 'She didn't get in that mess overnight, and she won't get out of it overnight, either.'"

"I don't want to be dependent on men all my life, like Mom," Jasmine said, looking first at me, then Mystery. "I want to be like y'all and own a business."

"Good. Remember, don't focus your thoughts on Chantel. Instead, focus your thoughts and energy on what you want in life and the person you want to be. Why don't you take some time tonight to write down your thoughts?" Lucille picked up her cup of coffee, took a sip and grimaced. "Goodness, I've talked so much my coffee is cold. Mystery, would you get an old lady some hot brew? Chocolate cake deserves hot coffee."

"Sure, Mama."

A knock on the back door triggered a knowing chuckle from Lucille. "Jasmine, you better cut another slice. I have a feeling that's Adam. He saw me bring in the cake. Mystery, you better pour another cup of coffee, too."

When I opened the back door, I asked, "Mr. C, did you smell that chocolate cake all the way from inside your store?"

His ears turned pink.

CHAPTER 28

Kaya hummed a perky tune while she and I tidied things before closing that evening.

"What's got you so chipper?" I asked while wiping the top of a glass counter. I still felt wrung out from the morning's scuffle.

"I'm happy. Jasmine is boxing up her stuff and moving to a new apartment tonight."

I looked up. "That fast? They only discussed it this afternoon."

She nodded. "She asked me to stop by a friend's liquor store after lunch to pick up some empty boxes. I piled a bunch of them into her car." Her brown eyes widened with a pleading look worthy of an Oscar. "Would you help her pack? I have class tonight. Papa will skin me alive if I miss a class."

Feeling wary about what this might entail, I asked, "Who else is helping?"

"Ms. Lucille and Mystery said they would help. She doesn't have much. No furniture. Y'all will be in and out in a jiffy."

Good Lord, that sounds like a Lucilleism. "What time?" I asked.

Kaya grabbed another bottle of glass cleaner and a roll of towels. "As soon as we close. I'll do the door."

I smiled to myself. As far as I was concerned, it was a win-win. With Jasmine living onsite, she'd be able to help or sound the alarm if something went wrong with Lucille.

A disturbing thought hit me like a cement block. "What about Damien?"

"Her madre's waitressing at the bar tonight. Jasmine said he usually goes there so she can slip him free drinks," Kaya said.

I followed Jasmine to an apartment complex that had seen better days. Lucille and Mystery drove behind me. While braking for a stop sign, I checked the rearview mirror. The red glow from my taillights highlighted the downward cast of Lucille's mouth. I judged by her tight-lipped expression that she disapproved of the neighborhood.

We parked and climbed out of our cars. I glanced around, wishing the lighting was better.

Jasmine led us down a cracked sidewalk, past metal stairs covered in peeling beige paint, to a first-floor apartment. She unlocked the metal door and said, "Hello? Anyone home?"

There was no answer.

Thank goodness we don't have to climb up and down the stairs. I went in behind her. The apartment smelled like overripe bananas. One small lamp lit the interior. Clothes lay strewn across the furniture and the floor. Used glasses rested without coasters on the furniture. Dirty dishes cluttered the sink and counter. *This would drive me over the edge.*

"Damien?" When there was no reply, Jasmine hitched a shoulder. "I guess he's not here. Sorry about the mess. I thought Mom was messy, but he's worse." She scrunched her face in a pee-yoo expression. "It looks like this every night when I come home."

We followed her to a small bedroom.

Jasmine turned on the light and gestured around the room. "Everything goes except for the furniture. It belongs to Mom. I'll get the boxes out of my car."

After Jasmine left, Mystery said, "Look at this room. Jasmine is as neat as a pin. How does she stand the disorder?"

"I don't know." I held a finger to my lips. "Shh, here she comes."

Jasmine gave us three of the four boxes she carried. "I need to get my stuff out of the bathroom."

Lucille picked up a blouse and began to fold it.

Mystery said between clenched teeth, "Just pile it in, Mama. We need to hurry. We'll fold everything when we put it away at the garage apartment. I don't want to run into that beast Chantel's dating."

The mere memory of the look of malice in Damien's eyes sent a shiver cascading down my body like an icy-cold waterfall.

Lucille's eyes widened with a look of alarm. "I'd forgotten about him."

We pulled clothes, still on the hangers, out of the closet and accordioned them into a box. I knelt and piled shoes from the closet floor into another container. Lucille emptied the drawers. Soon all three cartons were full.

"Give me your keys, Mama. Bree and I will put these in your trunk and get more boxes."

Lucille tossed her the keys and piled a crate on top of the one in my arms.

We followed Lucille into the living room, trying not to trip over the mess on the floor. We waited until she opened the door for us. I darted through the doorway and down the sidewalk with Mystery behind me. This was beginning to feel like a military rescue extraction. A quick in and out.

After we put the boxes on the hood of Lucille's Chrysler 300, I glanced around for Damien. *Don't get paranoid.* The parking lot was crammed full of cars, and I didn't know what type he drove. By the time Mystery unlocked the trunk, Lucille appeared carrying the shoes.

"My, my, this girl *loves* her footwear."

Mystery took the box of shoes and shoved it into the trunk. "She's a very thrifty shopper. That *young lady* can stretch a dollar like a rubber band."

After adding the other two boxes, I closed the lid. We grabbed four more cardboard boxes that sat on the ground beside Jasmine's 2012 Honda Civic.

Lucille eyed the car with apparent interest. "I wonder how Jasmine managed to buy this car? I know Chantel couldn't afford to get it for her."

"She saved most of her earnings for three years while she was in high school. A friend of mine bought a new car, so I talked him into selling it to her for five thousand dollars," Mystery said.

Lucille cocked a brow, looking impressed. "That's a good price. Did she have the full five thousand?"

Mystery and I exchanged glances, turned, and walked toward the apartment. I said, "We better get her stuff packed. It's getting late, and I haven't eaten yet."

Lucille shot us a knowing grin. "I thought so."

When we returned to Jasmine's room, we found her pulling books and other things from under the bed.

"Just in time," Jasmine said.

We filled three of the four boxes. Jasmine grabbed the last one and said, "I need to go through the dirty clothes hamper and grab my things. It's in Mom's room." She turned left and headed down a dark hall.

Each of us picked up a full container and headed to the car. We were closing the trunk when the scream reverberated across the apartment complex.

Jasmine! I raced back into the apartment, my heart pounding with alarm. Mystery and Lucille followed me.

Jasmine yelled, "I told you I don't have any. Let me go."

Rushing down the hall, I spotted an open door with a dim light on. *There wasn't any light down here before.* I slid to a halt inside the bedroom.

Damien held a struggling Jasmine down on the bed. "Tell me where you're hiding the money or I'll—."

I bellowed, "Stop!" and grabbed him by the shirt collar. The smell of booze enveloped me. "Let her go!" I yanked with all my strength.

He hollered, "Get off me," and threw back his arm.

I bounced off the wall and hit the floor. The coppery taste of blood filled my mouth. Pain sliced my tongue, sparking a fury that exploded inside me like a volcano. "You let go of her!" I scrambled to my feet, ready to lunge.

Before I could launch myself on the fiend, Lucille whacked him on the back with a baseball bat.

I was sure I heard a bone or two crack.

He howled and released Jasmine.

Curling into a ball, he moaned and rocked.

Mystery yelled, "Jasmine, grab your box and let's go."

Lucille rose to her full height and straightened her clothes. "Amen to that!"

I grabbed the bat before we hurried from the apartment. I feared he might follow us. We piled into our cars and wasted no time fleeing the parking lot. I kept checking the rearview mirror to see if Damien was behind us while I dabbed at my mouth with a tissue.

We caught a red light on Bob Wallace Avenue. My heart still banged like a cop with a battering ram trying to break down a door. *Where did Damien come from? He must've been asleep in the bedroom the whole time.*

Ten minutes later, we arrived at Lucille's house in south Huntsville. Mystery and I parked on the street. I sat a moment, trying to regulate my heart rate before exiting. *Too much excitement for one day.* I checked to see if I was still bleeding and scrubbed away a dried spot of blood near my lips.

Lucille backed up the drive and stopped close to the apartment door.

Jasmine did the same.

I admired the former detached garage while walking up the drive. Instead of the roll-up door I expected to see, the garage now featured a Wedgewood blue door centered between two double-hung windows. The entire building had been covered with beige vinyl siding. *I have to admit, it really does look like a small home. The two front windows even have matching blue shutters.*

Lucille was out of her vehicle and had popped open the trunk.

Jasmine seemed to be glued to her seat. Her wide-eyed stare and rapid breathing didn't bode well.

I opened the Honda's driver-side door and squatted to better assess the situation.

Jasmine gripped the steering wheel with shaking hands, her eyes shiny with unshed tears.

Her fear energy surrounded me. I raised my shields. *Adrenaline and shock.* I reached in and started rubbing her back, while crooning words of support.

Lucille opened the passenger door and slid into the seat. "What's wrong, Darlin'?"

Mystery leaned down, looking past her mother.

Jasmine broke into racking sobs. "He-he scared me. I thought he was going to kill me this time."

"Well, thanks to Mama, that didn't happen," Mystery said. "Mama, where did you find the bat?"

"Leaning against the dresser." She gave a haughty sniff. "I'm too old to be wrestling with men."

Jasmine wiped her eyes with a tissue. "I don't know what would've happened if y'all hadn't come with me."

Mystery asked, "Sugar, would you consider talking to Doc about all this? She's on our insurance plan."

Jasmine gave a quick nod. "Excuse my language, Ms. Lucille, but I've got a whole load of crap to talk about."

Lucille patted her arm. "Let's get you settled into your new home. I had deadbolt locks installed for your safety."

Jasmine's chin trembled. "Do you think he'll come looking for me here?"

I stopped rubbing her back. My knee popped when I stood. "He doesn't know where you live now."

Mystery added, "And don't you be telling Chantel."

"No way. She'd blab." Jasmine got out of the Honda and steadied herself with a deep breath.

"I don't think he'll come back to the shop, either, after what happened." I gave Jasmine a glance to remind her not to mention Pierre's part in the rescue to Lucille.

Once we were at the door, Lucille offered a beaming smile and handed Jasmine the keys to her new home.

Still trembling, Jasmine fumbled a bit before unlocking the door and turning on the light.

We entered a small combination living-dining room. The white paint and large ceramic floor tiles made the small space seem bright and cheery. I found it hard to believe that this pleasant space was the dark, scary garage stuffed with generations' worth of leftovers that Mystery had once confessed had fueled her childhood nightmares.

"Darlin', I know it's a bit bare, but I have a bunch of carpets and paintings that I saved in my attached garage," said Lucille. "You can pick which ones you like. I'm sure you'll want to use several throughout the apartment."

"Thanks, Ms. Lucille. I love it!"

The living area held a beige sofa long enough for napping, an end table, and a recliner, which faced a moderate-sized flat-screen television on a stand with a bookshelf on each side. The dining area had a retro Formica table for four with matching chairs. A small, fully equipped kitchen sat next to the dining area.

I walked into the kitchen and marveled. "Lucille, where did you find such a small four-burner range and oven combination? It's only two feet wide."

"Bob Wallace Appliance ordered it, the apartment-sized fridge, and the small-scale dishwasher for me. Aren't they cute as a button? By downsizing the appliances, it made more room for cabinets."

"Where did all the furniture come from, Ms. Lucille?" Jasmine asked while pulling open the dishwasher.

"When my parents and in-laws died, the stuff worth keeping went into this detached garage. Mystery took a few pieces of furniture, but her house was pretty full, so she didn't need anything else. I hired a contractor and moved the things I planned to keep for the apartment into my garage. I gave the rest away to The Salvation Army. I'm glad it's done, so I can park my car inside again."

Jasmine pulled Mystery and me by the hands. "Wait until y'all see the other rooms."

The bedroom held a double bed, a dresser, a bedside table, and a desk for a computer and to do homework. The walk-in closet was spacious compared to the one Jasmine had used in the apartment. The bathroom contained a sink with a cabinet, shelves for towels and supplies, a shower, and a toilet.

"You have everything you need," I said, smiling.

"There's more." Lucille's eyes gleamed. She opened a door that led outside to a small covered concrete patio, complete with a bistro set.

Jasmine's face glowed with delight. "I've got heaven on earth. I can't thank you enough, Ms. Lucille."

"All I ask is that you pay the rent on time, follow the rules, and keep my yard and landscaping looking good."

"Um, about the yard." Jasmine shifted from foot to foot, wringing her hands. "I've lived in an apartment my entire life. You may have to teach me how to use a mower and the other stuff."

Lucille gave her a kind smile. "We'll work on it this weekend."

CHAPTER 29

Mystery, Pierre, and I arrived at Tiffany's home. The cheery morning sun glinted off the windows, making the house seem wholesome again. Not fooled, I felt some trepidation about entering the scene of terror.

Tiffany greeted us with a pleasant smile, but the dark circles under her bloodshot eyes said more about her current state. "I'm so relieved to be back home and to have that horrid crime scene tape off the door."

We sat in the living room and explained to her in more detail our theories and why we wanted to search the house. I also took the opportunity to introduce Tiffany to Pierre.

Tiffany's eyes widened as she tried to pinpoint his location in the room. "Was he there the night that Jason…"

I nodded. Memories of those shadow figures flashed through my mind precipitating a shiver.

"I felt some level of protection that night," Tiffany said, rubbing her hands together, as if to warm them.

"Pierre shielded us. He was our spectral hero." I smiled up at him.

Tiffany's hand covered her heart. "There was a time I'd have thought you were both berserk, but I've seen too much. I know we discussed some of this on the phone, but I've been thinking, why not tell the police and let them do the search?"

"With your permission, I want Pierre to be the first to search your entire property. He can poke around in all sorts of places without having to open anything, cause a disturbance, or mess with evidence," I said.

Tiffany nibbled at the dry skin on her bottom lip. "If you find anything, how do we tell the police?"

I said, "Let's see what we find first." In other words, I had no idea.

Tiffany stared at the spot where her husband had died, looking uncertain. After a minute, she said, "Okay, but I want to start in Jason's office. I need help cleaning out his desk, anyway. We can do that while your, um, friend, I mean ghost friend, does the rest."

"Deal." I looked up at Pierre. "Please look everywhere. We're especially looking for something that might have been used to hit Victoria Spellman."

Mystery and I followed Tiffany up to the second floor. We entered the first room on the right, which had served as Jason's home office.

The room's double window faced the front lawn. Sunlight cascaded through the panes, spilling across the hardwood floor until it reached the edge of a large jewel-toned oriental rug. The remaining walls were lined with cherry base cabinets topped with green granite countertops. Bookshelves with under-cabinet lighting filled the space to the ceiling. Jason's ornately carved cherry desk occupied the center of the room A matching low hutch containing two rows of pigeonholes sat on top of the large desk.

"I love this room," I said, feeling a little awed. "Wish my home office had all this storage and these bookshelves."

Mystery scanned all the books with a wide-eyed, alarmed expression. "Lordy, I hope we find what we're looking for, so we don't have to go through every one of these."

"Me, too." Tiffany pushed her hair behind her ears. "I'll grab some empty boxes and be back in a flash."

Mystery looked at me. "Should we go ahead and start, or wait?"

"No telling what's in that desk. Best to wait."

Within minutes, Tiffany pushed through the door with several collapsed boxes and a roll of wide packing tape.

We set to work assembling the boxes.

"Any advice on how to begin?" I asked.

Tiffany placed the three boxes in front of her chair. "I suggest you start from the top and work down, beginning with the pigeonholes. Tell me what you find, then I'll check it and file it in the appropriate box. I have one I'm marking 'work,' the next one will be 'important,' and the third will be the 'shred' box. Jason's boss wants to make sure none of the company's files were brought home. They will be in folders with the firm's name on the outside."

I watched her label the boxes, the pungent smell of the marker scenting the air. "I bet the shred box will fill up first."

Methodically, Mystery and I examined the papers and notes, while Tiffany sorted the items into the correct boxes.

"I've been dreading this," Tiffany admitted. "It's so much faster with three of us working on it."

Ten minutes later, Mystery handed Tiffany the last of the notes stuffed in the hutch. "So far, nothing looks too important."

I pulled open a drawer. "Lots of office supplies here. We best put together another box."

Tiffany stood. "Be back in a sec." She returned with a smaller box and dumped the office supplies into it.

After thirty minutes of additional work, we were down to the last drawer, which was locked.

Tiffany rose from the chair and stretched. "I bet the key is on his ring. I'll go get it."

While she was gone, Mystery asked, "Do you think Victoria is jerking us around?"

I piled my hair into a knot and then released it. "We both know that Victoria's capable of anything."

Tiffany walked into the room. "Who's capable of anything?"

"Victoria," I said.

Tiffany shuddered. "Such a horrible woman, but she didn't deserve to be murdered." After trying multiple keys, she found the one that opened the file drawer.

Feeling excited, I reached in and grabbed a file crammed full of paper. "Let's take one at a time."

Fifteen minutes later, we'd examined all the files and found no incriminating information. Tiffany did discover a few case files that needed to be returned to the law firm.

Sounding defeated, Tiffany said, "Let's take a break. The restroom is the first door on the right. Meet me on the patio. We'll have some iced tea and discuss ideas of where to search for a secret compartment."

I was beginning to doubt there would be one.

The weather was perfect for sitting outdoors and sipping sweet tea. A male cardinal flitted from bush to bush, and a squirrel chattered from a nearby branch. The honeysuckle vine climbing a nearby arbor scented the air with a light sweet scent. Much sweeter than the Carolina Jasmine on Katie's fence.

Tiffany arrived carrying a tray with a pitcher and three tall frosted, ice-filled glasses. She poured the tea over the crackling ice and passed a glass to each of us. "Any ideas?"

I sipped the cold, sweet brew and said, "Let's pull out the drawers and check for items taped under them."

"We need to look for false bottoms, too," Mystery said. "Are you sure none of those papers showed any accounts or anything that could relate to our search?"

"I wish." Tiffany's shoulders hitched, then lowered when she exhaled a discouraged-sounding sigh.

After we'd drained our glasses, Tiffany piled everything back on the tray and headed to the kitchen. Mystery and I went inside and trudged up the stairs. Tiffany soon joined us.

We pulled out all the drawers. There was nothing underneath and no false bottoms.

Tiffany lay on the floor and scooted under the desk, looking for anything she might find. Flushed from the exertion, she crawled out and stood. "Nothing."

"Any other bright ideas, anyone?" Mystery crossed her arms and shot me a curious look. "Bree, what's so interesting in that box of office supplies?"

I reached inside and pulled out a Phillips head screwdriver. "Why would Jason keep a screwdriver in his desk drawer?" I walked over to the desk. "This hutch is attached by a bracket on each side that uses Phillips head screws." I pointed. "There are some scratch marks on the finish."

Mystery came closer and squinted at the marks. She moved around the desk examining it. "Look." She pointed at the side of the desk with the privacy panel. "I didn't notice before, but this side is at least an inch or more wider than the others." She plucked the tool from my hand. "Let's see what happens."

When the screws were removed, Tiffany and Mystery both grunted as they tried and failed to slide the hutch over. It was hung up on one side.

I leaned closer and squinted to see what was wrong. "Lift it up first, and then put it down on the other side of the desk."

Panting, Tiffany said, "This thing is solid cherry. The day the guys delivered this desk, I thought they would get a hernia bringing it up the stairs. I didn't realize it came apart."

We turned back to the desk and gaped at a small handle attached to a sunken drawer that the hutch had covered.

I said, "Place the hutch on its side."

When they did, we discovered that a section was hollowed out to accommodate the handle.

"So that's why he kept shooing me out of his office," Tiffany said with wonder in her tone. She grabbed the handle and pulled. A narrow box of thin wood slid out. When she loosened the tiny metal latch, a thin notebook lay nestled in the compartment along with some loose folded pages.

I pulled out the papers and unfolded the crackling pages before scanning them. With a triumphant smile, I said. "This may be information about offshore accounts. There are passwords and everything."

Tiffany's blue eyes twinkled with delight. "Ladies, we may have found my missing funds." She did a little happy dance before pulling out the slender notebook. "What is this?" She flipped it open. After reading for a few moments, she closed it. "Let's go downstairs and get comfortable. This could take a while."

Once we were downstairs in the den, Tiffany settled into a recliner to read the notebook. Her gaze never wavered from its pages. "This is Jason's diary." Her already fair complexion paled. "My goodness, I never knew Jason was so calculating."

"I wonder why he kept a diary. That's something a woman would do," I said.

Tiffany blew a stray hair out of her face. "Jason documented *everything*. He wrote down the gas mileage after each fill up, every date the yard guy added fertilizer, and one of his bosses told me that Jason's court cases were always thoroughly documented."

"Maybe he wanted evidence on Sierra in case she turned on him. What does it say?" Mystery asked, trying to read over her shoulder.

"Give me a minute." Tiffany's brow furrowed. "His writing is small and hard to read."

Mystery straightened, winced, and rubbed her lower back.

I sat reading the loose sheets in my hand.

Twenty minutes later, Tiffany said, "The short version is, Jason and Sierra have been an item since high school. They researched Sophie to determine her assets. He married her while finishing law school. After he passed the bar and went to work for a local law firm, he asked for a divorce. When Sophie refused to give him a divorce because she was Catholic, he and Sierra plotted her demise."

I felt queasy. "I can't imagine planning an innocent person's death that way."

"What else does it say?" Mystery asked.

"Let me read some more," Tiffany said.

"Well, I've finished reading mine. Jason has a bookoodle of money stashed in six different overseas accounts." I handed some of the papers to Mystery.

Never good with waiting, she stood and paced the room while we all continued reading. She nodded to herself several times while reading about the accounts.

I finished and looked up in time to see Tiffany lower the book.

"Oh, my!" A shocked look spread across her face. "Jason and Sierra did the same thing to Sophie that they did to me. They faked a haunting and convinced everyone she was going bonkers." Tiffany wiped her damp brow with her sleeve. "He put sleeping pills in her drink and later forced more down her. Before leaving to establish an alibi, he set the scene to look like a suicide."

The thought that Tiffany could have been murdered if she hadn't asked for our help made my stomach roil.

Tiffany flipped through several pages. "This section is about me. I'll read it later." She flipped through more pages and stopped to read. As she did, her brows shot straight to her hairline. "God help me, he tried to kill Victoria by hitting her head with a baseball bat."

"Why?" I asked, scooting forward on the sofa.

Mystery stopped pacing, now alert.

"Shush, let me read and I'll tell you."

A few interminable minutes later, Tiffany looked up again. "She found out about Sophie and figured out that he planned to kill me, too."

Mystery cocked her head, her brown eyes flashing with curiosity. "Sugar, I wonder how she put all of that together? I guess we may never know. I'd assumed all this time that he tried to kill her because she was going to block your patio extension and fountain."

Tiffany gave an emphatic nod. "He was furious about that, too."

I rubbed my chin considering everything I'd heard. "What I don't understand is why he married you for your money if he inherited Sophie's?"

Tiffany flipped back through the diary. "It's written in here. According to this, Sophie changed her will when he asked for the divorce. She gave everything to several charities in the area. The only money Jason acquired was a small life insurance policy to pay for her burial."

"That must've toasted his bun," Mystery said.

Tiffany poked a page with indignant fury. "Enough to spite her in death. First, he told her parish priest she committed suicide, so he wouldn't do the service, and then he didn't bury her in the family graveyard next to her parents." She slammed a fist on the arm of the recliner. "That rat!"

I nodded my agreement. "If you can discover where she's buried, I can check and make sure she's crossed over."

Tiffany's tight lips and the V formed by her brows made it clear what she thought of Jason. She slammed the diary shut. "Yes. Please make sure she's not stuck on this plane." She held up the notebook. "I know the police will want this, so I'm making a copy of everything before I turn it over to them."

"Great idea." I stood and looked over at Mystery. "If you don't mind, I'd like to read the whole diary, and I'm sure Mystery and Pierre would too. Can you make three copies?"

"No problem. Jason insisted on buying a fancy collating copy machine for his home office."

Before Tiffany could leave to complete the task, Pierre zipped into the room, bright-eyed with excitement.

"Ma chérie, j'ai trouvé l'arme du crime."

"Tiffany, hold up," I said. "Pierre says he's found something."

"It is a bat." He pretended to grip one and made a swinging motion. "Like you Americans use to play baseball." He shook his head. "Such a slow boring game. I prefer to watch le football."

"Actually, you found the attempted murder weapon, since Victoria was poisoned," I said.

Tiffany looked around. "What's he saying?"

"He found a baseball bat." I looked back at him. "Where?"

"Caché dans le garage." He expanded his chest. "After checking several places, I remembered that in America, most men hide their secrets in their office or the garage."

I cocked a brow. "Where do men hide their secrets in Paris?"

"I hid mine in my studio." He winked and grinned.

I relayed Pierre's message while we rushed down the stairs to the small garage behind the house.

Tiffany pushed the remote, and the door squealed open on its rusty chain.

Pierre floated through when it was half-way up.

I huffed before shaking my head with envy. "Show-off."

Looking confused, Tiffany asked, "Show off?"

"Pierre floated through the garage door," I said.

Her brows rose.

Mystery grinned. "Wish I could do that. I wonder what it's like?"

A faint musty smell assaulted my nose causing me to sneeze.

Pierre pointed at a pile of boxes topped with a couple of paint cans. "It is in the big rectangular box on the bottom. It took a while, but I found it."

I rubbed my chin. "I wonder why he didn't get rid of it? That would be the safest thing to do."

"Who knows? He grew up poor, so he had a hard time letting go of things." Tiffany stepped back. "Let's finish the copies before we call the police."

Twenty minutes later, we had everything copied. Tiffany stashed her copy in a hidden safe. Mystery and I put ours in the hidden storage area of Hot Stuff's trunk.

"Who should I call? 911?" Tiffany asked.

I handed her a card. "Call Detective Ricci. He's in charge of Victoria's murder case. If this keeps up, I'm going to have to put him on speed dial."

CHAPTER 30

Mystery, Tiffany, and I were seated in the living room talking, when the doorbell chimed Beethoven's Fifth.

Pierre stuck his head through the door. "C'est la police."

His English isn't always perfect but it's much better than my French. His tendency to revert to French when excited makes it harder for me to understand him at times.

Tiffany rose from her chair, looking a bit unsteady. "Y'all need to help me explain to Detective Ricci how we found the murder weapon."

"Attempted murder weapon," I said. "I wonder if Chris came with him?" I exchanged a worried glance with Mystery before nodding toward Pierre, who levitated nearby. I wasn't sure how a living man and a ghost might interact when they both had a romantic interest in me.

When Pierre looked my way, I pointed a warning finger at him and said with my best school teacher tone, "Please behave! I think Ricci is afraid of spirits."

He shrugged his shoulders. "What am I supposed to do about it? I am not a therapist."

Tiffany opened the door and greeted the two detectives before leading them the short distance to the living room.

Ricci scanned the room with interest.

Chris smiled at me and nodded.

Ignoring my warning, Pierre carried a decorative bowl in front of the detectives and placed it on a nearby table.

Color drained from Ricci's face, leaving him as white as the sand on Alabama's Gulf Coast.

Pierre looked quite pleased with himself. He flitted back and forth in front of Ricci, I'm sure to annoy me.

Ricci backed up.

Did he see Pierre or just sense him?

Chris's mouth dropped open. "Is there a ghost present?" From the look on his face, he'd resisted saying, *or am I going crazy?*

My shoulders, which had involuntarily risen to my ears, lowered as I exhaled my pent-up breath. "Yes, it's Pierre, an artist I met in Paris. He attached himself to one of his paintings, the one hanging over my fireplace." Unsure what else to do, I made the introductions.

Chris nodded. "Excellent work. I love that painting. It looks like Brianna."

Pierre threw back his shoulders and smiled. "This detective has good artistic taste."

I chuckled and passed on Pierre's response.

Detective Ricci hadn't made a comment. He sidestepped to a nearby chair and sank into it.

Chris placed a reassuring hand on his shoulder. "My partner suffers from phasmophobia, the fear of ghosts."

"So that's why you turned pale when you watched the video of what happened at Tiffany's home," Mystery said.

The mirror over Chris's shoulder revealed my flush to be bright pink. I looked down and cleared my throat. When I looked up into Chris's steady gaze, I said, "I'm sure it's obvious by now that I can see and communicate with earthbound spirits. I've been able to do so from birth."

Chris walked toward me. "Thought so. You do a pretty good job of hiding it." He flashed me a reassuring smile. "No worries. We're good." He leaned over and whispered in my ear, "My granny saw them, too."

Pierre shot closer and frowned. "What does he mean by, 'We are good'? I do not trust this detective. He looks at you with désir."

I ignored Pierre's jealous outburst and gave Chris a grateful smile. "Glad to hear it."

"Now that we've gotten the ghost business out of the way, our explanation of what we found and how we found it will be easier," Tiffany said, sounding more at ease.

The three of us tag-teamed while explaining what we found, and Pierre's role in the search. Pierre puffed out his chest and looked quite pleased with himself.

Chris took notes. When we finished, he capped his pen and asked, "Where are these papers?"

Tiffany stood and gathered the diary and loose sheets from a nearby side table. She handed them to Ricci, who'd extended his hand to receive them.

Ricci flipped through the diary and glanced at the papers. He gave a low whistle before passing them to Chris. "Mio Dio, y'all hit the motherlode! Can you show us the desk?"

Tiffany said, "Sure, it's upstairs."

Chris raised a finger to stop her. "We also need to see the garage where Pierre found the bloody baseball bat?"

"It's out back," I said. "Because Pierre could look into the box without touching anything, the evidence has been preserved."

Ricci said, "Give us a moment to decide how to handle this situation." They stepped back into the foyer and conversed in hushed tones, occasionally casting a glance our way.

Ricci rubbed his hands together, looking determined. "Someone needs to take me to examine the desk."

Tiffany raised her hand.

He nodded. His gaze skipped across us. "My partner will call in the crime scene folks. He'll need someone to take him to the garage to show where the bat is hidden." He inclined his head. "I'm assuming that will be you, Brianna, since you can converse with the um, ghost."

I smiled and felt my face flush again.

Ricci said, "I also need each of you to write out your witness statements leaving out the, um, ghost's role in the discovery."

Mystery said, "Sugar, I'm not sure how we can manage to leave out the haint part. Give me the form and I'll do my best."

Tiffany raised her hand again. "I have a solution. It may help that Jason mentioned in the diary that he'd hidden the bat inside the garage. That man documented everything. Of course, Pierre is the one who discovered the exact location."

He floated closer and gave a courtly bow.

I shook my head. *Frenchmen.*

Ricci smiled for the first time since arriving. "Good to know.

That will give us a logical reason to search the garage."

Tiffany crooked her finger. "Follow me, Detective. It's not far."

CHAPTER 31

Pierre hovered over the sidewalk, arms crossed, jaw rigid with frustration. I'd extended his ban to include my property, after I caught him hovering outside my window the previous night, while I was undressing.

I lounged on my front porch swing, reading the Sunday paper. I did my best to ignore him. A sweating glass of iced tea rested on a nearby table. The honeysuckle-scented breeze rustled the Boston ferns hanging between the columns supporting the front porch.

I huffed. "Oh, okay. You are no longer banned from the property." I added malice to my tone. "If I catch you levitating outside my bedroom window again, I'll reinstitute the ban in a heartbeat." Spirits have poor boundaries, but this love-stricken Frenchman seemed worse than most when it came to me.

"Ahh, nothing like a relaxing Sunday afternoon." I yawned, patting my mouth. "I'm even considering a nap."

Pierre's jaw relaxed a bit. "You probably need one ma chérie. You've been working day and night lately. If you like, I can join you."

I shot him a don't-go-there look.

Mystery's ring tone blasted on my phone.

I answered, "Why are you disturbing my peaceful afternoon?"

"You told me to call if Tiffany and I found Sophie Blake's grave."

I stopped the motion of the swing and sat straight. "That was quick."

"Do you want to go check out the situation today? Tiffany's available."

I weighed my options: nap or solve a mystery. "Who's driving?" "Tiffany offered."

"No. No way!" I made a slashing motion with my hand. "Absolutely not. I nearly have a panic attack just watching that little woman pull into a parking slot in front of our shops."

Mystery gave an empathetic chuckle. "Me, too. I told her I'd drive since I know the location."

"In that case, count me in." I looked at Pierre. "Want to go check out Sophie's grave to see if she has crossed over?"

He flexed his bicep. "Bien sûr. You ladies may need my protection."

I rolled my eyes. *Frenchmen.* "Pierre is coming, too."

Mystery turned into a cemetery full of flat gravestones. Artificial flowers in vases attached to the markers provided small pops of color. A handful of well-placed sculptures were all that disturbed the horizontal plane.

I left the car and scooted into the cemetery's office to find out what section held her grave. When I returned, Pierre ghost-sat on the hood.

He shrugged. "I was making the ladies cold."

I was in the car buckling the seatbelt when Tiffany asked from the backseat, "Why did Jason bury Sophie *here*?"

"Sugar, who knows why that man did anything. Sometimes newer cemeteries give good deals to attract business." Mystery started the car.

"The lady I spoke with said she was in section twelve."

Mystery pulled away from the curb and crept along the narrow roads.

I pointed. "Over there. That's her ghost. I recognize her from the photo Jasmine found during her research."

"Where? This is frustrating. Why can't I see ghosts, too?" Tiffany asked, straining to see.

"Sugar, most of us can't see haints," Mystery said with a wistful tone.

Tiffany slid back into her seat and crossed her arms. "Don't y'all find it strange that all the members of the Rocket City Paranormal

Society can't see earthbound spirits either?"

"Not really," I said. "Those of us who can see them are too busy trying to hide the fact from spirits with poor boundaries. Once they know I can see them, they stick around, like Pierre."

Pierre turned and stuck his tongue out at me.

"And then there are the ghost-crazy folks. They can also be a pain."

We parked and gathered near the rear of the car. A light breeze helped to dispel the heat from the bright sun.

"How do we handle this?" Mystery asked while shouldering her purse.

A malevolent looking specter emerged from the ground in front of a nearby grave.

He floated in a menacing way toward us. I nodded toward the scary spirit. "I'm more interested in how we're going to handle *him*."

Mystery stared where I'd indicated. "Him, who?"

"A mean-looking ghost."

His evil eyes locked onto us. Floating closer, his bony, claw-like hands reached out. "What are you doing in my cemetery? Leave!" Each word was coated with acid.

I looked for Pierre. He was nowhere in sight. "No help from him."

"Him who?" Mystery asked.

"Pierre disappeared." I tried to keep panic from my voice.

Sophie looked from us to the predatory poltergeist. "Watch out! He hurts people."

I nodded to her. "Thanks for the warning. What's his name?"

Sophie's brows inched up. "You heard me?"

I said with growing alarm, "His name!"

"Whose name are you asking about?" Tiffany's voice had risen several squeaky octaves.

The ghost drew closer.

"Names have power in the world of the supernatural." I pointed. "We have a threatening ghost coming toward us." I gestured for Tiffany to get behind me.

She wasted no time complying. "What are you going to do? Where is he? Is the ghost close?" She looked around, trying to see what was happening.

Mystery knew the drill. She moved next to Tiffany. "Shush! Let her concentrate."

"Seth Harbinger," Sophie said.

Seth turned and hissed at Sophie. "Mind your own business. I'll deal with you later."

Fear raced down my spine. My racing heart commanded me to run. My feet didn't move. My head said, *Where is Pierre?*

Seth began circling us.

I shifted to face him. Mystery and Tiffany followed my example by staying behind me.

Enough of this crap. Inhaling a deep breath, I gathered my energy. I shoved the palm of my hand toward him. "Seth Harbinger, back off!"

An invisible force pushed the ghost back at least three feet, knocking him flat on the grass. The round-eyed look that replaced his formerly slitted eyes relayed his surprise.

"Pierre! Where are you?"

He popped into view in front of me.

"Where the heck have you been?" I asked, not taking my eyes off Seth, who was upright once again.

"I was admiring the statuary. Nothing like Rodin's Garden, of course." His tone was smug.

I pointed at the frightening specter behind him. "We have a problem. Can you help?"

Pierre whirled. After taking in the situation, his hands tightened into fists. "Are you threatening ma femme?" He rocketed toward Seth.

His woman?

Seth zoomed backward and dived into the ground in front of a headstone.

I felt my knees give from the expenditure of energy, so I propped myself against the car. Visions of Victoria slashing Jason before throwing him to his death flitted past. *I need to visit Mom and learn more about handling aggressive ghosts like Seth and Victoria.*

Pierre leaned over Seth's grave. Reaching in, he yanked his head above the ground. "If you are intelligent, you will stay down there and leave people alone. Do not make me come back here. You will not like it."

Seth bobbed his head.

Pierre released him.

Seth sank down out of sight.

Swaggering back to us, as only a French ghost could, he said, "Bullies are brave until it comes to someone bigger."

I brushed a stray hair from my face. "I'd say you're a good bit bigger. Thanks, Pierre."

He did a gallant bow. "No one annoys you while I am around." He looked at me, his expression softening. "Are you well, ma chérie? Do you need an embrace?"

I held up my hands in a stop gesture. "Thanks to you, I'm good. A hug isn't necessary." My still-panicked heart felt like it was beating at the rate of a hummingbird's wings. I took a deep calming breath and said, "We need to talk to Sophie."

When we reached her, I could tell she was curious. Her gaze shifted from Pierre, to Mystery, to Tiffany, then to me.

"I'm not sure who you are or why you're here, but thanks. Seth has been terrorizing me since I came here. He runs off all the visitors." She shrugged. "Not that I ever get any." She smiled up at Pierre. "Thanks for putting him in his place. He deserved it."

Pierre flashed an embarrassed smile and cocked his head toward me. "Nobody is going to hurt ma dame if I can prevent it."

His lady? We're going to have a talk about his possessive nature.

"I wouldn't be dead if I'd married a man like you." Regret filled her eyes. "Instead, I got conned by a monster who killed me and put me *here."* She said the word "here" like he'd dumped her body in a muddy swamp.

I stepped forward and explained to Sophie that my friends weren't psychic. "I'm going to report what you and Pierre say to me."

Everyone nodded.

After introducing the group to Sophie, I gestured toward Tiffany. "This is Jason's second wife and almost victim. You ladies need to talk."

For the next thirty minutes, using me as a go-between, Jason's wives shared information about their marriages and his death. Jason and Sierra's modus operandi hadn't changed much from Sophie to Tiffany.

I thought, *Lucille would say, if it's not broken, don't fix it.* Curious, I asked, "When and why did you change your will?"

"I'd reached the conclusion that Jason had married me for my money. I was stupid and didn't insist on a prenup. When he asked for a divorce, I went to my attorney the next day. He arranged for a mental health exam and a report to prove that I was of sound mind. After that was complete, we rewrote my will." She looked over at Tiffany. "I had no idea that I was setting the stage for him to go after you. I'm sorry."

After I'd relayed the message, Tiffany gestured toward us. "If it hadn't been for these ladies and Mystery's assistant, Jasmine, I'd also be dead." Tiffany rubbed her hands together, looking ready to change the subject. "I agree we both married the same homicidal jerk, but I'm ready to move on." Tiffany pulled a notebook and pen from her purse. "Let's talk about how to spring you from this cemetery and get you to your final resting place of choice."

CHAPTER 32

After my Monday morning walk with Mystery, I was having a cup of java with her and Jasmine before opening our stores. When we heard squealing brakes and the screech of tires in front of Mystery's store, we all flinched.

"That can only be Tiffany," Mystery said.

We all hurried into the retail area in time to see that a gray-haired woman with an enormous purse had her back plastered against the store's window. I could tell by the up and down heave of her shoulders that she was probably hyperventilating.

My hand covered my stomach, which felt like a flipped pancake. "I swear, I don't understand how Tiffany passed her driver's test."

"I don't understand why she doesn't have dents or scrapes on her Volvo. Do you think maybe it's a magical car?" Jasmine asked, a speculative look on her face.

"You're still reading those fantasy books, aren't you?" I asked, amused that she wanted to endow the Volvo with magical qualities.

"Yeah. It's my favorite genre. Here she comes."

Tiffany smiled and greeted the woman before knocking on the door.

Jasmine unlocked it and stood aside.

Tiffany popped through the doorway, sending the bell into a tizzy. She held her arms wide. "You are looking at one relieved woman!"

Mystery, Jasmine, and I exchanged confused looks.

"Sierra has been arrested once again, only this time for

conspiracy to murder. To make it even better, the police and my accountant were able to recover all of my lost assets."

Mystery leaned on a counter, looking delighted with the outcome. "We aim to please."

"Let me tell you, it's been an adventure," Tiffany admitted. "I've come to pay the charges for your additional services."

The gray-haired woman straightened, gripped the purse to her chest, and hurried down the sidewalk.

Mystery walked to her office and returned with an invoice.

Tiffany squinted while looking down the page. She pulled her purse closer and pawed around inside until she pulled out a bedazzled glasses case. After a quick look around, she placed them on her nose and reread the invoice. "Much better. I kept getting headaches, so I gave in and purchased these cute little reading glasses.

Don't y'all be telling anyone I wear them. A lady is entitled to a few vanities."

Jasmine zipped her mouth with a gesture. "Your secret's safe with me."

"This looks accurate, except you didn't charge for yesterday at the cemetery."

Jasmine looked from one to the other of us. "What happened yesterday? You went to a cemetery?"

I relayed the events at the graveyard.

Jasmine did her neck thing. "You went off on a ghost adventure without me?"

Mystery glared at her. "Weren't you studying for exams yesterday?" She refocused on Tiffany and said, "Yesterday was about helping Sophie. No charge."

"Thanks. Put it on my Visa." Tiffany patted Jasmine on the shoulder. "I'm racking up my bonus points for a cruise this fall."

"I want to go on a cruise someday," Jasmine said with a faraway look in her eyes.

"You will," I said. "Right now, you need to focus on finishing college."

"It's much easier now. I can study without interruptions and get a good night's sleep."

"Were you living in a dorm?" Tiffany asked.

"With my mom and her latest boyfriend. I moved out a few days ago into Ms. Lucille's garage."

Tiffany's mouth dropped open. "Garage?"

I wanted to laugh at the horror in Tiffany's expression.

"Sugar, my mother renovated a detached garage into a furnished apartment. I saw it several days ago and it's adorable."

Tiffany removed her glasses. "That's wonderful, Jasmine. I remember my first place. I was so excited."

"It's like a whole new world for me—my own place. You should stop by some time and see it. I could use some decorating advice. Ms. Lucille has some carpets and paintings for me to look through."

Tiffany's smile widened. "I'd love to help. I have some items I'd planned to donate that you might want. I decided on a whim to redecorate my bedroom. I have an Austin Horn comforter set with coordinating drapes if you want to look at them. No obligation."

"That would be great. Thanks." Excitement brightened Jasmine's brown eyes.

The two pulled out their phones and began discussing possible times to look at the carpets.

I couldn't believe the transformation in Jasmine. It was like the young woman had hope and a future ahead of her. *Since Jasmine's mother can't help, I need to snoop around and find out what else she needs for a first apartment gift. Maybe some towels and washcloths.*

After Tiffany and Jasmine set a date and time and confirmed it by phone with Lucille, Tiffany put away her phone. "I have a proposition."

Mystery quirked a brow. "Oh? What did you have in mind?"

Tiffany slid onto a nearby stool. "I want to work for you on a commissioned basis."

"I'm not sure what you mean," Mystery said, standing straighter. "Doing what?"

"I know lots of folks who have old houses with ghosties. I can set up the contracts. You, Jasmine, and Brianna can do the investigations and the clearings, with my help, of course. I don't want to miss out on all the fun." Tiffany planted her hands on her hips. "I can also help with the advertising of the ghost tours. I looked online. You don't even have a website. You can use more business, can't you?"

"It's an interesting proposition, but I don't want to be known only as a local haint chaser. When I bought the business from my old boss, it came with a whole slew of search programs. Jasmine and I would like to expand our background searches for companies." She explained in detail about new hires, secret clearances, and property searches. "I need a broader, steadier base of income that has nothing to do with the paranormal," Mystery finished.

"I see your point." Tiffany nodded, fingering her glasses. Diversification makes sense. You will need two sets of business cards." Tiffany put the glasses in her purse before tapping the glass with her French manicured index finger. "Keep in mind, I have lots of connections in this town and can also set up contracts for title searches and employee background checks." She winked. "Of course, you may have to hire additional employees in the future."

"Clay Wilkes has started working for Mystery, so he can help," Jasmine said, her voice full of excitement.

"Isn't he that cute red-headed guy who was at the meeting the other night?" Tiffany asked.

"That's him. He seems really nice. He's a computer major, so he can help with the website." She cracked her knuckles, earning a wince from Mystery. "If we have a website, we can do online sales."

Tiffany smiled. "Great idea." She nudged Jasmine. "I joined the RCPS, too. You'll have to help me pick out some ghost hunting stuff. Nothing too technical." She looked ready to bounce in her seat. "I can't wait until the next meeting. Will it be here at the Mystery Shop?"

"No!" Mystery said, making a slashing motion.

Jasmine's eyes widened. "Come on, Mystery. Please!"

"Absolutely not. Clay and his buddy almost came to blows in here." She pointed at Jasmine's mouth. "Girl, don't you be giving me that pouty lip look."

Jasmine crossed her arms and emphasized the pout.

"Sugar, I'm immune." Mystery walked several feet away and crossed her arms.

"I guess Mystery will miss all the fun at the next meeting," Tiffany said with a conspiratorial wink. "If I'm going to work here, we'll have to work together on the marketing plan."

Jasmine gave Tiffany a curious look. With a disbelieving tone, she asked, "Have you ever done marketing before?"

Tiffany threw her head back and belly laughed. When she'd gained control and had wiped away her laugh-tears, she said,

"Jasmine Williams, you must think I'm a spoiled rich kid who never worked. I have a BS in business and was in marketing and sales for years. My husband, Wendell, sold several lucrative patents for millions. When all the money started rolling in, I stopped working."

Jasmine crossed her arms tight across her chest. "If you don't need to work, then why do it?"

"Believe it or not, I'm bored, and it's been lonely since Jason's death. Heck, working with y'all has been the most exciting thing that's happened to me in years. I think it's time to dust off my skills and put them to good use."

"What percentage of the profits would you want on the contracts you procure?" Mystery asked with a cautious tone.

"Twenty percent."

"Ten," Mystery countered, raising her chin.

"Fifteen," Tiffany said.

"Deal."

They shook hands.

"What about your time spent on paranormal investigations and clearings? You don't need to attend those. Setting up contracts and marketing would be your job description."

"No charge. I'm hooked. It would be like a hobby for me. Of course, I'm not guaranteeing to attend each one," Tiffany said.

They shook hands again.

Tiffany said, "A friend of mine who's an attorney in Jason's old firm might be willing to write a contract for us. He owes me a favor."

"That's fine, but there is one restriction that must be included."

"What?"

"You're banned from driving any company vehicle."

CHAPTER 33

I left Mystery's shop and settled down in my office for a quick break. I had twenty more minutes before opening time.

Pierre hovered in the corner, looking bored.

I picked up my copy of Agatha Christie's *Big Four*, thinking, *At this rate, I'll never finish this novel*. I opened the book to where I'd placed a Sherlock Holmes bookmark and was pleased to see I'd made it to Chapter Nine. Hercule Poirot was investigating Mr. Paynter's death.

I took a sip of coffee, slouched down in my chair, and propped my feet on a nearby box. Ten minutes later, I sat straight, placing both feet on the floor. "Oh my gosh!" A strange sensation crawled over me. *How did I miss it?*

Pierre jolted to attention. "What is it, ma chérie?"

I waved Pierre closer before picking up the phone to call Mystery. When she answered, I said, "I know who killed Victoria Spellman."

"I'm on my way," Mystery said with an excited tone.

Mystery and I sat at the conference table, while Pierre floated nearby.

"What clued you in?" Mystery asked.

I recounted my walk with Katie and the discussion of the flowers on her fence. I held up the book. "In this novel, the victim was poisoned with Carolina jasmine."

"Jasmine!" Mystery said, looking incredulous. She pulled her phone from her purse and googled the plant. "It says here that a teaspoonful can kill a person. Death is caused by a paralysis of the muscles responsible for breathing. The face takes on a mask-like appearance, and the pupils will be fully dilated after death."

I nodded, my mind flashing back to that fateful morning when we'd found the body. "That's what Victoria's face looked like, remember?" Another memory dropped into my head. I pointed at my purse. "Hand me that, please."

Mystery grunted surprised by its weight. "You carrying gold bullion in there?"

I frowned while digging through the handbag. "The good thing about a purse this size is it holds a lot. The bad thing is I can never find anything." I searched for a few more minutes. "There it is! On the bottom as usual." I pulled a wrinkled, folded envelope out and held it up. "This is the letter Victoria wanted Father Garrison to read at her funeral. There's been so much going on that I forgot it was in here."

Mystery cocked her head. "I can't believe we both forgot it all this time."

"What does it say?" Pierre asked, floating closer.

I perused it. When I finished, I gave a low whistle before saying, "No wonder Father Garrison didn't read it. Victoria intended to reveal all the dirt she'd gathered on people over the years to the congregation. It covers the entire suspect list that we investigated, including Jason. It would have made things so much easier. I wish I'd remembered this letter sooner. Do you think we should turn this over to the police?"

"It's evidence." Mystery rubbed her chin. "She may have threatened to reveal everyone's secrets if they harmed her. What was Katie's secret?"

"Victoria was blackmailing her because she caught her being unfaithful. She hinted that she suspected Katie might have poisoned her husband! If Katie did, I bet we can guess how." I picked up my phone. "I'm calling Chris."

CHAPTER 34

Mystery and I sat in a conference room at the police station while Pierre circled the space. An oversized whiteboard was attached to one wall. To me, the handwriting scrawled on the surface looked like artsy chicken scratches. The room's well-stocked coffee station would have tempted me, but the acrid smell of burnt coffee caused my nose to twitch. Locating the source, I stood, turned off the burner before the glass pot exploded, and placed the blackened pot in the sink. "I wonder how many of these they break a year?"

Ricci strode into the room with Chris at his heels. "Usually ten." He sniffed the air and scowled. "You'd think adults could do better."

The two men pulled out chairs and sat. Ricci straightened his Sponge Bob tie.

Chris shot a discreet wink to me while he readied a legal pad to take notes.

Pierre saw it and frowned. "Why is this detective flirting with you? Does he not understand our arrangement?"

I glared at Pierre. "We have no arrangement."

Ricci drummed his fingers on the table while assessing the situation. He looked straight at Pierre. "Is your um, pet ghost here?"

"Pet ghost!" Pierre tossed the pile of papers at the end of the table in the air. They floated delicately to the ground.

Ricci leaped from his chair and backed against the wall, looking left and right.

I whirled to face Pierre. "Shame on you."

"He called me your pet ghost." He pounded his chest, chin held high. "I deserve respect."

"True. Get over it or leave. We need to catch a murderer." I crossed my arms and faced Ricci. "You insulted Pierre. He deserves some respect from you."

Eyes bulging, Ricci apologized.

Chris watched the whole interaction with a curious expression. I hadn't yet explained the ghostly infatuation.

Holding up his hands, Pierre said, "Okay, tell Ricci I am not going to hurt him. I only want to make sure you stay safe. We can work together if he never refers to me as your," He made quote signs with his fingers, "pet."

I passed on the message to Ricci.

Ricci managed a reluctant nod. "I'll try, but please stay over there somewhere." He gestured toward the far corner of the room. "I know my fear is unreasonable, but I can't help it."

"Can you see him?" I asked.

"I get occasional glimpses sometimes," Ricci said.

Chris uncapped his pen. "He saw his grandmother after she died when he was a kid."

Ricci shot Chris a blabber-mouth look.

Pierre said, "Ghosts are like people; not all of us are bad. Some, like me, are just trying to find justice and gagner l'amour d'une belle femme."

I relayed the message, leaving out the part about winning my love.

"I'll keep that in mind, but for now, please keep your distance," Ricci said, looking pale and fidgety.

I reached into my purse and handed him Dr. Stone's card. "I've been thinking about this problem. Dr. Stone does psychological profiling for your department. She won't think you're crazy, because she understands about ghosts."

Ricci picked up the card, looked at it, and placed it in his blazer's pocket. "I'll think about it."

I leveled my most serious look his way. "There are ghosts everywhere. Call her."

"That information does little to allay my fears." He resumed his seat and said, "Start at the beginning."

I started with my first talk with Katie and concluded with my latest chapter in the Agatha Christie novel. I counted off the critical points on my fingers. "She has a motive, a means and a probable opportunity."

Mystery once again pulled up the information about Carolina jasmine on her phone and let the detectives read it. When they finished, I pulled out the letter Victoria had wanted Father Garrison to read at her funeral and explained how I'd acquired it. "This should get your attention."

As the two detectives read, their interest was obvious. Ricci rubbed a finger across his lips, while Chris's brows rose and fell as he read.

"This is circumstantial. We interviewed her. She was out of town when the victim was killed. How did she deliver the poison?" Ricci asked.

"I don't know yet, but I have a plan to find out," I said.

Ricci frowned, his eyes narrowing. "Whatever it is, I don't like it."

I crossed my arms and stared him down.

"I'm listening," Chris said.

Ricci cocked a surprised brow at his partner but said nothing.

I told them each step of my idea and explained why I thought it would work.

"I don't like it. It's too dangerous," Ricci said, the corners of his mouth turned down.

Chris rubbed his chin with a thumb and forefinger. "It might work."

Ricci whipped his head in Chris's direction. "Have you lost your ever-lovin' mind? She's a civilian."

Chris eyed me with a speculative up and down. "We wire civilians all the time; besides, Katie is what? In her seventies?"

He has a point, but she's still pretty spry. "I'm sure I can outrun her," I said.

"Bree, if you do this, don't eat anything. She could try to poison you," Mystery said, looking concerned.

After fifteen minutes of arguing our point, Ricci reluctantly agreed.

Two hours later, I smoothed the front of my emerald green blouse over the wires taped to my abdomen and glanced back at the white van parked down the street. "Can you hear me?"

The van's lights flashed once.

I looked down at Prissy. "Stay calm. Remember, we can handle this." The dog whined and pulled toward the house. "Pierre, best you hang around in case something goes wrong, but not too close. She believes in ghosts, so I don't want you to spook her." I realized what I said. "No pun intended."

My knees felt like they might give way as I walked up the three stairs to Katie's porch. *What was I thinking? Mom will kill me if I get hurt.* I tried to swallow, but my throat felt tight. I managed a deep breath and rang the doorbell. Prissy danced from paw to paw beside me.

Phoebe barked in sharp excited yips on the other side of the door. The two dogs knew it was play time.

Katie opened the door with a confused look that she managed to transform into a smile. "This is a pleasant surprise."

I pasted on a tight smile. *Calm down.* "I hope this isn't inconvenient, but I realized I don't have your number, so here I am, on your doorstep."

Phoebe squeezed past Katie. The two dogs greeted each other with whines and wagging tails.

Katie smiled like an indulgent grandmother at their antics and chuckled.

"I was hoping we could set up some playdates for our dogs. Prissy is so small that I hesitate to take her to the dog park. I'm afraid one of the bigger dogs might hurt her."

Katie stepped out onto the porch. She frowned and shook her head. "I won't take Phoebe there either. Some of those folks don't have a lick of control over their dogs."

"If now isn't a good time, I can give you my number and we can arrange another one," I said, half hoping she'd reschedule.

"Goodness, no, I'm glad to see you. I've been curious about how the murder case is coming along." Katie held the door open wide and stepped to the side. "Come in."

I tried to swallow, but my mouth was dry. Chris had advised me to stay outside if possible. *Think!* "Can we sit on the porch? It's so pretty, and I've been cooped up inside for most of the day." *No way am I leaving the line of sight of that van.*

"Why, sure. I spend a good bit of my time on the porch in the morning and afternoon when the heat and humidity isn't too high.

In fact, I was snipping coupons out here before my daughter called." A warm smile lit her face. "She likes to check on me daily."

Katie closed the door and gestured me toward a wicker chair nudged against a round glass-topped wicker table. The white paint was beginning to peel in places. "You can catch me up on Victoria's case while Phoebe and Prissy play. Darlene wants this mess to be solved, sooner rather than later. The poor dear has financial troubles."

"I got that impression when we last spoke." *Time to turn up the heat.* I shot Katie my best I-know-what-you-did look to throw the older woman off her game. "I've learned a good bit in the last week. I'm sure the case will be solved in a few days."

Katie narrowed her eyes and bared her yellow teeth, in a poor imitation of a smile. "Good, I'm anxious for Darlene and Susie to be my new neighbors." She eyed me with suspicion and paused, raising a finger. "I'll be back in a jiff with something for us to drink and nibble on."

I pulled out the chair that faced the van and brushed yellow pollen off the cushion before sitting. *Dang stuff gets everywhere.* I cast a nervous glance toward the van. *Stay calm. Don't hyperventilate, and remember, if something goes wrong, say, "hot", and the detectives will come running.* I unleashed Prissy and the two dogs started playing, running up and down the length of the wide porch.

A stack of coupons sat across the small table next to a pair of large scissors.

Katie returned carrying a small round tray with two glasses full of ice, water bottles, and some muffins. She placed the tray on the table and pulled out her chair. She settled into her seat and folded her hands on the table in front of her.

The scene was idyllic. Baskets full of a variety of blooms hung between the columns, swaying in the gentle breeze. The sweet scent of Carolina jasmine filled the air. The dogs were alternating between wrestling, and then lying beside each other. They currently lay panting on the other side of the wide porch.

My gaze flicked to the pair of scissors near Katie's elbow.

Katie picked up a bottle of water. "Thirsty?"

I nodded and accepted it. My mouth was so dry my lips were sticking together. When the seal popped, I thought, *At least this is safe to drink.* I'd gulped down half the bottle when a disturbing thought hit me. *What if she has injected something into the bottle?* Feeling queasy, I capped it and put it on the table. I managed a small smile. "I'm feeling dehydrated. I had three cups of java this morning. If I drink any more caffeine today, I may jump clear out of my skin. Cold water is just what I needed."

Katie nodded and slid one of the two glasses filled with ice toward me. A thin layer of clear liquid pooled on the bottom of the glass she offered me. The one still on the tray didn't have liquid on the bottom.

Katie's eyes gleamed. "Don't you want ice?"

I crossed my fingers out of sight and shook my head. "Sensitive tooth."

"I've heard Jason is dead. Is it true? I haven't seen an obituary in the paper yet." Katie steepled her fingers and peered over them. "When you get my age, the obituaries become the most important part of the news. I like to see who I've outlived."

I gave a conspiratorial nod and leaned forward. "As the old saying goes, he's deader than a doornail."

"How do you know? Did the police tell you?" Katie asked, her tone sharp. She filled her glass with water and took a sip.

A drop of perspiration trickled down my side while I pondered how to answer. I decided on the truth. "I saw him die."

Katie sat back, her eyes popping wide. "For land's sake!" She leaned closer, a curious spark in her eye. "I never did like that guy. What happened? Was it gory?"

Since I knew Katie believed in ghosts, I recounted Victoria's attack on Jason. She looked more and more alarmed as the story progressed. She kept looking around her, perhaps thinking Victoria would appear at any moment.

She's scared of Victoria's ghost. I don't blame her. That specter has already attacked her twice in the churchyard.

Katie touched her parted lips with her fingers. "How do you know it was her?"

I looked deep into Katie's eyes, not wanting to miss her reaction. "I can see ghosts."

Katie jerked her head back, giving me an open-mouthed, incredulous stare. "You're yankin' my chain." She paused. "Are you serious?"

I nodded.

"Why did she kill him?"

"I suspect for revenge. She knew Jason hit her with a baseball bat in the churchyard, and then dumped her behind the bushes."

Katie's shoulders lowered several inches. She took a sip of water and then bunched her brows. "That woman was a hissy fit with a tail on it when she was alive. She's not much better dead." Katie slammed her glass on the table, water sloshing over the side. "Maybe she'll go where the sun don't shine, now that she's gotten rid of her murderer."

I waited, saying nothing. I'd read in several crime novels that the silent technique worked wonders to get a suspect to reveal information.

Katie mopped up the water with a napkin. "This won't help Darlene. It's going to be hard to prove Jason murdered Vickie, since he's dead. The police can't get a confession out of a ghost." She shook her head. "I was so hoping this would be over soon."

"Not true," I said.

Katie's lips parted. "What do you mean?"

"Jason hid a diary in his desk. In it, he admitted to the crime."

Katie's expression took on a relieved look as she placed the wet napkin back on the tray. Her gaze traveled toward a bumble bee buzzing around the closest hanging basket, sampling the nectar of the various flowers.

"The police even found the *alleged* weapon hidden in the garage at his house. The baseball bat is being processed for fingerprints and other things as we speak." I decided to let her deduce what *other things* meant.

Katie scrunched her nose like she'd smelled death. "Well, I'll be darned." She sat back in the chair, her fingers gripping the edge of the table. "I'm glad that's all settled. Darlene can inherit the estate and move in next door. It will be so wonderful to have nice neighbors for a change."

Matching her behavior, I sat back in my chair, too. I hooked an elbow over the back, trying to look nonchalant. "Unfortunately, that only proves Jason *attempted to murder* Victoria."

Katie stiffened in her seat like she'd entered rigor mortis. "What foolishness are you carrying on about? You said the diary proves he hit Vicky, and the police found the murder weapon. That's murder, not attempted murder."

I stared at Katie for a few moments, watching her squirm. "Victoria didn't die from the head wound."

Katie cleared her throat and touched her fingers to her lips.

I thought, *Strange, she didn't ask how Victoria died. Probably because she knows.*

Katie pushed the plate with baked goods toward me. One muffin stood separate from the others. It was the one closest to me, "Try one of my morning glory muffins. It's my grandmother's recipe. She was a wonderful cook."

I eyed the muffins, which were browned to perfection. *They do look tasty, but I don't trust anything that you've made.* It was then the idea hit me. *Baked goods!* I suspected Katie had poisoned Victoria with Carolina jasmine. I didn't have a clue how, until now.

"I bet Victoria liked these muffins."

Katie blushed, looking pleased. "The old biddy loved them. She'd steal them off this very table every time I'd put them out to cool."

Bingo! "I see," I said with an accusing tone while shooting her a condemning look.

"Do you know how Victoria died?"

Katie sat back and crossed her arms. "No. How would I know that?"

I leaned closer and said, "She was poisoned."

Katie blanched. "Well, I never." Her hand covered her heart. "Surely, you're not accusing me? I was in another state when Victoria was killed."

"To be more accurate, you were in Tennessee when she *died*. Before you left town for your birthday, did you put Carolina jasmine in some muffins, and then leave them on this table for her to steal?" I asked.

"You're crazy! Jason murdered Victoria with a baseball bat. I didn't have anything to do with it. All this talk of poison is pure foolishness." She had her hands on the arms of the chair, ready to spring into action.

"You were married to a botanist, so you'd know how much jasmine to use."

"I don't know what you're talking about." Katie said, her brow furrowing with either anger or worry or both.

"Jason tried to kill Victoria, but he didn't. She would've survived the head wound if the poison hadn't killed her."

Katie's normally pleasant features transformed into the face of a predator. She snatched the scissors and launched herself across the table at me, stabbing with an overhand thrust.

I scrambled to stand. The scissors' point tugged at the fabric of my blouse.

The chair hit the porch with a bang.

I backpedaled to dodge another downward swipe from Katie.

"Get away from me with those scissors. Hot! Hot!"

Katie advanced. She held the scissors like a knife. Her gaze was on my stomach like she planned to stab me. "How did you figure it out?"

I backed away. *Good grief, she's gone over the edge.* "Hot!"

Katie jabbed, trying to gut me. She missed. "The old biddy deserved to die. She blackmailed me for years about a stupid one-night stand."

Pierre stepped between us. Katie walked through him and shivered. "What was that?" She looked around.

I saw the two detectives and Mystery over Katie's shoulder. They sprinted toward the porch.

Hurry up! There's a cold-blooded granny trying to kill me.

I dodged another slash of the scissors by sucking in my abdomen. *That was close.* "Pierre, do something!"

"Who the heck is Pierre? You hallucinating?" Katie followed my every move with eyes feverish with rage.

He turned the table over. The tray flew into the air, dumping the muffins. The glasses fell to the porch. Shards of glass sparkled in the sun.

She whirled, looking for her foe. "Who did that?"

"Your husband's dead. Why kill Victoria now?" I asked, trying to distract her. I didn't take my gaze off her weapon.

She glanced over her shoulder at me. "She kicked Phoebe. Nobody kicks my baby and lives." Katie turned; her face contorted. She shifted her hold on the scissors. Screaming at the top of her lungs, she ran at me.

Pierre pushed a porch chair between us, delaying her attack while I backed out of range.

Trees began to sway.

The sky darkened, hiding the sun.

The air grew colder.

My panicked exhalations formed clouds of condensation.

When the window panes frosted over, I knew trouble was on the way.

Trouble by the name of Victoria.

Mystery cupped her hands and yelled, "Run before she cuts you to smithereens!"

Katie paused. Her terror-filled eyes scanned the area. It was only then that she noticed the two detectives approaching the porch. She ran for the front door.

Pierre slammed it shut.

Her eyes widened until white showed all around her pupils. She backed away, clutching the scissors.

Both dogs cowered and whined.

Katie barred my path to the steps. Desperate, I turned and leaped over the low azalea bushes, twisting my ankle when I landed. *Ow!*

I scrambled to my feet and hollered, "Prissy, come."

A panicked-looking Mystery stood on the sidewalk, motioning for me to hurry. "That woman's batshit crazy."

I hobbled toward her, as Prissy streaked across the lawn with Phoebe chasing behind her.

Ricci and Chris slid to a stop on the grass and backed away from the porch, staggering against the howling wind.

Chris yelled, "What's happening?"

"It's Victoria!"

Pierre joined us. "Move across the street. I have a feeling this will be terrifiant."

"Good idea." I relayed the message to Mystery while picking up Prissy. I held her close and limped across the street.

Mystery scooped up Phoebe and screamed a warning to move back to the two detectives, before joining Pierre and me across the street.

A screeching Victoria flew low over the detectives, knocking them to the ground. She raced toward Katie like the roar of a bitter gale. Her bony fingers were like claws. Her eyes blazed red.

Katie must have sensed her, because she screamed and turned to run. She fell over a chair and huddled behind the table Pierre had turned over.

The poltergeist reached the porch and stopped. She reached out.

"I will flay you to death."

A vortex of moaning shadow shapes sprang from a steaming crack on Katie's green lawn.

"They're coming for Victoria the way they did Jason," I said, covering my ears. I didn't want to hear the screams.

Pierre shielded us once again. "Mon Dieu! They are back."

They surrounded Victoria.

She turned in a circle looking for an escape.

Two of the demons latched on to her with long black fingers.

Victoria screamed and fought with the ferocity of a cougar.

The rest moved in surrounding her.

There were too many of them.

She shrieked once more before disappearing into the glowing crack.

It closed with a snap and a sizzle.

The reek of brimstone filled the air. I steadied myself with a hand on Mystery's shoulder. I could feel her trembling.

"That was ...horrible," she said.

I nodded. "I hope I never see them again."

"Amen! Those demons are scary. Why did they come for Victoria?" she asked.

"Murdering Jason marked her soul," I said while trying to soothe my trembling dog. "My theory about her seeking safety on sacred ground seems to have panned out."

"So, it was her need for revenge that got her in the end," Mystery said, staring at the place where the earth had opened.

"Is this what will happen to the man who murdered moi?" Pierre asked.

I shrugged. "Probably."

He smiled. "Good. He stole my life with you."

Mystery asked, "What's he saying?"

"It's private," I said.

A stunned-looking Ricci sat up on the grass. Chris stood and brushed off his pants before offering him a hand. They both walked over to examine the area where the crack had opened and closed.

The screech of the table moving on the porch drew everyone's attention.

Chris raced up the stairs and wrestled a struggling Katie out from behind the table. For a woman her age, she put up quite a fight.

Fortunately, she'd lost the scissors while scrambling to hide.

We hurried back to Katie's lawn to witness her take-down. When Chris had managed to pull her out, he cuffed her hands behind her back. Ricci, who'd recovered from his shock, mounted the stairs to the porch to read her rights to her.

"I'll sue you for false arrest," Katie screamed, trying to incapacitate Chris with a vicious kick of her pink-sneakered foot. "You have no proof of anything."

Ricci turned Katie to face him. "Brianna was wearing a wire under her blouse. We heard it all and saw you try to kill her." He pointed at the mess on the porch floor. "Chris, take everything that was on that tray as evidence. I want all of it analyzed for Carolina jasmine."

All the fight left Katie. She slumped and seemed to age several years within moments.

Mystery stroked Phoebe. "What do we do with this adorable dog?"

"Good question." Remembering that Katie wore hearing aids, I yelled, "Who do you want me to call to pick up Phoebe?"

Katie looked up, tears streaming down her face. With a hoarse voice, she said, "Keep her for me. I know you'll take good care of her until I can bail out of jail. Her bed and food are in the house." A bitter expression turned the corners of her mouth down. "My son-in-law won't allow dogs in his precious home."

I gave her a thumbs up and turned to Mystery. "I'm bummed about this. I liked Katie. She has so much spunk." *At least I did until she tried to kill me.*

"I didn't hear anything she said after I left the van." Mystery shivered. "When I saw her chasing you with those scissors, I thought she'd gut you for sure."

I donned my best indignant expression. "Mystery, are you saying I'm so out of shape that I can't outmaneuver a woman in her seventies?"

Looking embarrassed, she said, "It was a small area. Thank goodness Pierre intervened when he did. Did Katie say why she killed Victoria?"

"That wicked woman had kicked Phoebe. Lucille would say it was the last straw." I shifted Prissy from one arm to the other. "When do you plan to tell Darlene?"

She sighed. "I'm dreading that task. When I get back to the shop. I'm sure she'll be pleased to claim her inheritance, but finding out Katie murdered her mother will be a blow. I think Katie was more like a mother to Darlene than Victoria ever was."

Mystery and I took Phoebe to her master and allowed the dog to lick her tear-stained cheek.

Katie smiled. More tears filled her eyes. "I love you, Phoebe." She looked at me. "I know I have no right to ask, but if things don't turn out well, will you keep Phoebe or find her a good home?"

"I'd love to have her," Mystery said. "I have the shop next to Bree. The two dogs can visit each other."

"Thank you." Katie slumped, looking exhausted. "I need to sit down."

I righted a chair for her, wondering if she had a premonition about her future.

CHAPTER 35

"It is hard to believe that a week has passed since those so-memorable events on Madame Katie's porch," Pierre observed as he rode with me to Sophie's funeral. "Will Mystery keep Phoebe? She and Prissy do well together. I had thought you might keep la petite."

"I considered it. Prissy acts like Phoebe is a long-lost sister. I never realized that the little tyke could be lonely. Then I considered the doubled expenses and decided Mystery and Phoebe needed each other."

Pierre shook his head with a look of wonder. "Katie looked vigoureuse when she pursued you with those scissors. Sans doute Detective Ricci was surprised when she had a massive stroke and died in la salle d'interrogatoire."

I had an involuntary shiver. "Tony called me beyond freaked out because he was in that small room trying to resuscitate her when a crack appeared in the floor and those shadow figures came to claim her. Chris told me he found Tony huddled in a corner, shaking uncontrollably."

Pierre scrunched his brow. "Why can you see me and not the others?"

I shrugged. "Beats me. Some people have the gift. I suspect Ricci occassionally sees whisps of ghosts, but everybody saw the demons."

Pierre cocked his head. "What does beating you have to do with the situation?"

I chuckled. "It's an expression that means, I don't know."

"Then, why did you not say so?"

Frustrated, I said, "To get back on the subject, I fear Tony may be marred for life." I rubbed my arms. "I know I'll never see life and death quite the same."

"So, it is Tony now?" He crossed his arms. "When did you and Detective Ricci become meilleurs amis?" He raised his chin.

"We're not best friends. The ability to deal with what we've seen makes for unusual alliances. I only hope Dr. Stone can help him cope through this. He promised me he'd call her."

"From listening to you and Mystery, if anyone can help that man, my Euro is on her," Pierre said.

I chuckled at his choice of words. "Ghosts don't have money. Mom always said, you can't take it with you. She never understood my dad's fixation on cash."

Pierre glanced at the clock on the car's computer screen. "If we do not hurry, we will be late."

A few minutes later, I turned right into a quaint, small private cemetery. A white funeral tent stood in one corner shaded by a large oak tree.

When I reached the tent, Mystery, Tiffany, and Jasmine were already seated on a row of chairs in front of a gleaming silver casket. I slid into the empty seat between Mystery and Tiffany. Pierre floated behind me.

"What took you so long?" Mystery asked.

"This and that."

Tiffany nodded to a bent, white-haired priest. "We're all here."

Father Murray introduced himself and read from a well-worn Bible in an Irish brogue. When he finished, he made the sign of the cross and sprinkled holy water over the new metal casket that sat suspended over a six-foot hole.

Tiffany whispered, "I bought Sophie a new casket and a vault. That cheapskate put her in a crummy wooden box with no vault. When the funeral home dug it up for transfer, it started falling apart."

Pierre asked, "What is a cheapskate?"

I whispered, "Un avare."

Jasmine did her neck thing. "Sounds like Jason."

Father Murray shuffled over to Tiffany, took her outstretched hand and patted it. "Thanks for all you've done. I feel terrible that I denied a faithful parishioner a Catholic burial based on false information. Perhaps everything in life isn't so black and white."

The priest left, tottering toward his black sedan.

Tiffany handed us each a pink rose. We rose from the wobbling metal chairs and made our way over the uneven surface to the casket, where Sophie had levitated during the entire service.

Jasmine nudged me. "Where is she?"

"Floating above the head of her coffin," I said.

One at a time, we said goodbye to Sophie, before adding the roses to the spray of spring flowers atop the coffin.

Pierre floated over and kissed both of her cheeks. "Did that cochon at the other cemetery bother you again?"

Sophie looked confused. "What's a cochon?"

I laughed. "It means, pig."

She smiled. "Nope. You scared him good."

"Do you plan to cross over now?" he asked.

"I'm ready, and I feel the tug. I wanted to say goodbye first."

Sophie floated off the casket, placed a translucent hand on it, and smiled again. "Thank you. You have no idea what this means to me." She looked toward the bright light that appeared. "I see my parents. They're waiting for me."

Jasmine nudged me again. "Is she saying or doing anything?"

"I'll tell you later. She's preparing to cross over," I said, marveling at the sparkling light. "There she goes," I said, waving.

Pierre joined us and waved along with my friends as Sophie's turned and floated toward the light.

My pulse quickened when Sophie flowed into the brightness that soon faded.

"Mon Dieu!" Pierre said, his tone full of wonder.

"Is she gone?" Tiffany asked.

I nodded, tears welling in my eyes. "It's moments like this that make it all worthwhile."

THE END

ABOUT THE AUTHOR

Shirley B. Garrett, Psy.D. is a three-time Silver Falchion finalist. She uses her former career as a psychologist to create realistic characters and plots. Dr. Garrett is also an artist in the mediums of watercolor, oil, and acrylic. She enjoys ballroom dancing, traveling, and hiking with her husband, Bob. Her bibliocat, Pookie, supervises all writing efforts between catnaps.

Dr. Garrett is available to speak at book clubs, conferences, and conventions.

https://www.shirleybgarrett.com
Facebook.com/ShirleyBGarrett
Twitter.com/ShirleyBGarrett

Made in the USA
Columbia, SC
29 June 2022